3

HANDICAPPED ENGLISH

HANDICAPPED ENGLISH

The Language of the Socially Disadvantaged

By

JOHN NIST

Department of English
Auburn University
Auburn, Alabama

CHARLES C THOMAS • PUBLISHER
Springfield • Illinois • U.S.A.

Published and Distributed Throughout the World by
CHARLES C THOMAS • PUBLISHER
BANNERSTONE HOUSE
301–327 East Lawrence Avenue, Springfield, Illinois, U.S.A.

© *1974, by* CHARLES C THOMAS • PUBLISHER

ISBN 0–398–02800–1

Library of Congress Catalog Card Number: 73–199

With THOMAS BOOKS *careful attention is given to all details of
manufacturing and design. It is the Publisher's desire to present books
that are satisfactory as to their physical qualities and artistic possibilities
and appropriate for their particular use.* THOMAS BOOKS *will be true
to those laws of quality that assure a good name and good will.*

Printed in the United States of America

BB-14

For

MARISA

whose heart speaks all the lects of love.

PREFACE

THIS BOOK DEALS with the greatest single problem facing the public school system in the United States today—namely, that of the interference of a *native* language with the learning of the *national* language. The results of this interference are all too apparent in society at large: isolation and alienation for native–language speaking minority groups; inferior performance in reception, transmission, reading, and composition among at least 40 percent of all students in the classrooms of America; and above all else, the vicious circle of *un*equal educational opportunity and its attendant degradation of joblessness and poverty. The underlying cause of these negative results, of course, is a "mass psychological murder" that is being committed against the children of the socially disadvantaged and the culturally deprived: Negroes in urban ghettos and on tenant farms; Spanish–speaking Americans of Puerto Rican, Cuban, and Mexican descent; poor whites in Appalachia and the rural South; Indians on Government reservations; *mestico* speakers of creolized pidgins in Hawaii; and orphans in many foster homes and impersonalized institutions. So great is the extent of the problem of handicapped English that it embraces at least thirty to fifty million Americans of all ages, races, religions, and ethnic backgrounds.

Handicapped English: The Language of the Socially Disadvantaged is organized into seven chapters.

Chapter 1 defines the problem of handicapped English and shows that it is *not* the outgrowth of pathological speech disorders, either somatically or psychosomatically induced. Handicapped English, in short, is a *cultural* rather than a *physiological* phenomenon. And it exists oftentimes *where least suspected*—not just in the substandard performance of disadvantaged schoolchildren, but in the formal compositions of college and university students and in the "semantic pollution" of professional writing.

Chapter 2 traces the language growth of the child, both as a receiver–transmitter and as a conceptualizer. This delineation of the child's acquisition of his language emphasizes the concept of *resonance,* implemented in the period (2 to 12 years) within which the child optimally learns his own geographical dialect and social–class lect. In detailing the stages of the child's acquisition of language and the phases of his conceptual growth, the importance of *phenotypical modeling* among the following three kinds of language is stressed: *ancestral, native, national.*

Chapter 3 analyzes in detail the three levels of social–class lects in Modern American English: *acrolect,* or the prestigious standard; *mesilect,* or the all–pervasive manifestation of the vernacular; and *basilect,* or the totally nonprestigious and socially disadvantaged "vulgar." From such analysis, it becomes apparent that speakers of the basilect, which is of course a native language rather than the national language, suffer from an inadequate segmentation of reality and from an inappropriate image of themselves and of the linguistic roles which they should or might assume.

Chapter 4 delves deeply into the inadequate segmentation of reality among speakers of the basilect and finds their language deficient in the semantic variables of Modern American English, as well as in designative, implicative, and pragmatic ranges of meaning. Such an inadequate segmentation of reality, furthermore, relates directly to the deficiencies inherent in what Basil Bernstein has called the "restricted code" of the basilect.

Chapter 5 probes into the inappropriate image of the self and into the linguistic roles which this same self must assume. Such probing, in turn, reveals that speakers of the basilect suffer from a deficiency in Aristotle's categories of observation—first, from a high and negative emotive function as *transmitters,* and second, from a low and negative conative function as *receivers* of messages. Victims of their own "restricted code," speakers of handicapped English fail to master forms of mitigation and politeness, cannot handle the full range of the styles or keys of discourse, both spoken and written, and nurture a poor image of themselves which frequently results in either will–less lassitude or hostile belligerence. Linguistically, they often tend to react automatically and within a very narrow range of English structures.

Chapter 6 undertakes to study the various causes of handicapped English, paying special attention to environmental deprivations rather than to biological inheritance. These environmental deprivations of necessity include the lack of appropriate language models within the period of resonance, the lack of richness and variety in the play materials available at home, the failure to receive emotional security from parents, the stunting influences of closed systems of communication and of imperative modes of behavior control in positional, status–oriented families, the cultural warfare inherent in the conflict of value systems in the public schools, and the peer–group reinforcement of environmental deprivations. In this chapter, moreover, the "linguistics of white supremacy" comes in for some measure of discussion.

Chapter 7 offers what I have called some "pretensions at pedagogy," some conclusions of a linguist–critic who admits that he is no expert in the field of public–school education. The current problem of "lect engineering" figures heavily in this chapter, which deals in detail with the following three major proposals: (1) *eradication* of all forms of the basilect in Modern American English; (2) *cultivation* of a multilectal mastery of Modern American English by members of socially disadvantaged communities; and (3) *inculcation* of functional knowledge about, performing mastery of, and emotional respect for all forms of nonstandard English by speakers of the acrolect standard. Since the achievement of Proposal 1 is not possible before Proposals 3 and 2, in that order, have first been effectuated, these latter proposals are discussed in great detail, together with general rules and specific suggestions for the promotion of optimal language teaching in the United States.

Furthermore, since the achievement of Proposal 1 involves a complete overhaul of the present American public school system, it is not treated in anything like the detailed depth which any future adoption of it as a course of educational policy would deserve. For those readers who are interested in the possibilities of the eradication of the basilect through a system of nationwide preschool nurseries, their attention is directed to Fred M. Hechinger's volume, *Pre-School Education Today* (1966). This collection of essays is a beginning presentation of that educational strategy which eventually will be seen as the *sine qua non* for the elimination of handicapped English in the United States.

If it is true that we must love one another or die, it is also true that without a really equal educational opportunity for *all* American children (regardless of race, creed, ethnic origin, or socio–economic status), we cannot truly love one another. To think otherwise, is the height of national folly—and hypocrisy.

And now to close these remarks upon a series of personal notes.

First of all, I must thank the Administration of Auburn University for having granted me research funds and reduced teaching time so that I could prepare the present study. I am especially grateful to Dr. Ben T. Lanham, Jr., Vice President for Administration, and to Dr. W.R. Patrick, Head of the Department of English.

Next, I am indebted to countless scores of speakers of the basilect, who so willingly let me tape–record their speech, their reading, and their "free expression."

I am especially thankful for my association with the splendid teachers of English in the State of Hawaii, teachers with whom I lived and worked in close association during the summer of 1967. They were most generous to me in their modeling of present–day creolized versions of the various pidgins of the Islands.

And then I am deeply grateful to Professor Alexander R. Posniak, a resonant speaker of several languages and a close personal friend. He initiated the concept of the distinctions to be made among ancestral, native, and national languages, a concept which I have used, hopefully, to good effect throughout this study.

Nor can I forget Mr. Payne Thomas, my publisher. He has encouraged me throughout the entire course of this project.

And last, and most important of all, I must thank my wife, Marisa. It was she who quite literally called me back from death to life. It is her call of love, therefore, which is ultimately responsible for my ever having written the book at all.

Auburn, Alabama JOHN NIST

CONTENTS

HANDICAPPED
ENGLISH

Chapter 1

THE PROBLEM DEFINED

THROUGHOUT THE LAST THIRD of the twentieth century, the American public in general will become increasingly aware of what linguistic specialists in particular have now known for some time—namely, that the substandard performance of socially disadvantaged students in the schools of the United States constitutes the single greatest problem facing the educational system of the country. In the overly cautious words of Michael F. Shugrue (1968, p. 142), Secretary for English in the Modern Language Association of America, "The education of the disadvantaged is probably the major educational issue in the United States today." Why "overly cautious"? Because under a mask of stupidity and resentment seethes a hidden self–contempt among the children of isolation and alienation which constantly threatens to geyser up into open cultural warfare in the classrooms of America, simply because America has been unwittingly committing *mass psychological murder* through self–fulfilling prophecies of failure (all too soon turned into reality) upon the socially disadvantaged speakers of handicapped English. This mass psychological murder, in turn, results in the vicious circle so clearly depicted by Frederick Williams (1970, p. 2); development disadvantage produces educational disadvantage, which produces employment disadvantage,

3

which produces economic disadvantage, which produces the
originating developmental disadvantage.

Isolation and Alienation

All of the various forms of disadvantage inherent in the
vicious circle depicted by Williams are the cumulative effects
of isolation and alienation, two of the cardinal crimes of an
advanced technological society which cares more for profits
than for people, more for irrelevant creeds than for relevant
action, more for paying lip–service than for serving lips—and
tongues. In the historical evolution of the multi–ethnic and
polyglot cultural spectra in the United States, such isolation
and alienation are—ironically enough—only further intensified by the uniform ambition of the frequently well–meaning
but even more frequently misguided members of the political,
economic, and educational Establishment: make every student in the public schools of America speak and write, listen
and read, think and feel like a socially advantaged WASP
(white Anglo-Saxon Protestant) cruising down the mainstream
of equal opportunity and shared affluence.

What makes this ambition so self–defeating in performance,
of course, is its utter blindness to the fact that hundreds of
thousands of American students either do not have the where-
withal to become linguistic WASPS, *given their present
course of instruction*, or simply do not want to. The blindness
of this ambition, moreover, is exceeded only by its abysmal
ignorance of language itself, an ignorance which has led the
eminent American dialectologist Raven I. McDavid, Jr. (1971,
p. 83) to remark: "In Detroit, even superior students have
undergone the brain–washing of courses in 'corrective speech'
if their native pronunciation has been that of Oklahoma."
In other words, the educational executors of this ambition
frequently cannot tell the difference between a culturally
induced geographical dialect and an organically suffered
speech disorder. Little wonder is it then that many of these
same educational executors fail to perceive the relationship
between social isolation and alienation on the one hand and
an almost militant refusal by the speakers of handicapped
English, so isolated and alienated, to abandon it on the other.

WHAT IS "HANDICAPPED"?

If social isolation and cultural alienation do indeed produce handicapped English among millions of Americans enduring poverty and degradation in black urban ghettos, on rural tenant farms, in Southern and Appalachian ignorance belts, in the border towns of California Chicanos and Lone–Star–State Tex–Mexicans, on Indian reservations maintained by the Federal Government, and in countless orphanages supported by state and local funds and by the private charity of anonymous donors—then this crucial question demands an answer: "What does the term *handicapped* mean?"

Handicapped Speech

First of all, despite the misapplication of the term in all the "corrective speech" classes that erroneously (and arrogantly) seek to substitute one geographical standard for another, handicapped English does *not* mean an *organic* speech disorder, whether somatic or psychosomatic in origin. When a humanistic linguist uses the term *handicapped* as a modifier of *English*, therefore, he does *not* mean to characterize such nonstandard performance in the language as *pathological*.

Handicapped English, consequently, must be distinguished from the following speech disorders, which truly are pathological: brain–injury disorders like those caused by bulbar polio, encephalitis, neurosyphilis, chronic subdural hematoma, intracranial aneurysm, cerebral abscess, and glioma; the four types of aphasia (motor, auditory, alexiac, and agraphiac) caused by high–frequency deafness, mental deficiency, cerebral palsy, and infantile schizophrenia; the two types of semantogenic, psychodynamic, and organic stuttering (*clonic,* repetitive and *tonic,* continuous); the choreic speech induced by rheumatic fever; the various forms of dyslalia produced by such structural anomalies as cleft palate, harelip, hypertrophy of the adenoids, open bite, recessive jaw, prognathic mandible, and high palatal arch; the various voice disorders (dysphonia and aphonia) resulting from deformities of the glottis; and last but not least, the several different forms of communication breakdown directly related to organic (conduction, perception, nerve) and inorganic (psychogenic, hysterical) deafness.

If handicapped English is not the outgrowth of pathological speech disorders, neither is it the result of nonpathological speech defects *per se*. In the words of Robert West (1971, p. 307), such nonpathological speech defects may occur as follows:

> Allowances being made for children in the speech learning period, the speech of a given person may be regarded as defective under the following conditions: (a) when his voice is not loud enough to be easily heard in the practical situations of his vocational and social life; (b) when his speech is partially or wholly unintelligible because of inaccurate articulations; (c) when his speech is partially or wholly unintelligible by reason of serious lapses of grammar, syntax, or word use; (d) when, for any reason, his speech is intrinsically unpleasant to listen to; (e) when his utterance is so different in rate, rhythm, pitch, loudness, timbre, or individual sounds of speech from that of the average speaker of his age and sex that the differences serve to distract the hearer's attention from what is being said to how it is said; (f) when his speech is accompanied by extraneous mechanical or vocal sounds or by distracting grimaces, gestures, or postures. The *perception of speech*—hearing—is defective when it is inadequate for the individual's educational, vocational, and social needs. . . .

If these speech defects outlined by West are not sufficient in and of themselves to constitute handicapped English, then they certainly are attributes of that phenomenon—attributes which tend to deepen the basic isolation and alienation of socially disadvantaged people. Such isolation and alienation, moreover, result in the two chief characteristics of what is meant by the term "handicapped": (1) an inadequate segmentation of reality and (2) an improper (or inappropriate) image of the self and the various linguistic roles which this self must assume. The first of these characteristics will be discussed in detail in Chapter 4; the second, in Chapter 5.

Meanwhile, speakers of handicapped English do suffer from some or all of the six nonpathological speech defects categorized by West—a fact which is easily demonstrated throughout the published research papers on this subject. Under category (a), for example, it is well known that socially disadvantaged children "often answer with a nod or one–word reply for fear of not being able to answer correctly in the school culture" (Ponder, 1967, p. 26). When they do answer in extended discourse, moreover, they often mumble their words, break their sentences with hesitation noises, and keep volume down in order to avoid being heard as wrong. As hearable extensions of (a) into categories (d) and (e), the performances of Negro school children in Butler County, Alabama, 97 percent of whom *will never leave the county,* are marked by a staccato intonation in which word groups occur like words in a series; by a high incidence of baby talk, lisping, and breathiness; by a distractive musical intonation in dipodic jazz rhythm; by a frequent jamming up of sentences by making the /#/ juncture induce not enough silence between structures; by a distractive speed in the pace of delivery, together with a tendency toward a monotoned voice melody; by word– or syllable–calling instead of true reading; and by such a poor command of paralinguistic signals that it produces a kind of lassitude in expression which borders upon an utter lack of volition (see Nist, Nov. 1969, p. 11). The overall impression caused by such performances, of course, is that of an emotive function which is high through its very negation of emotion. The function so foregrounded, consequently, draws distractive attention to itself.

This drawing of distractive attention to some manifestation of its performance is a marked feature of handicapped English. In the field of geographical dialects and social–class lects, for example, it is certainly true that we all "talk funny," a linguistic truism eminently illustrated in the Central Midland speech of President Eisenhower contrasted with the Eastern New England variety of President Kennedy, or in the West Texas Southern of President Johnson contrasted with the cosmopolitan California version of President Nixon's North Central American English. But whereas all four of these recent Presidents talk or talked "funny," they do or did so *with prestige rather than with stigma.* In other words, the peculiar ways of talking funny among these four Presidents have never constituted their own barriers to communication among the public at large.

The same value judgment, unfortunately, cannot be made about handicapped English: its various ways of talking funny *do* constitute their own barriers to communication. Why? Because they distractively draw attention away from the speaker's *message* and concentrate it in that vehicle of the message known to linguistic science as the *code*. And one of the surest methods for achieving such a distraction of attention may be found in the nonstandard pronunciation patterns of handicapped English.

The deviant pronunciation patterns of handicapped English are not confined to any one section or social group in the United States. Nonstandard and distractive phonology, moreover, transcends the dividing lines of race, religion, social class, occupation, and economic income. If disadvantaged black schoolchildren in Butler County, Alabama (see Nist, Nov. 1969, p. 11) tend to drop phonemes of friction in final positions, thereby ending monosyllables on open vowels or glides, then many educated white adults in the South today still shift the maximum lexical stress of words like *police, insurance, efficiency,* and *guitar* to the first syllable—a distractive habit of phonological realization stigmatized as a social shibboleth (see McDavid, 1967, p. 9). Whereas lower–class immigrant speakers of English in New York City tend to substitute /t/ for /θ/ and /d/ for /ð/, even upper middle–class Brooklynites sometimes have trouble making the distinction between the vowels in words like *Boyd* and *bird, coil* and *curl, Hoyt* and *hurt.* The tendency among black Northern ghetto speakers of American English to reduce two syllables involving a stop to one easily pronounced syllable—so that /rahm/ = *rotten,* for example—is notorious. By way of contrast, so strong is the "Kanaka" (native Hawaiian) influence in the pronunciation patterns of the fiftieth state that even middle–aged college graduates in Honolulu, especially under the pressure of emotional excitement, will revert to their creolized pidgin of childhood and drop /r/ and /l/ in word–final positions.

Distractive as such nonstandard pronunciations are, they do not begin to match the disruption–of–communication force exerted by the grammatical deviations of handicapped Eng-

lish. In other words, a distractive grammar is a greater stig-
matizer of handicapped English than is a distractive
phonology. Why? Because a distractive grammar is a stronger
indicator of the lack of linguistic sophistication induced by
social isolation and alienation. Speakers of such a distractive
grammar, which generates structures and usages that stray
rather markedly from the norms of some widely accepted
standard, more often than not may be characterized as follows
(see Bernstein, 1970): (1) They will be the rhetorical users
and victims of a *restricted,* as distinct from an *elaborated,*
code, which will be *position-* or *status-*oriented, rather than
*person-*oriented. (2) Seekers of social solidarity in preference
to the realization of individual achievement and personal fulfillment, they will elevate "we" above "I" and seek to communicate in the intimate and/or familiar styles of affective
empathy. (3) Reared in a *closed,* as distinct from an *open,*
role system, which orients them more to the object mode
than to the person mode, they will seek to establish a *limiting*
rather than an *exploring* conceptual order and will therefore
be severely hampered in their ability to cope with ambiguity
and ambivalence. (4) Relying heavily on the closed system
of communication inherent in facial expressions, bodily gestures, intonation patterns, and paralinguistic signals, they will
speak with a low amount of verbal planning and through
an impoverished repertoire of rigid syntactic structures. (5)
Suffering from a subnormal command of cause–and–effect
relationships and lacking in time–oriented moral patience,
they will rely on *imperative* modes of social control rather
than on *appeals* modes and will therefore choose *power*
instead of *language* as a means of exercising influence over
the behavior of others. (6) Dominated by *assigned,* as distinct
from *achieved,* rules for personal behavior and motivated
more sharply by *fear–boundedness* than by *love–freedom,*
they will tend to use persons as objects, seek to remove
ambiguity rather than to create it, and experience cultural
conflict when confronted with the problem of switching from
a restricted code to an elaborated one while in the educational
institutions of America.

The grammar that such speakers of handicapped English

use, moreover, will—more likely than not—be characterized (and stigmatized) by such nonstandard features as these (see McDavid, 1967, pp. 9–10): (1) Omission of markers for the noun plural, as in *three goat* and *four pear*. (2) Omission of markers for possession in the noun, as in *Mr. Brown hat*. (3) Analogical use of absolute genitives like *ourn, yourn, hisn, hern,* and *theirn*. (4) Substitution of *them* for *those* in demonstrative function. (5) Analogical formation of compound reflexives in the possessive rather than in the objective, as in *hisself, theirselves*. (6) Use of compound demonstratives like *this here, that there, these here,* and *them there* before, rather than enclosing, their substantives. (7) Improper inflection of comparisons, like *wonderfullest* and *lovinger*. (8) Use of double comparisons as psychologically intensive expressions, as in *more prettier, more better, most ugliest,* and *most best,* or even *bestest*. (9) Violation of person–number concord in both the present and the preterit forms of the verb *be*—e.g., *We was wondering where them kids is*. (10) Violation of person–number concord in the present forms of the verb *do,* as in *I does* and *he do*. (11) Omission of the *-ing* of the present participle. (12) Omission of the allomorphic markers of the preterit tense: /t ~ d ~ ɪd/. (13) Omission of the allomorphic markers of perfective aspect in the past participles of historically "weak" regular form: /t ~ d ~ ɪd/. (14) Omission of appropriate forms of the verb *be* in statements before both predicate noun phrases and predicate adjectives, as in *He a good boy* and *They ready*. (15) Omission of appropriate forms of the verb *be* in statements before both present and past participles—e.g., *He going with us* and *The window broken*. (16) Omission of the phonemically enclitic contractions of *has* (/s ~ z ~ ɪz/) before *been,* as in *He been drinking*. (17) Substitution of *been, done,* or *done been* for *have,* especially in the third person singular—e.g., *He done been finished*.

Important as these seventeen grammatical stigmata of handicapped English are in marking their speakers as socially disadvantaged, they do not even begin to tell the full extent of what is meant by the terms *handicapped* and *disadvantaged*. To try to alleviate the economic and educational ills attendant upon these terms by means of a symptomatic "correction" of these so–called grammatical "errors" in the classrooms of America is to try to cure a patient dying of cancer of the stomach by giving him a mouthwash for halitosis. So bad has this curative "correction" been that it has resulted in *functional illiteracy* for about one–third of all Negro students graduating from the high schools of New York City, in a clearly below–normal level of reading for more than forty percent of the elementary school children in the United States at large (see Lefevre, 1964, pp. 15–23), and in such widespread inferior command of the written word that more than half of the American people will never become fluent in composition, even after the benefits of a high school diploma and/or a Bachelor of Arts degree.

As Doris R. Entwisle (1970) has demonstrated, the social stratification and the social mobility inherent in the various forms of American English result in the differential mobility that may be popularly called the "life chances" of the individual. Since socialization in language is the *sine qua non* for all other forms of socialization, it necessarily follows that educational opportunities and their resultant social mobility depend in large measure upon the linguistic habits developed by the individual *during the first eight years of his life* (see Ervin and Miller, 1968; Braine, 1971). And it is a well–known fact that socially disadvantaged children usually do not become functionally literate at an early age. Consequently, this arrestment or retardation in literacy is the linguistic handicap which intensifies their original social deprivation, so that the poverty cycle and their poor language performance become mutually convertible. As Davenport Plumer (1970, p. 298) has shown in one brilliant diagram, a poor language learning environment produces the handicapped English, which results in the poor school performance that almost inevitably leads to dropout, unemployment, poverty, and ultimately the originating poor language learning environment. Functional illiteracy, of course, is a key factor in the poor school performance of the socially deprived (Entwisle, p. 125):

> If an individual fails to become sufficiently literate, all other parts
> of the educational process break down. The child who cannot read
> well acquires a scanty store of information; his ineptness in reading

directions causes him to show up poorly on standardized tests, and then he is put into "slow" or "basic" sections in school; he is handicapped in assimilating and interpreting all the events in the world around him by his clumsiness in reading. In effect it is as though he reaps compound interest on his initial deficit; his skills of perceiving, of learning, and of attention are stunted because less and less success is experienced. Less and less success leads to less and less expectation of success by him and by his teachers, and the whole deficit snowballs. . . .

This snowballing deficit, so accurately observed by Entwisle, bears eloquent testimony to the fact that the public schools of America frequently do not help the socially disadvantaged child, but rather hinder him, in overcoming his language handicaps. Because of this hindrance, furthermore, his inadequate segmentation of reality and his inappropriate image of himself and of the linguistic roles he must play persist, in crippling fashion, beyond graduation or dropout and succeed in punishing his adult life with a kind of "psychological deafness."

Reading Difficulties

Insofar as reading is concerned, such psychological deafness usually results in a retardation of from one to five years, a retardation induced by what Carl A. Lefevre aptly calls a lack of "sentence sense." This lack of sentence sense is the primary cause of the "crippled reader" (Lefevre, 1964, pp. 15, 23), who tends to read literally word–by–word, or arbitrarily by nonsignificant word groups and sentence fragments. Often mistaking introductory clauses for complete sentences and dependent structures for independent ones, the "crippled reader" may be characterized in his partial dyslexia as follows:

Lacking a sure grasp of the printed sentence as the common building block of the paragraph and of the more extended forms of written discourse, the crippled reader cannot comprehend what he "reads" as organized, coherent form. Instead, he tends to register only arbitrary, random elements, and even to miss important language structures altogether in the material the writer sets before him. He sees a subject without its verb, a verb without its subject; he combines subjects with the wrong verbs and verbs with the wrong subjects; he attaches expanding phrases to the wrong sentence elements, or "reads" them by themselves, without any structural context. In this process he may retain a large number of isolated words, particularly if his basic reading instruction stressed memorizing single words; he will do better on the vocabulary than on the comprehension of a test passage (Lefevre, 1964, p. 23).

In oral performance, these crippling features of partial dyslexia will often be accompanied by hesitation noises, erasure backups, omission of structure or function words, metathesis within difficult words, mispronunciation through echoic anticipation, misplacement of junctures, faulty use of terminal intonation contours, monotonously narrow range of emotive paralanguage, and frustrated collapse into insecure sighs, moans, and groans or into frightened or hostile silence.

Such performance, in which mere word–calling often replaces true reading, is not confined to the socially disadvantaged lower classes. In other words, subnormal reading, like all other attributes of handicapped English, is not the necessary offspring of poverty *per se*. Abraham Lincoln, for example, was poor, poor as the proverbial church mouse, but he was not socially disadvantaged, simply because he was not linguistically deprived. With this distinction ever in mind, then, it is easy to understand why emotionally disturbed white upper–middle–class teenagers in Columbus, Georgia, read on the performance level of emotionally secure but poor black children of half their age in Auburn, Alabama: the degree of language deprivation, and therefore of true social disadvantage, in both groups is roughly about the same.

Limited Composition Skills

As with reading, so with composition: markedly inferior performance is not the sole possession of the poor. Indeed, as any instructor in English can testify, students in Freshman Composition at the college or university level are notorious for their inability to write with an adequate use of detail, variety of development, clarity of organization, suitability of tone, choice of effective diction; for their failure to properly sequence their paragraphs and to smoothly transition between them; for their lack of mastery in writing sentences that are economic in expression, varied in form, appropriate in function, and graceful in style; for their violations of simplicity, sensory appeal, and sincerity in description; for their becoming victimized by such "problems of competence" as these: use of a wrong morphological form, improper shift in the subject of a sentence, improper shift in any feature of the verb system (tense, mood, voice, aspect), faulty reference, violation of subject–verb or antecedent–referent agreement, malapropism, dangling modifier, improper use of sentence fragment, comma splice, fused or run–on sentence, violation of parallelism in structures, failure to distinguish direct discourse from indirect, unsupported categorical statement, inadequate or improper documentation, and plagiarism (see Nist, 1969a, pp. 84–151). These same students, of course, have difficulty with such minor matters as spelling, punctuation, and the mechanics of expression.

The "psychological deafness" which contributes to the handicapped English of inferior composition is not confined to any one social group in the United States today. Economic income, age, race, sex, and cultural opportunities for personal fulfillment are, however, important factors in the determination of substandard expression in writing. In other words, all other factors being equal, white girls from high–income families will write better than black boys from low–income families, and older girls better than younger. The biggest obstacle to effective composition, in fact, is the same one that obstructs effective speech in English—namely, the interference of a native foreign language. Hence, though painfully amusing, the following examples of "hilarious mistake" in English composition are eminently forgivable—their authors are foreign users of the language, ill–at–ease in the medium:

From *Thailand:*
My old is 20 years.
From *Nigeria:*
Our medium of instruction is English. I can read writte and speak English frequently.
From *Hong Kong:*
Sorry bordering you so much.
From *India:*
Excepting an early reply.

From *East Pakistan:*
> I am a fresh Bachelor of Engineering and have active habits.

From *India:*
> I am at present a student of B. E. final year Electrical and I shall pass out in the month of July 1st week.

But flawed as these written expressions are, they are more than matched by the following twenty excerpts from actual letters received by the Department of Public Welfare in Phenix City, Alabama:

1. Please send me my elopement as I have four months old baby and he is my only support and I need all I can get everyday to buy food and keep him close.

2. Both sides of my parents is poor and I can't expect nothing from them as my mother has been in bed for a year with the same doctor and won't change.

3. Please send my wife's form to fill out.

4. I have already wrote to the President and I don't hear from you, I will write to Uncle Same and tell him about you both.

5. Please send me a letter and tell me if my husband made application for a wife and baby.

6. I can't get my pay. I got sex children. Can you tell me why this is?

7. Sir, I am forwarding my marriage certificate and my children, one is a mistake as you can see.

8. Please fien out for certain if my husband is dead as the man I am living with won't eat or do anything until he noes for sure.

9. I am writing to tell you that my baby was born two years ago and he is two years old. When do I get relief?

10. I am annoyed to find that you branded my children illiterate. Oh! the shame it is—it is a dirty trick, as I married their father a week before they were born.

11. In answer to your letter, I gave birth to a boy weighing ten pounds. I hope this is satisfactory.

12. I have no children as my husband was a truck driver and worked day and night when he wasn't sleeping.

13. In accordance with your instruction, I have given birth to twins in the enclosed envelope.

14. You have changed my little boy to a girl. Does that make any difference?

15. Unless I get my husband's money soon, I will be forced to lead an immortal life.

16. I am glad to say my husband who was reported missing, is now dead.

17. I want my money quickly as I can get it. I've been in bed with my doctor for two weeks and he doesn't seem to be doing me much good. If things don't improve, I will have to send for another doctor.

18. My husband had his project cut off two weeks ago, and I haven't had any relief since.

19. I am a poor widow and all I have is in front.

20. Both my husband and I are sterile, is there any chance of our children inheriting this?

Despite the high interest of their unconscious humor, what makes these excerpts potentially so dreary is their advanced state of *semantic collapse*. Lamentable as it may be that native speakers of English should write about as poorly as the foreign students of the language quoted earlier, what is particularly disheartening about these welfare letters is their almost incredible Edith (Mrs. Archie) Bunker naïveté. In other words, it is not nearly so much the grammatical errors, the malapropisms, the misspellings, the rhetorical blunderings, or the sheer illogicalities in these excerpts that brand them as examples of handicapped English, as it is the "psychological deafness" which makes them and—above all—their transmitters impervious to the cleansing laughter of a sophisticated and Mercutio–like self–awareness.

SOME FACTORS IN SEMANTIC DIFFICULTY

Social Disadvantage

Why do the authors of these welfare letters write so poorly, so much like foreign students of the English language? Because of the language interference inherent in their social disadvantage. Although many of the causes of handicapped English must wait until Chapter 6 for a detailed discussion, certain characteristics of social disadvantage may be listed now. As Edgar Dale (1967, p. 31) has indicated, the theory and the research of Martin Deutsch, Gertrude Whipple, Roger Brown, Ursula Bellugi, John B. Carroll, and Basil Bernstein have isolated the following statements about culturally deprived children (who grow up to be culturally deprived adults) and the social disadvantage that linguistically handicaps them:

1. Models of excellence in use of vocabulary or sentence structure are not easily available to these deprived children.

2. They come from broken rather than intact homes. Often there is a nonexistent or weak father image.

3. Underprivileged children stay closer to home, in their own neighborhood. Their physical ranging is limited.

4. They have a negative self–image.

5. Their auditory span, their capacity for sustained attention is less than [that of] middle– or upper–class children.

6. They use a smaller number of less varied words to express themselves.

7. Their sentences are shorter and more categorical. There are more incomplete sentences.

8. These children meet limited variability in the kinds of problems they face, have no opportunity to be challenged by the complexities faced by middle–class children.

9. Home tasks tend to be motoric, not motivated by distant goals. There is emphasis on the immediate.

10. There is probably less listening to TV or radio, but here the data are limited.

11. There is a lack of manipulable objects in the home.

These eleven statements listed by Dale are classics in the study of social disadvantage, supported by tons of published evidence based upon impeccable research. What the statements mean in a somewhat simplistic summary is this: Handicapped English is the result of "noise" interference in the lives of the socially disadvantaged. This noise interference, as implicitly indicated in the preceding eleven statements, occurs in such varying forms as a damaging negative emotive function, an inadequate performance model, an impoverishment of perceptual experience, and a reduction of the privilege of choice through avoidance of confrontation with plurisignificance and multivalence. But regardless of the form taken by the noise interference, this phenomenon is a crucial factor in the process of handicapping a child's language and therefore must be studied in some measure of detail.

Matrix of Communication

As Davenport Plumer has indicated, noise interference constantly besets the socially disadvantaged child and hinders him in his attempts to master a standard version of English, one that is widely acceptable among educated speakers of the language. On the basis of his own deep study of the research relating to social disadvantage, Plumer (1970, p. 287) posits the following three conclusions:

> (a) Urban slum children do live in an environment characterized by a high noise–to–signal ratio. (b) As a group these children do show marked problems of auditory and visual discrimination, of auditory and visual memory and of attention to auditory and visual stimuli. (c) These problems of perception, memory, and attention are associated with reading retardation, as is the problem of audio—visual integration.

In short, Plumer is saying that noise interference in the lives of poor slum children is a necessary, if not sufficient, cause of their inadequate segmentation of reality—one of the two primary attributes of handicapped English.

Whenever children who are handicapped by an inadequate segmentation of reality seek to use their handicapped English, they enter the *matrix of communication* that relates to the sending of messages in any language or nonstandard version thereof. As first discussed in the brilliant theory of Roman Jakobson (1960), this matrix operates by means of six *dimensions* and seven attendant *functions,* and is extremely helpful in pinpointing the source of metaphorically extended noise interference in the handicapped English of the socially disadvantaged. But first, a detailed study of the matrix itself.

As understood by modern linguistic science, the equilibrium of verbal exchange is maintained by an organic–like union among these six dimensions of communication, grouped into two triads as follows: (1) *addresser, message,* and *addressee;* (2) *context, code,* and *contact.* In this process of verbal exchange, according to Jakobson (1960, p. 353):

> The ADDRESSER sends a MESSAGE to the ADDRESSEE. To be operative the message requires a CONTEXT referred to ("referent" is another, somewhat ambiguous nomenclature), seizable by the addressee, and either verbal or capable of being verbalized; a CODE fully, or at least partially, common to the addresser and addressee (or in other words, to the encoder and decoder of the message); and finally a CONTACT, a physical channel and psychological connection between the addresser and the addressee, enabling both of them to enter and stay in communication.

By way of summarizing Jakobson's analysis, these six dimensions in the matrix of communication may be visualized as follows:

Dimensions of the Matrix of Communication

CONTEXT

ADDRESSER-----**MESSAGE**-----ADDRESSEE

CODE

CONTACT

As the foregoing schematic chart implies, the addresser is the person sending the message, whereas the addressee is the person receiving the message. The context is the cultural situation to which the message refers. The code, on the other hand, is the language (whether natural, as in English, or abstractly specialized, as in the formulas of mathematics) in which the message is cast. The contact, however, is the vehicle of the code, just as the code is the vehicle of the message—that is, the contact is the means by which the code is conveyed: for example, by air waves, radio, telephone, television, letter, telegram, or printed book. The message itself, of course, is whatever the addresser wants to convey to the addressee, such as information, emotional mood, attitude toward subject, or tone toward audience. Many times the message becomes something that the addresser does not want to convey to the addressee—for example, a hypocritical pattern of behavior, a shrewish temperament, a lack of respect for age, an inadequate command of the grammar of the language, or an insensitivity to the immediate context situation. The message, furthermore, differs from the other five dimensions in the mattrix in that it supports two basic functions, whereas they support only one each (see Nist, May 1966).

The function assigned to any dimension in the matrix of communication is that which *foregrounds* itself for human awareness; other functions may exist in each dimension, but if they do, then they remain secondary to the basic one. Hence the basic function of the addresser or the sender of the message is *emotive*. When asked what he thinks, the average man will reply by telling how he feels. Emotion, therefore, is the catalytic impulse from which most human beings speak. If George asks his wife Grace to close the window and does so in a courteous manner, she will probably reply in kind and close the window: emotional neutrality for emotional neutrality. But if he says, "Grace, will you close that damn window!"—she will probably answer like this: "Don't you swear at me!" And the window will probably remain open, a victim of negative emotive function, until George and Grace finally end their verbal sparring.

By way of contrast to the emotive function of the addresser, the function of the addressee, seen so clearly in the two examples of Grace's response to George's message, is *conative*. The term *conative* means that the receiver of the message must ultimately *believe that the message is valid in terms of his own conduct*. Derived from *conation*, a term that means the aspect of endeavor in certain Semitic verbs, *conative* deals with the will. In other words, the addressee or receiver of the message must will to understand the communication before he can will to believe in its ultimate validity for the pragmatic conduct of his own life. If that conduct calls for a linguistic response, then the addressee becomes the addresser, with his own emotive function.

The context in which both the addresser and the addressee operate, of course, is the total cultural situation to which the message relates and in which it achieves validity, or fails to do so. Hence the function of the context is *referential*. The words of the message, that is, represent objects in the world outside the discourse—or within it. Like a kaleidoscope, the context is constantly shifting shades of meaning and colors of expression. Mr. Smith, for example, does not tell a story to his bowling alley buddies in the same way he does to his wife's bridge club; the context situations are different, even through his basic message is the same. Rude people can and do cut others out of their conversation simply by talking about persons, places, and events that are outside the context of commonly shared experience.

Since the code is the language, natural or artificial, in which the message is cast, its function is *metalingual* or *glossing*.

If the addresser does not have a good command of the code, he may send a ridiculous message, as did King Levinsky when once asked how it felt to be knocked out by Joe Louis. "How should I know?" said the Maxwell Street Chicago strong boy, "I was in a transom!" By the same token, if the addressee does not understand some key term in the code, then he may have to ask for a clarification in order to understand the message. Thus a father frustrated with his teenage daughter's slang may sigh and say, "Just what do you mean by an *L-7?*" Similarly, everytime a person looks up the meaning of a word or a phrase or an idiom in a dictionary, he is extending his mastery of the code and its metalingual or glossing function.

Because the contact is the physical and psychological channel by which the message is conveyed from the addresser to the addressee, its function is *phatic* or *medium expressive*. Babies babble and coo as a natural outlet for phatic function. Grownups at cocktail parties engage in banal chit-chat as a means of establishing social rapport. Junior comes into the house after school and yells, "Mom!" When she answers, "Yes, dear, what is it?"—more likely than not he will say, "Oh, nothing." And then he goes into his clubroom and works on a model airplane until dinner. Once he has established contact by means of phatic function and therefore once he is emotionally secure that Mom is in the house, then Junior can go about his normal routine without any more fussing of the addressee.

The message itself, or the statement sent from the addresser to the addressee, is unlike the other five dimensions in the matrix of communication in that it has two basic functions instead of one: (1) *pragmatic* and (2) *esthetic*. If the message is sent as an immediate means to an end other than itself, as in George's polite request, "Grace, will you please close the window?"—then the message is pragmatic in function. If, on the other hand, the message is sent as an immediate end in itself, an end which seeks permanence and infinite reiterability as its key artistic attributes, as in the great soliloquies of Shakespeare's tragedies, then the function of the message is esthetic. Pragmatic function, therefore, produces *communication;* esthetic function, *communion* (see Nist, May 1966). Implicit in the foregoing discussion, of course, is a summary visualization of the matrix of communication, shown below with its six dimensions and their seven attendant functions:

The Matrix: Dimensions and Functions

CONTEXT
Referential

ADDRESSER-----**MESSAGE**-----ADDRESSEE
Emotive　　　　Pragmatic　　　　Conative
　　　　　　　　　or
　　　　　　　Esthetic

CODE
Metalingual

CONTACT
Phatic

What this schematic chart visualizes, then, is this: if the orientation is toward the addresser, and the expression of his mood or attitude, the function is emotive. Orientation toward a response from the addressee, seen so clearly in employment of the vocative and of the imperative, constitutes the conative function. If the addresser and the addressee check the context to guard against an ambiguous meaning there, then they are resorting to the referential function. If they check the contact in order to establish, prolong, or continue the communication, they are using the phatic function. If they check the code, on the other hand, then they are engaged in the metalingual (or glossing) function. These five functions, furthermore, all share the same basic attribute: they are *pragmatic.* That is, they are all involved in the use of language as a means to an end other than itself. The function of the message, by way of contrast, may be an immediate end in itself. This function of the message is thus potentially *esthetic* (or poetic). Such an esthetic function, when employed, is the basis for the behavior of language as artistic communion as distinct from mere pragmatic communication. The reality of meaning, by implication then, is like that of style: double in nature, depending on whether meaning permeates the message as a pragmatic means or as an esthetic end.

Crucial Locus of Meaning

As already indicated elsewhere (Nist, 1971b, p. 326), the *crucial locus of meaning* within the matrix of communication is the point where verbal exchange either succeeds or fails. It may be within the addresser and his emotive function or within the addressee and his conative function. It may lie outside both the sender and the receiver of the message in the context and its referential function, or in the code and its metalingual function, or in the contact and its phatic function. Or the crucial locus of meaning may lie in the message itself and in either its pragmatic or its esthetic function.

Now by means of metaphorical extension, anything which impedes any of these functions may be called "noise." In other words, if the listener cannot hear the speaker well, he loses meaning through *contact noise.* If he does not know some of the speaker's key terms, he loses meaning through *code noise.* If he does not know some of the items that the speaker is referring to, he loses meaning through *context noise.* If he fails to understand whether the speaker's intention is pragmatic or esthetic, he loses meaning through *message noise.* If he overreacts to the speaker's emotive function, he loses meaning through *addresser noise.* If he brings too much personal connotation into his response to what the speaker is saying, he loses meaning through *addressee noise.*

Examples of Semantic Deficiency

It is precisely because the socially disadvantaged are beset with all the various kinds of noise in the crucial locus of meaning that they are so handicapped in their use of English. Indeed it is because of such a variety of noise interference that the socially disadvantaged are, above all else, deficient in the semantic component of their language. This semantic deficiency is demonstrated in essay after essay published in recent anthologies in sociolinguistics, for example, those edited by Bright (1971); Everetts (1967); Fishman (1968); Halsey, Floud, Anderson (1961); Postman, Weingartner, Moran (1969); Reed (1971); and Williams (1970). It is further substantiated as a phenomenon in society at large in the third edition (1972) of S.I. Hayakawa's classic *Language in Thought and Action*. Indeed as will be shown in far greater detail in Chapter 5, speakers of handicapped English (see Nist, Nov. 1969, p. 3) are semantically deficient in Aristotle's ten categories of observation: substance, quantity, quality, relation, place, time, posture or position, state or condition, action, and passivity or affection.

The socially disadvantaged, therefore, do not associate and differentiate items of experience as well as others; they do not develop abstract systems of thought, cause–and–effect relationships, moral patience and a time–oriented conscience as well as others; they are demonstrably deficient in their control over the connective system of English and hence fail to understand relations among items in the cultural context. Speakers of handicapped English often lack "instrumental metaphor" as a means of gaining leverage on meaning. And frequently they fail to relate to more culturally advantaged speakers of the language, either through will–less lassitude or hostile belligerence. In short, as a crucial stigma of their semantic deficiency, speakers of handicapped English suffer from this first great flaw in mastering a language in order to comprehend and dominate the world about them: THE INADEQUATE SEGMENTATION OF REALITY.

The semantic deficiency inherent in this inadequate segmentation of reality is both the cause and the result of this central fact—namely, that speakers of handicapped English tend to be culturally deprived in the following semantic variables (see Landar, 1966, Ch. 10) of the language: situational stimuli (S), behavioral responses (R), external events (E), internal events (I), nonlinguistic contexts (N), linguistic-contexts (L), linguistic tokens (T), linguistic types (ΣT) components (C), literal frequency factor (F), and metaphoric nonfrequency factor ($\bar{F}$). Although the detailed argument in support of this claim of cultural deprivation in the semantic variables must wait until Chapter 4, it can nevertheless be said now (see Nist, Nov. 1969, pp. 4–5) that speakers of handicapped English often do not get either adequate or appropriate situational stimuli from their parents and/or their language models; instead, they often receive negative and emotion–warping behavioral responses from those same parents and/or language models.

In addition, it is notorious that speakers of handicapped English frequently lack a varied and rich set of external events in their immediate surroundings—for example, few toys, small range of friends with similar impoverished experiences, restriction of mobility. As a consequence of this extreme deprivation in external events, which finds that some black children in Miami, Florida, for instance, have not seen the Atlantic Ocean, speakers of handicapped English suffer from insecurity in an ego–shattering set of internal events. As a result of this suffering, furthermore, speakers of handicapped English are usually markedly impoverished in both nonlinguistic and linguistic contexts, and have a very weak transmissional and conceptual control of linguistic tokens, linguistic types, components, literal frequency factor, and metaphoric nonfrequency factor.

As a deepening continuation of their semantic deficiency, speakers of handicapped English show an extremely immature mastery of linguistic signs, nonlinguistic referents, and interpretive references. Why? Because they do not have an adequate control over the three different ranges of meaning or kinds of semantic structures: (1) *implicative,* or the relationship of linguistic signs to linguistic signs; (2) *designative,* or the relationship of linguistic signs to their nonlinguistic referents; and (3) *expressive/pragmatic,* or the relationship of linguistic signs and nonlinguistic referents to the interpretive references in the behavioral responses of their users. Since speakers of handicapped English are usually very deficient in their control over these three kinds of semantic structures or ranges of meaning (see Nist, Nov. 1969, pp. 4–6), their grasp of syntax and morphology in implicative meaning is generally deviant and nonstandard or subnormal; their vocabularies and powers of referential conception are limited and anemic in the area of designative meaning; and their behavior in pragmatic meaning is stigmatized by low motivation, short attention span, poor comprehension of complex linguistic structures, failure to relate properly to the contextual function of a message, and an inability to believe in the validity of the message in terms of their own conduct. In short, as culminating stigmata of their semantic deficiency, speakers of handicapped English often, though certainly not always, have a high and negative emotive function as addressers and a low and negative conative function as addressees. They suffer, that is, from this second great flaw in mastering a language in order to comprehend and dominate the world about them: AN INAPPROPRIATE IMAGE OF THEMSELVES AND OF THE VARIOUS LANGUAGE ROLES WHICH THEY MUST ASSUME. This flaw will be discussed fully in Chapter 5.

So crucial are the two attributes of semantic deficiency in the production of handicapped English that an inadequate segmentation of reality and an improper image of the self and its various language roles pervade twentieth–century American culture like carbon monoxide in a Los Angeles smog. Because of these two attributes, in some unguarded moment, any one—whatever his race, education, social class, economic income, or cultural background—can fall a victim to handicapped English. Especially is this true in the realm of semantic deficiency. Thus the malapropist Mayor of Chicago can urge his campaign workers on to higher and higher *platitudes of achievement,* while *creeping stagnation on a high plateau* continues to trouble the thinking of Wall Street, and college and university students persist in writing such opaque gems of the critical coma as these (see Corbett, 1965, p. 526):

> Entrance requirements have gone so high that nobody can get into college, and the reason that nobody can get in is that everybody is going.
> Abstinence is a good thing if practised in moderation.
> It was the painter Donatello's interest in the female nude that made him the Father of the Renaissance.
> (Examination question: *Identify "Skylark."*) Skylark is the merchant of Shakespeare's play. When we first see him he is on the Rialto, which is the business end of Venus.

An active verb shows action, and a passive verb shows passion.
(If *pro* is the opposite of *con*, give examples.) Progress and Congress.

In Bernard Shaw's play *Mrs. Warren's Profession* her profession is the Oldest Profession but she is not really a Lost Woman. She is just mislaid.

The food in the cafeteria is absolute poison and they give you such small portions. It's about time the students spoke up about this unspeakable situation.

In Shakespeare's comedies every Tom, Dick and Harry is named Sebastian.

Socrates died from an overdose of wedlock, but before he went he had the crowned heads of Athens shaking in their shoes. It was a good thing for them he was determined to stay and die even if it killed him.

The world's greatest problem today is the H–Bomb. That's dynamite!

A virgin forest is a place where the hand of man has never set foot.

Hilarious as these excerpts are for the sheer incongruity of their expression, they are also pathetic in the very ineptness which that incongruity inflicts upon their content. That incongruity and that ineptness further reveal that the socially advantaged authors of such handicapped English have fallen victims to semantic deficiency, both in their inadequate segmentation of reality and in their improper image of themselves and the language roles they must assume. This sort of victimization, furthermore, is almost invariably accompanied by the conflict between a naïve interior seriousness of purpose and a sophisticated exterior laughter in effect. It is as though Dogberry and Bottom have inherited center stage to evoke the beatitude of cynical wit and belittling humor in a world of groundlings.

That conflict between interior seriousness and exterior laughter, however, foregrounds this often neglected fact: bad writing can become a better teacher than good writing, *especially when it is recognized as bad.* Why? Because the psychological divorce from bad writing can cause laughter in the student, and laughter is of extreme importance in the development of a sense of proportion and balance. When man first laughed at himself, then he discovered that he indeed does have a soul that sets him apart from the animals, who tend to be enslaved by the inflexible and automatic seriousness with which their genetic inheritance endows them. When students of English composition first laugh at their own writing, or at some deliberately miserable facsimile thereof, then they discover that they are capable of attaining stylistic grace. This discovery, in turn, is the necessary initial phase in their achievement of rhetorical maturity through the overcoming of the semantic deficiency inherent in inadequate segmentation and improper image.

But such a psychological divorce from bad writing is rarer in America than many defenders of the current system of education in the country would suppose. The handicapped English of formal composition crops up everywhere, like the proverbial weeds at harvest time. The lack of rhetorical maturity inherent in semantic deficiency is no respecter of person or status. Indeed it calls clamorous attention to itself in the following brief essays written by black eighth–graders in Auburn, Alabama, on the classic question that ends Frank R. Stockton's short story "The Lady, or the Tiger?"

Once there was princess who had to made a chose of two doors. One door had a lady the other door had a tiger in it. If he chose the door with the tiger the tiger would kill him. If he chose the door with the lady the lady would marry him. He chose the door with the lady in it. And they got married and live happiness very after.

The Lady Tiger

After the man was trial the King put the man in the pen. He had two choice to open one of the door. Because behind one door their were a tiger and behind the other door their were a beatiful lady. The King said if he open the door with the tiger he would be eaten alive. But if he open the door with the lady he would have marry her and live happy ever after.

The Lady Or th Tight

The lady came out of the door because if the tiger came out the would have eaten the Man up. The lady came out because the Man did not get eaten up. The princess told the Man which door the Man was in, Because she didn't want the tiger to eat up the handsome man. The reason she told the man what door the lady was in because she didn't wanted the tiger to eat the man up. The princess wanted the lady to come out so the man to marry the lady. When the man and the lady got married the man came to the castle to see the princess.

"Which One"

Once there was two door, And one of the door there was a lady behind one and a hangory tiger. As the man approached the two door everyone was silent. As he wen't toward the right you could here a pen drop. And he open the door and the greedy tiger came out jumps on the man, and started bitting the man around the throat. The people all left the arena. From then on it was sad.

When the people open the door, the Lady came out with frighten, The princess jump up out of her chair and scream no no, and everyone in the arena cheer with happiness. So the lady came out, and ran to the boy she love.

In addition to their obvious deviations from the norms of so-called "standard" American English, the foregoing five one-paragraph essays (the first and the fifth are untitled) are rhetorically immature and semantically deficient in their lack of analysis of motive, in their wishful thinking and attendant circular reasoning, in their failure to distinguish direct discourse from indirect, in their belaboring of the obvious dilemma by sheer repetition of the story's surface facts, and —above all else—in their terrible inability to expressively develop a true discourse (with a beginning, a middle, and an end) based upon the organization of vividly imagined details. It is as though their young and socially disadvantaged authors had been struck as inarticulate as parrots.

If the five black eighth-graders in Auburn, Alabama, who wrote the foregoing one-paragraph essays on "The Lady, or the Tiger?" can claim social disadvantage as their excuse for handicapped English, then the five white twelfth-graders in Tampa, Florida, who penned the following passages of moral observation on the medieval Latin proverb *Radix malorum est cupiditas,* cannot. They come from middle-class homes, with annual family incomes between twelve thousand and twenty thousand dollars, and attend a so-called "elite" high school.

1.

Love of money brings many a man's downfall. Life forever flows on and the tragic downfall of man flows with it. The story "King

Midas and the Golden Touch" shows an example of cupidity. Have-ing turned his daughter to stone was Midas's downfall. Many a king beggar and thief has had money bring nothing but unhappness.

People have a love for money which is only human nature. The more money you recieve the more you want. "Silas Marner" is an example of the Love of money brings a man's down fall.

 . . . Paul's mother had a love for money but the family was to poor to live in the class they where living in. Paul's father had no luck either. Paul's mother said luck was something you make money with. Possibly she could thing of nothing else but money. Possibly this is why her heart was solid in the center.

2.

"The love of money is the root of evil" is a true but primary form of a statement. It is not so much the love of money itself but the oppurtunity or what it can obtain for the holder. In the beginning man had no money in any form. But still he did evil. Even today in some parts of the world, evil is prevailing not on money itself but its meaning.

Through many of the minds of our teen–agers at this present time has ran thoughts of thieft, srewdness and infinatly others, of ways of maintaining money and the power of it. Many of the crimes both pardonable and unpardonable have been committed for the want of money. . . .

Paul wanting to prove to his mother that he was lucky. But without her know it untill he had filled his need of wealth.

The love for money had caused Pauls downfall and his death. If money can be obtained there is not a human in the world who would not work for it and the positions held by the holder of it. Since time begain posession of a sorce of wealth has constantly been seeked after.

3.

Any person is suceptable to the idea of cupitity, but it also can cause a person's downfall. If, for example, a man and his family had a very low income, and always in need of more money, and has never been able to afford the finer things in life. Then the man gets a better job and a much larger income. Now they can afford more luxuries. Soon the family will not accept what it was like to be poor. Their demand for more money increases. The man can't make enough money to suit his family. This causes him to become very nervous, so he worked harder. Because he works harder he becomes more and more run down, causing him to have a heart attack and he dies, leaving the family with know money and essen-tially the way they started, poor. There greediness and cupitity cause the mans downfall.

4.

The statement "the love for money is the root of evil" has been illustrated again and again thoughout history. We have found examples of though life stories. Like John Dillinger, his down fall was because of his greed for money that made him change to be a gangster and was later killed by the F.B.I.

Paul found that if he rode his rocking–horse hard enough that he could see who would win the race 95% of the time. When he starts this at first he put little money on the horse but he later puts mor money on the horse he has picked. But when his mother finds that she has been giving money she begins to spend it like water. This was to keep the whisperinng that all of them heard most of the time because they had been poor.

5.

Money, no matter what form, is essential to the existance in any society. This form of exchange allows you to buy your bread, your drink, and any other nesesities that may be burdened upon you. However, a constant striving for this commodity can, at times, prove to be disastorous.

An example of this can be seen in what happened to Marie Antoinette. Marie, after the death of her husband Louis XVI, was made queen of France. Because of her lavish tastes she needed large amounts of money to maintaine here exspensive way of life. In order to obtain these large amounts of money she would tax, quite heavily, the peasents of France. The peasent, having taken all the taxation he could and tolerated the neglect on political issues by the queen, revolted and Marie Antoinette lost her head. . . .

Although the essays of these five socially advantaged white twelfth–graders are true discourses (with a beginning, a middle, and an end), they are rhetorically not much more mature than the meager one–paragraph efforts of the five socially disadvantaged black eighth–graders. In fact, the greater ambition inherent in these five essays (only excerpts from which have been quoted) merely serves to betray their basic semantic deficiency in greater detail and at a more leisurely pace. That semantic deficiency, in turn, is stigmatized by such failures at formal written competence as these: "scattergun misspellings" that call distractive attention to the bleeding texture of the mutilated code, egregious grammatical blunders like wrong verb forms, incomplete constructions, improper forms of the possessive, faulty references, and misuses of tense and aspect; damaging rhetorical violations of overall unity, coherence, and emphasis; ludicruous lapses in logic, idiom, and figures of speech; embarrassing wallowing in sententious cliché and self–satisfied sermonizing. So semantically deficient are these five essays that they bear, ironically enough, eloquent witness to the fact that the two chief enemies of man in his attempts to become fully human are simply these: (1) the tyranny of the literalist mind and (2) the fanaticism of the moral will. These two enemies of man have succeeded in making the psyches of the five teen–age authors of these essays as open and as flexible as cannon balls.

EXTENT OF THE PROBLEM

Implicit in the foregoing discussion is the fact that handicapped English, especially in the attribute of semantic deficiency, is a far more widely distributed social phenomenon than is generally suspected. So pervasive indeed is this inability to use the language well that it extends far beyond the inarticulateness of poor black school children, the rhetorical immaturity of advantaged white high school students, the hilarious illogicality of advantaged college students of all races, and the tragicomic written "blunderdom" of adult welfare recipients. Indeed as George Orwell has shown in his classic essay "Politics and the English Language" (1945), dying metaphors, verbal false limbs, pretentious diction, meaningless words, euphemism, and inflated style make even some of the professional writing of Great Britain look like the semantically deficient composition of the socially disadvantaged. Handicapped English, in other words, is no respecter of continents or of international varieties of the language.

Verbal Pollution in Professional Writing

To prove his point about the universality of the problem, Orwell quotes the following five passages as representative samples of English handicapped by both its staleness of imagery and its lack of precision:

1. I am not, indeed, sure whether it is not true to say that the Milton who once seemed not unlike a seventeenth–century Shelley had not become, out of an experience ever more bitter in each year, more alien [*sic*] to the founder of that Jesuit sect which nothing could induce him to tolerate.

Professor Harold Laski (Essay in *Freedom of Expression*)

2. Above all, we cannot play ducks and drakes with a native battery of idioms which prescribes such egregious collocations of vocables as the Basic *put up with* for *tolerate* or *put at a loss* for *bewilder*.

Professor Lancelot Hogben (*Interglossa*)

3. On the one side we have the free personality: by definition it is not neurotic, for it has neither conflict nor dream. Its desires, such as they are, are transparent, for they are just what institutional approval keeps in the forefront of consciousness; another institutional pattern would alter their number and intensity; there is little in them that is natural, irreducible, or culturally dangerous. But *on the other side*, the social bond itself is nothing but the mutual reflection of these self–secure integrities. Recall the definition of love. Is not this the very picture of a small academic? Where is there a place in this hall of mirrors for either personality or fraternity?

Essay on Psychology in *Politics* (New York)

4. All the "best people" from the gentlemen's clubs, and all the frantic fascist captains, united in common hatred of Socialism and bestial horror of the rising tide of the mass revolutionary movement, have turned to acts of provocation, to foul incendiarism, to medieval legends of poisoned wells, to legalize their own destruction of proletarian organizations, and rouse the agitated petty–bourgeoisie to chauvinistic fervour on behalf of the fight against the revolutionary way out of the crisis.

Communist pamphlet

5. If a new spirit *is* to be infused into this old country, there is one thorny and contentious reform which must be tackled, and that is the humanization and galvanization of the B.B.C. Timidity here will bespeak canker and atrophy of the soul. The heart of Britain may be sound and of strong beat, for instance, but the British lion's roar at present is like that of Bottom in Shakespeare's *Midsummer Night's Dream*—as gentle as any sucking dove. A virile new Britain cannot continue indefinitely to be traduced in the eyes or rather ears, of the world by the effete languors of Langham Place, brazenly masquerading as "standard English." When the Voice of Britain is heard at nine o'clock, better far and infinitely less ludicrous to hear aitches honestly dropped than the present priggish, inflated,

inhibited, school–ma'amish arch braying of blameless bashful mew-
ing maidens!

Letter in *Tribune*

As Orwell justifiably claims, each of the five writers from
whom he quotes "either has a meaning and cannot express
it, or he inadvertently says something else, or he is almost
indifferent as to whether his words mean anything or not.
This mixture of vagueness and sheer incompetence is the
most marked characteristic of modern English prose, and
especially of any kind of political writing. As soon as certain
topics are raised, the concrete melts into the abstract and
no one seems able to think of turns of speech that are not
hackneyed: prose consists less and less of *words* chosen for
the sake of their meaning, and more and more of *phrases*
tacked together like the sections of a prefabricated
hen–house."

Since the code used by each of the five authors so heavily
criticized by Orwell is in itself grammatically standard English, then the logic implicit in Orwell's argument surely
results in this conclusion: handicapped English does not
inhere in the code *per se*, but rather in the failure to properly
use the code in the development of the message. When Bernstein (1970), therefore, speaks of restricted and elaborated
codes, he is really speaking of restricted and elaborated *messages*—or the rhetorical mastery of codes.

Eloquence in "Handicapped" English

Nowhere can this basic distinction be better illustrated than
in the brilliant use of so–called "broken" English in the
farewell address of the condemned Bartolomeo Vanzetti
(1888–1927). Indeed the simple eloquence of this immigrant
Italian fishmonger, as reported by Philip D. Strong in the
New York *World* of May 13, 1927, proves that when the soul
is incandescent with its own passion, a man may talk in grammatically handicapped English and still speak a rhetorically
deathless prose (see Weeks, 1958, p. 226):

> If it had not been for these thing, I might live out my life,
> talking at street corners to scorning men. I might have die, unmarked,
> unknown, a failure. Now we are not a failure. This is our career

and our triumph. Never in our full life can we hope to do such
work for tolerance, for joostice, for man's onderstanding of man,
as now we do by an accident.

Our words—our lives—our pains—nothing! The taking of our
lives—lives of a good shoemaker and a poor fish peddler—all! That
last moment belong to us—that agony is our triumph!

So beautiful are these two brief paragraphs by Vanzetti that
only a pompous pedant would object to the ungrammaticality
of plural *these* with singular *thing*, of singular *moment* with
plural *belong*, of the infinitive forms *live* and *die* serving
as past participles, of indicative *can* substituting for subjunc-
tive *could* (in which immediate aspect poses as nonimmediate), and of present *do* working for future *shall do* or
will do. As indicated by Strong's pronunciation spellings of
justice and *understanding*, Vanzetti "talks funny," with a
heavy Italian accent, but he does so with stylistic grace and
artistic polish. Though "broken," his English is actually not
handicapped; it achieves both an adequate segmentation of
reality and a proper image of the self and the language role
it must assume in this hour of political martyrdom.

Victims of Handicapped English

Millions of native speakers of American English, however,
neither speak nor write their language with the same sort
of stylistic grace and artistic polish that characterize Vanzetti's
valedictory statement to reporter Strong. Whether masters
of so-called "standard" grammatical forms or not, these native
speakers of the language fail to achieve an adequate segmentation of reality in their rhetorical control of the message.
Whether culturally deprived and socially disadvantaged or
just the opposite, these native speakers of the language fail
to develop a proper image of themselves and of the various
linguistic roles which they must assume. Semantically
deficient above all else, these native speakers of the language
are the victims of handicapped English. Just how many millions of them there are in the United States today is a matter
for painstaking research. But an extremely conservative
estimate of the number of *hard core* victims of handicapped
English in America runs to between thirty million and fifty
million speakers of the language.

Further intensifications of the problem of the extent of handicapped English in America inhere in the following facts: (1) Socially advantaged and well-educated speakers of the language frequently fall victims to handicapped English through such various expressions of linguistic accident as these: inattention to details, sheer physical fatigue or mental boredom, emotional hyperbole, sloth at revision, overzealous didacticism, literal–mindedness, moral fanaticism. Let it be emphasized that the author of this present study is no exception to such self–induced victimization. (2) The public schools and institutions of higher learning in the United States have failed to properly diagnose the problem; they have therefore failed to offer effective remedies to achieve a solution for it. (3) The big question of liberal linguists on whether "different" equals "inferior" has concentrated an inordinate amount of attention on the code *per se* and an insufficient amount on the rhetorical mastery of the code in the organization and the delivery of the message. In other words, there has been too much professional *talk* about the model and the price of the car, and not enough pragmatic *action* to demonstrate whether indeed the car has an engine and can carry the would–be communicator anywhere worth going. (4) The resultant great debate among liberal linguists at one extreme, a reactionary public at another extreme, and conservative educators somewhere in between, has produced more heat than light on the very terms "different" and "inferior"; a cool appraisal of the various kinds and degrees of relationship between the phenomena signified by the terms has thus become difficult and subject to partisan attack.

A Challenge

But the challenge to make such a cool appraisal of the kinds and degrees of relationship between "different" and "inferior" is both clear and imperative. Clear because no amount of critical obfuscation can hide the fact that handicapped English exists in many forms and at all levels of American society. Imperative because the "semantic pollution" injected into the linguistic environment of the United States by both the users and the abusers of handicapped English threatens the very survival of the Republic. The inflicter of its own cultural deprivation and social disadvantage, handicapped English is perhaps the number one national menace: through its hamburger–guzzling and horse–opera–applauding tastes comes the vulgarization of a world in which George F. Babbitt is the windy and yet inarticulate heir of Shakespeare.

To meet this challenge, the next six chapters will try to draw upon the best available evidence in both theory and empirical fact, ultimately in order to suggest a series of solutions for the various social problems that are connected with handicapped English. And there is no better way to begin meeting this challenge than by undertaking a study of the child and his language.

Chapter 2

THE CHILD AND HIS LANGUAGE

As DWIGHT BOLINGER (1968, Ch. 1) has said, *man was born to speak.* Indeed man's talent for speaking is the one gift that, more than any other, separates him from the animals. Porpoises and chimpanzees, for example, are extremely intelligent, but their intelligence is severely limited by the fact that they cannot talk and therefore cannot abstractly conceptualize or "think." Hence they do not build a culture and fashion a civilization. Only man can do those things (see Nist, 1971a, p. 336), because only man has "the gift of gab." So important is this gift that it means that man became *Homo sapiens* only after he had first become *Homo loquens.* In other words,

$$Homo\ loquens \longrightarrow Homo\ sapiens$$

Since "man speaking" produces "man reasoning," it was a wise Englishman who once said, "How can I tell what I think till I hear what I say!" And since thought is impossible apart from some code to carry that thought, the subject of language is perhaps the most important and fascinating for man to study: it lies closest to his evolution toward a full humanity.

THE CHILD AS RECEIVER AND TRANSMITTER

Competence and Performance

In that evolution toward a full humanity, every child in the United States learns the linguistic medium of his national culture and civilization—that is, American English of some variety or other—by applying his innate *instinct* (or *capacity*) for language–learning to the modeled systems and structures of that linguistic medium in order to achieve both a *competence* and a *performance* (see Chomsky, 1965, pp. 3–62). This relationship among the language to be modeled, the child's innate instinct, and the resultant competence and performance may be illustrated in the following schematic chart (Diagram 1).

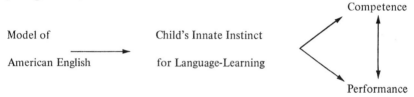

DIAGRAM 1. LANGUAGE-LEARNING.

As the above chart shows, the child's innate instinct (see Lenneberg, 1967, Ch. 4) is like a computer into which is fed the modeled version of American English, both as *abstract systems* and as *concrete structures* generated by those systems. Thus the arrow leading into the child's innate instinct (or capacity) for language–learning emerges in two arrows, one leading to competence and the other leading to performance. The child's competence is his interiorization of the modeled performance into a set of habits that operate by means of the grammatical rules which he has abstracted from the specific version of American English so modeled in the performance. The child's performance is his exteriorization of both the habits and the rules (see Twaddell, 1967) into individual acts of utterance in his specific version of American English. The overwhelming importance of the parental (or some surrogate equivalent) modeling to the child's achievement of his specific version of the language will be discussed in detail in the last third of this chapter, but in the meantime the following observation clamors to be heard: IN THE LINGUISTIC AREA OF THE CHILD'S **GENOTYPICAL** CAPACITY TO LEARN ANY NATURAL LANGUAGE, COMPETENCE TAKES HIERARCHICAL PRECEDENCE OVER PERFORMANCE; IN THE LINGUISTIC AREA OF

THE PARENT'S **PHENOTYPICAL** MODELING OF A
SPECIFIC NATURAL LANGUAGE, PERFORMANCE
TAKES HIERARCHICAL PRECEDENCE OVER COM-
PETENCE.

As Diagram 1 and the foregoing discussion imply, performance is the basis for the abstract interiorization that becomes
the child's competence, and is therefore the ultimate proof
that the child has mastered the habits and the rules of his
language—or failed to do so, which is often the case. But
another look at the schematic chart shows that competence
and performance are mutually interpenetrative; that is why
the arrow between these two terms is double–headed. This
bifurcation indicates that language–learning is an organic
activity, one in which the total union is greater than any mere
mechanical or mathematical summation of its parts. In that
principle of organicity lies much of the mystery, the miracle,
the majesty of man's creativity in his native tongue. And as
Jespersen (1964, p. 122) has indicated, there are times when
nobody can be more creative in English than a child:

> Schuchardt has a story of a little coloured boy in the West Indies
> who said, "It's *three* hot in this room": he had heard *too* = *two*
> and literally wanted to "go one better." According to Mr. James
> Payne, a boy for years substituted for the words *"Hallowed* be Thy
> name," *"Harold* be Thy name." Many children imagine that there
> is a *pole* to mark where the North Pole is, and even (like Helen
> Keller) that polar bears climb the Pole.

To keep such creativity within the bounds of convention,
most adults act as linguistic superegos for their children. One
way in which adults so act is in the simplification of their
own performance for the purpose of helping children to master
the code, both as receivers and as transmitters of it.

Parental Simplification

Since language is absolutely necessary for the building of
a culture and the preservation of a society, and since the
building of a culture and the preservation of a society are
absolutely necessary for the preservation of the individual
(see Hertzler, 1965, Ch. 1), American adults are—or should
be—deeply involved in the transmission of English to their
children. As Bolinger (1968, p. 4) has demonstrated, in that

transmission parents tend to simplify the programming of the child's innate instinct (or capacity) for language–learning in the following six ways: (1) by overarticulation, (2) by exaggerated intonation, (3) by slower pacing in the rate of speaking, (4) by use of simple sentence structures, (5) by avoidance of substitute words, and (6) by repetition of key words and phrases. These six ways of simplification may be illustrated as follows:

Overarticulation

MOTHER: Would you like a pea–nut but–ter and jel–ly sand–wich, dear?

CHILD: Yes, Mother. I like pea–nut but –ter and jel–ly.

Exaggerated Intonation

MOTHER: Daddy's going to take us to the *beeaach!* Won't that be *fuunn?*

CHILD: Yes, Mother. I like the *beeaach!* That's *fuunn!*

Slower Pacing

MOTHER: *(Slowly)* Can you say, "Daddy's———go-ing——bye-bye——to—Phila–del–phia?

CHILD *(Slowly, in imitation of Mother)* Daddy's ——go-ing——bye-bye——to——Phila–del–phia.

Simple Sentence Structures

MOTHER: Will the big bad wolf eat up Grandma?

CHILD: No, Mother; Grandma will hide in the closet.

MOTHER: But big bad wolves eat up little Grandmas.

CHILD: Not in *Little Red Riding Hood.*

MOTHER: You are just too smart.

Avoidance of Substitute Words

MOTHER: Where is your train? Show me your train.

CHILD: *(Showing his train)* Here is my train, Mother.

MOTHER: Very good. Now where are your blocks? Show
me your blocks?

CHILD: *(Showing his blocks)* Here are my blocks, Mother.

Repetition

MOTHER: Say, "Night–night, Teddy Bear. Night–night,
Teddy Bear."

CHILD: Night–night, Teddy Bear. Night–night, Teddy
Bear.

MOTHER: Say, "Night–night, choo–choo train. Night–night,
choo–choo train."

CHILD: Night–night, choo–choo train. Night–night,
choo–choo train.

In the foregoing illustrations, overarticulation produces a
striking variation in the pronunciation of the key ingredients
of the sandwich: *pea–nut but–ter* and *jel–ly*. In similar
manner, exaggerated intonation heightens the pitch and pro-
longs the articulation of both *beeaach* and *fuunn* to show
that they are the emotion–evoking words in the discourse.
The child, of course, responds to them by repeating their
heightened pitch and prolonged articulation, just as the child
responds by imitating the mother's slower pacing in speaking
rate in the next little drama. Even as this slower pacing is
a help to the child's understanding of the statement, so is
the use of simple sentence structures in the dialogue about
Grandma and the big bad wolf. As is obvious from her speech,
the mother avoids saying *Will Grandma be eaten up by the
big bad wolf?* and *But good little Grandmas are eaten up
by big bad wolves*—precisely because constructions in the
passive voice are more difficult than those in the active, and
she is engaged in the process of simplifying English for her
child. So is the mother who avoids using substitute words
like *it* for *train* and *them* for *blocks*. Such simplification by
avoidance of substitute words is closely linked to the last
illustrated means of making the child's learning of English
easier—namely, repetition. As a matter of fact, repetition as
a method of word–formation in English is known as *reduplication*. Reduplication, in turn, is one of the central features

of "baby talk," as heard in the use of such terms as *pooh–pooh* and *wee–wee* and *tinkle–tinkle* as euphemisms associated with the discipline of toilet–training. When speaking with their young children, most parents use reduplication and word– and phrase–repetition as a means of simplifying the acquisition of the language. As will be shown later in this chapter and especially in Chapter 6 ("Causes of Handicapped English"), an undue amount of "baby talk" on the part of parents may result in the linguistic handicapping of their children. Unless used carefully, simplification of English can produce a kind of Laurel–and–Hardy system of transmission, overdone in effort and comic in effect.

Stages of Acquisition

Running parallel with the desire of parents to simplify the learning of English is their children's evolutionary growth in both competence and performance. As Jespersen (1964, p. 103) has indicated, "A child's linguistic development covers three periods—the screaming time, the crowing or babbling time, and the talking time. But the last is a long one, and must again be divided into two periods—that of the 'little language,' the child's own language, and that of the common language or language of the community. In the former the child is linguistically an individualist, in the latter he is more and more socialized." Drawing upon the research of Carroll (1960), Lenneberg (1967, Ch. 4), and Braine (1971), psycholinguists can analyze the three periods in a child's language development, spoken of by Jespersen, as follows:

1. THE SCREAMING TIME. From birth to about 2–3 months the child exercises his vocal apparatus and lets his immediate physical needs be known in cries which most mothers can distinguish as indicating such things as discomfort, pain, hunger, anger, and fear.
2. THE CROWING OR BABBLING TIME. From about 3 months to 10 months the child continues to exercise his vocal apparatus in a kind of *phatic communion* with the world, in which he produces nonphonemic sounds in his attempt to express his emotive function. These sounds, of course, occur in random and nonsequential order—that is, they do not add up to the transmission of any English words.
3. THE TALKING TIME. From about 10–12 months to four years

the child is in Jespersen's "little language" phase of learning English. During this time the child comes to master, in both reception and transmission, the distinctive structures that relate to the phonology, morphology, and syntax of his language. That is, he learns both word–forms and word–orders and the distinctive sound shapes of both. In the period between about four years and eight years, the child deepens his awareness of "the common language or language of the community" and moves steadily from *egocentric* speech to *socially directed* speech (see Piaget, 1926).

These, then, in broad outline are the three times of a child's linguistic development.

Since the talking time is obviously the most important for the study of a child's stages of acquisition of English, it must be looked at in some measure of detail. Including the period of 6 to 10 months in the crowing or babbling time as a key period of transition first to language comprehension and then to language transmission, the six central stages of a child's acquisition of English run as follows (see Bolinger, 1968, pp. 4–7):

1. INTONATIONAL. In this stage (ca. 6–10 months) the child has no vocabulary or wide range of phonemes (basic class units of *distinctive* English sounds), but he does begin to understand intonational contours as they relate to *sentence sense*. As Lenneberg (1967, p. 279) says, "Perceptually, the child reacts also to whole patterns rather than to small segments, and so the intonation pattern of a sentence is the more immediate input rather than individual phonemes." Gradually (ca. 8–10 months) the child learns how to intonationally state, request, question, and exclaim—even though the so–called "gibberish" he babbles is not English (Nist, November 1969, p. 6).

2. HOLOPHRASTIC. In this stage (ca. 10–18 months) the utterance equals the thing, as in *Mama, Dada, Mapank, Dadapank, Whassat?* and *Allgone!* During this stage the child knows no syntax; the world, therefore, is the deed. Or in Chomskan terminology, the child rewrites the sentence as the word: S→W (see Lenneberg, 1967, p. 292).

3. ANALYTIC. In this stage (ca. 18–24 months) the child begins to speak true sentences, even if primitively based upon what Braine (1963) has called functor "pivot" words. The child, that is, begins to play with *substitution*, thereby creating *enate* constructions (those of analogous structure, but of different meanings, as in *John walks* but *Mary runs*) generated from partially mastered models—for example: *Mama pank, Baby pank, Dada kiss, Baby kiss, Mama*

go bye–bye, Dada go bye–bye. Enation, or the process of making analogous structures with different meanings, is therefore a key characteristic of the analytic stage in the child's learning of English. Even in two–word statements, as Lenneberg (1967, p. 293) has indicated, functional distinctions are emerging, as in such nonrandom concatenations as these: *find it, fix it, drink it, here sock, here milk, here allgone, more wawa, more nut, more up.*

4. SYNTACTIC. In this stage (ca. 24–36 months) the child invents a variety of sentence types. The child, that is, begins to play with *transformation,* or the process of deriving secondary structure(s) from primary or basic one(s). Since *singulary* transforms—those derived from only *one* underlying basic structure—emerge during the third year of the child's life (see Braine, 1971, pp. 40–44), it is during this period that topic–comment constructions become true subject–predicate constructions and that the negative, the imperative, the yes–no interrogative, the *wh*–word interrogative, and the verb–contraction constructions become permanent additions to the child's growing syntactic repertoire. It is during the syntactic stage that such statements as the following delight parental ears: *No more milk, No doggie fun play, Get train on tracks, Give doggie baf, He gots to* (for *He's got to*), *Mommy come home? Why not we can't dance? Why not baby eat? Why you won't let me?* The absence of verb auxiliaries and the indicative word–order characterize most of the child's questions in this stage.

5. STRUCTURAL. In this stage (ca. 36–48 months) the child learns how to make larger units from smaller units, how to set smaller arrangements within larger arrangements, as in *Baby sit in Daddy chair, He said it was locked, This truck is painted red, That horsie got tied up, I got left behind, His son died by the war, It already has sand on by Jonathan* (see Braine, 1971, pp. 43–44), *I want an icecream cone at Dipper Dan's, I'm going swimming when we get to Florida, Will Mama Risa dance with me? I had a good time at nursery school today* (personal observation). Beginning with pre–passive forms like *This is torn,* the child learns to make *agnate* constructions (those of different structure, but of similar meaning, as in *John hit Bill* and *Bill was hit by John*) and develops his ability to create *generalized* transforms—that is, derived sentences based on two or more underlying kernel or basic sentences, as in all coordinating and subordinating constructions. (For a thorough discussion of both enation and agnation, see Gleason, 1965, pp. 196–221.) In a process of overlearning that turns competence rules into performance habits (see Carroll, 1971), the child deepens his mastery of the structural stage in speech until he is about eight years old (Carol Chomsky, 1969, would extend this period for mastering some constructions until about age ten); in writing, until he is about fourteen (see Gregory and Tingle, 1967, *passim*).

6. STYLISTIC. In this stage (4 to 8 years) the child develops a repertoire of constructions to choose from—for example: kernel or basic sentences; singulary transforms; generalized transforms of restrictive modification upon noun phrases; elliptical deletion transforms. Since elaborate generalized transforms of nonrestrictive modification are the formal constructions of mature English composition, most often found in print, they are among the last to gain entrance into the repertoire of choice. Individual acts of choice, of course, are largely determined by the child's discourse needs and the constructions that are best suited to the emphasis of his message: pragmatic or esthetic, literal or figurative, seriously sincere or mockingly sarcastic. If the child joins in on this kind of sing–song, then he has arrived at the stylistic stage: *Johnny's got a girl! Johnny's got a girl! Nyah–nyah nyah–nyah nyeah–nyeah!* Since it is in the stylistic stage when the child usually begins to read and write and since it is in this stage when he truly "overlearns" his spoken language, it cannot be too strongly stressed that the child generally continues—unless socially disadvantaged by linguistic deprivation—to deepen his mastery of the stylistic stage, in both speech and writing, until the advent of adulthood. If he is extremely intelligent and sensitive to his native English and to the rhetorical strategies and tactics of dealing with his audience, then his spoken and written mastery of the stylistic stage continues to grow and develop throughout his entire lifetime. Shakespeare is perhaps the most eminent example of such growth and development in the entire history of the language.

These, then, are the six central stages in the child's acquisition of English. They are alike, moreover, in that they are all *grammatical* and/or *rhetorical.* While the child is passing through these stages, he is also engaged in mastering various phases in his acquisition of English phonology.

Phonological Phases

Parallel with the foregoing six stages in the child's grammatical and rhetorical acquisition of English are five phases in the *ease of discrimination* by which the child learns to master the pronunciation of English phonology (see Leopold, 1961). These five phases may be named and characterized according to their relative difficulty as follows: (1) *voicing,* the easiest phase of articulation for the child to master; (2) *nasalization,* the next most easy phase; (3) *friction,* a moderately difficult phase; (4) *duration,* the next to the most difficult phase; and (5) *point of articulation,* the most difficult phase for the child to master. Since each of these phases is of great importance to any understanding of the child's phonological development, each one must be examined in detail.

First of all, there is voicing—the resonant hum heard in the pronunciation of the nine simple vowels (see Trager and Smith, 1957, p. 27) of Modern American English: the /i/ in *pit*, the /e/ in *pet*, the /ae/ in *pat*, and the /a/ in *pot;* the /ɨ/ in *just* (adv.) and the /ə/ in *just* (adj.); the /u/ in *pull*, the /o/ in *pole*, and the /ɔ/ in *pall*. This same kind of resonant hum may also be heard in the following fifteen consonant sounds of the language: the initial /b/ in *buy*, /m/ in *my*, /v/ in *vie*, /ð/ in *thy*, and /d/ in *die;* the initial /z/ in *zoo*, /n/ in *new*, /l/ in *Lou*, /r/ in *rue*, /j/ in *Jew*, /g/ in *goo*, /y/ in *you*, and /w/ in *woo;* and the terminal /ž/ in *rouge* and /ŋ/ in *sing*. This resonant hum, or voicing, of course, is absent in the remaining nine consonant sounds of Modern American English (see Trager and Smith, 1957, pp. 29–35): the initial /p/ in *pie*, /f/ in *fie*, /θ/ in *thigh*, /t/ in *tie*, and /s/ in *sigh;* the initial /c/ in *chew*, /š/ in *chew*, /h/ in *who*, and /k/ in *coo*. Since vowel sounds do not encounter any obstruction in their articulation, they are easier for the child to articulate than are any of the consonants. Voicing is thus a redundant factor in the vowels. In the consonants, however, voicing is a product of *laxness* in articulation. Such laxness, as distinct from the *tension* needed to articulate /p f θ t s c š h k/, means that voiced English consonants are easier for the child to learn. As Ervin and Miller (1968, p. 73) have remarked, the child normally acquires "initial consonants before final or medial consonants, and consonantal contrasts often apply to initial position before other positions." With the vowels, of course, the child normally masters the classic triangular opposition of high–front /i/ with high–back /u/ with low–central /a/ before any other system of vocalic contrasts.

The second phonological phase in the child's ease of discrimination is nasalization or the process of articulating consonant sounds through the nose. In Modern American English the three nasal sounds are the terminal /m/ in *ram*, /n/ in *ran*, and /ŋ/ in *rang*. These nasals form a basic contrast with their voiced *oral* opposites—namely, the terminal /b/ in *rib*,

/d/ in *rid,* and /g/ in *rig.* The orals, that is, are formed in the same respective regions of the mouth as are the nasals, but these same orals are *not* released through the nose. Since voicing and nasalization are the easiest features for the child to master in his learning of English phonology, it is hence no accident that *Mama* is one of his first holophrastic utterances.

The third phase in the child's ease of discrimination is friction, or the process of articulating consonant sounds by partially obstructing the flow of breath through the mouth, but without quite shutting it off. Frictional obstruction characterizes the following phonemes (minimum class units of significant sound) in Modern American English: the initial /f/ in *fie,* /v/ in *vie,* /θ/ in *thigh,* and /s/ in *sigh;* the initial /z/ in *zoo,* /c/ in *chew,* /š/ in *shoe,* /j/ in *Jew,* and /h/ in *who;* and the terminal /ž/ in *garage.* Just as many a foreigner has trouble with English /θ/ and tends to make it /t/ and with English /ð/ and tends to make it /d/, so many a child generally finds it somewhat difficult to articulate the English sounds of friction. That is why many a child says *tee* for *see, Whassa?* for *What's that? kittut* for *kisses, fif* for *fifth,* and *el* for *elves.* Mastery of the consonantal sounds of friction, then, is a middle phase in his growth in the ease of discrimination.

The next most difficult phonological phase for the child is duration, or the redundant factor of tension in the vowels. As distinct from the simple and so-called "short" vowels, duration produces the complex and so-called "long" vowels (see Trager and Smith, 1957, pp. 20–26) in Modern American English, or the vocalic sounds that most adults make when they articulate such words as *beet* /biyt/, *boot* /buwt/, *bait* /beyt/, *boat* /bowt/, *bite* /bayt/, *bout* /bawt/, and *boy* /bɔy/. Since these representative complex and so-called "long" vowels are formed by the application of tension on the simple vowel by means of a semivowel glide (either /y/, /w/, or /h/), their duration is rather difficult for the child to master at first. That is one reason why a youngster will often call a *bomb* a *bum* or a *light* a *lot,* or say *ba–ba* for *bye–bye* and *rod* for *ride.* In Modern American English the following principles are governors of the length of human articulation:

(1) stressed syllables tend to have more duration than do unstressed syllables; (2) stressed syllables with complex vowels as their peaks tend to have more duration than do stressed syllables with simple vowels as their peaks; (3) stressed syllables ending on *continuants* tend to have more duration than stressed syllables ending on *stops* (/p b t d k g/) or on *affricates* (/c j/); (4) stressed syllables ending on *voiced* continuants (/m v ð z n l r ž y ʍw/) tend to have more duration than stressed syllables ending on *voiceless* continuants (/f θ s š h/); (5) stressed syllables under the intonation of high emotive function or rhetorical emphasis tend to have more duration than do stressed syllables under the intonation of low emotive function or no rhetorical emphasis.

Just as the child has trouble in mastering the five principles governing duration, so he has difficulty in gaining control over the point of articulation in his transmission of messages in English—in fact, the most difficulty of all. By *point of articulation* is meant the exact spot where the tongue strikes or where the breath is released when an English phonemic sound is formed. These spots are the *lips*, which form the *labials* /p b m/; the *lips and teeth together*, which form the *labiodentals* /f v/; *between the teeth rows*, which forms the *interdentals* /θð/; *on the dental ridge*, which forms the *alveolars* /t s d z n l/; *on the hard palate* moving toward the dental ridge, which forms the alveopalatals /c š r j ž/; *on the soft palate*, which forms the *palatals* /h k g y/; and *on the velum* or way back in the throat, which forms the *velars* /ʍw/. Because the child has the most trouble with the point of articulation in the transmission of his English sounds, it is the phonological phase in his mastery of the ease of discrimination that gives him the most difficulty. Thus a freckle-faced tike will often say *fwock* for *flock*, *twee* for *three*, *swits* for *switch*, *sawn* for *song*, *mouf* or *moush* for *mouth*, and *jettut* for *lettuce*. As Leopold (1961) has demonstrated, the child tends to substitute stops for fricatives (/p/ for /f/, /t/ for /s/ and /θ/, /d/ for /z/ and /ð/ etc.), and generally has a rough time mastering all the variations of the liquids /l r/. Complete control of /l/ usually does not come before 36 months; of /r/, usually not before 48 months. But then adult speakers of English from the Orient have a tendency to confuse these two sounds throughout their entire lives, producing such delicious errors as *flied lice* for *fried rice.*

From the foregoing discussion, then, it is apparent that the child who grows up speaking Modern American English as his native tongue tends to make mistakes in his articulation of the language *in reverse order* of the ease of discrimination. He makes his mistakes, that is, as follows:

Incidence of Pronunciation Errors

1. *Point of articulation:* cause of most errors.
2. *Duration:* cause of next most errors.
3. *Friction:* cause of medium amount of errors.
4. *Nasalization:* cause of next fewest errors.
5. *Voicing:* cause of fewest errors.

As for the child's acquisition of the various local features within the ease of discrimination that produces the incidence of pronunciation errors, it is fairly certain at this time that the child learns the sound patterns of his native English according to the main outlines depicted in the brilliant phonological theory of Roman Jakobson (1962). In Jakobson's views (see Jakobson, Fant, and Halle, 1963), Modern American English—like all other natural languages on earth—operates phonologically by means of a series of *binary* contrasts: for example, vocality *vs* consonantality, orality *vs* nasality, laxness *vs* tension. These binary contrasts, in turn, become the "distinctive acoustic features" (see Chomsky and Halle, 1968, pp. 176-177) of the language. Of course the child gradually absorbs his native American English phonology by learning to *discriminate* those contrasts that are truly phonemic in effect—commencing with the grossest contrasts (e.g., vocality *vs* consonantality) and finishing with the most delicate of contrasts (e.g., stridency *vs* mellowness in the fricatives). Although no definitive study of the child's step-by-step mastery of the distinctive acoustic features as yet exists, the following hypotheses about that mastery seem to be tenable (Ervin and Miller, 1968, p. 73):

> (a) The vowel–consonant contrast is one of the earliest, if not the earliest, contrast [sic] for all the children. (b) A stop-continuant

contrast is quite early for all children. The continuant is either a fricative (e.g., /f/) or a nasal (e.g., /m/). (c) When two consonants differing in place of articulation but identical in manner of articulation exist, the contrast is labial *vs* dental (e.g., /p/ *vs* /t/, /m/ *vs* /n/). (d) Contrasts in place of articulation precede voicing contrasts. (e) Affricates (ch, j) and liquids (1, r) do not appear in the early systems. (f) In the vowels, a contrast between low and high (e.g., /a/ and /i/) precedes front *vs* back (e.g., /i/ and /u/). (g) Consonant clusters such as /st/ and /tr/ are generally late.

Morphophonemics

Despite his errors in learning the phonology of Modern American English, the child nevertheless comes rather rapidly to master the regular ways in which the rules of the language make the plural forms of nouns and the past–tense forms of verbs (see Berko, 1958). In the terminology of linguistics, the child masters the *morphophonemics* (the varying sound shapes that a basic unit of English meaning may take within different phonemic environments) of his language by following the ways in which his elders mount a pattern of regular convention upon a pattern of regular arbitrariness:

MOTHER: *(Holding up a drawing)* Now this is a *Wig–Wug*. If there were two of him, what would they be called?

CHILD: They would be called *Wig–Wug*/z/.

MOTHER: Very good. *(Holding up a new drawing)* Now this is a *Wick–Wack*. If there were three of him, what would they be called?

CHILD: They would be called *Wick–Wack*/s/.

MOTHER: Very good. *(Holding up another new drawing)* Now this is a *Winch–Wunch*. If there were four of him, what would they be called?

CHILD: They would be called Winch-Wunch/ɨz/.

MOTHER: Excellent! You got them all right, my dear.

As has just been illustrated, the child in the foregoing dramatic sequences has demonstrated his mastery of the *allomorphs* (the varying phonemic or significant sound shapes which a *morpheme* or basic unit of meaning may take, according to the phonological demands of its immediate environment) of the regular plural in Modern American English. These allomorphs, of course, run as follows:

Allomorphs of the Regular Plural in English
/s/ in voiceless, nonsibilant environments
/z/ in voiced, nonsibilant environments
/ɨz/ in all sibilant environments: /s z c š ž/

In an analogous manner, the child learns the allomorphs of
the regular past tense in his language as follows:

Allomorphs of the Regular Preterit in English
/t/ after all voiceless consonants except /t/
/d/ after all voiced consonants except /d/
/ɨd/ after the previous exceptions: /t d/

Just as the child learns to master both the plural forms of
English nouns and the preterit forms of its verbs, so he also
learns to master the basic sentence types and the intonation
patterns that accompany them. In fact, by the time he enters
the first grade, at about age six, he is a linguistic adult in
the *spoken* version of Modern American English.

How has the six–year–old child arrived at this kind of linguistic sophistication? By an application of imitation, demonstration, circumlocution, and translation. By responding to
his parents' simplification of English through overarticulation, exaggerated intonation, slower pacing of speaking
rate, use of simple sentence structures, avoidance of substitute
words, and repetition of key words and phrases. By passing
through the intonational, holophrastic, analytic, syntactic,
structural, and stylistic stages of language acquisition. By
learning to regularize the morphophonemics of English as
an end result of his development in the ease of discrimination
among such key transmission features as voicing, nasalization,
friction, duration, and point of articulation. In short, the child
has learned his native American English through an *informal*
daily immersion in it. And of all the ways to learn (e.g., *formal,*
technical), the informal is the best; it places *the least burden*
of self–consciousness upon the learner.

THE CHILD AS CONCEPTUALIZER

If the child were no more than a receiver and a transmitter
of English, then he would be little better than a parrot or

a computer. The child, however, is also a *conceptualizer* in language. What he hears and says, that is, relates to *meaning*, to the encoding and the decoding of it. In other words, from the moment of birth the human consciousness of the child *experiences* the stimuli of the world about him and then *differentiates* and *associates* those stimuli into *categories of thought* that will eventually seek *expression* by means of words, sentences, and the rhetorical skills that govern the organization of a discourse (see Vigotsky, 1961).

CONTINUUM OF EXPRESSIVENESS. As J.N. Hook (April 1966) has indicated, the child develops in a *continuum of expressiveness* that occurs in this order: (1) experiences, or the sensory receptions and emotional perceptions of the child; (2) *differentiation and association,* or the logical separating of unlikes from unlikes and the grouping of likes with likes into categories of ever–increasing abstraction; (3) *words,* or the referential assignment of a relationship between vocal symbols (and eventually their written abstractions) and objects in the world about the child; (4) *sentences,* or the grammatical assignment of a relationship between vocal symbols and vocal symbols, which ultimately assigns a relationship among the objects designated by the vocal symbols (and eventually their written abstractions); and (5) *rhetoric,* or the stylistic control of words, sentences, and larger units of discourse for the sake of either informing the mind or influencing the behavior of the addressee.

Stages of Conceptual Development

Within this continuum of expressiveness, the child develops his ability to conceptualize through three distinct stages. As first named and characterized by Piaget (1926), these three stages (see Piaget and Inhelder, 1969) of the child's conceptual development run as follows:

1. PRE–OPERATIONAL. In this stage (from birth to about 5–6 years) the child grows in his ability to represent the external world by means of vocal symbols. His main concerns are with *manipulating things* and *attaching names* to them (see Swain and Gregory, 1967, p. 92).

2. CONCRETE OPERATIONS. In this stage (from 5–6 years to 12–14 years, depending upon the rate of maturation) the child grows in

his ability to *manipulate symbols internally.* No longer dependent upon tangible manipulation of things or upon trial–and–error action, the child can now "think through" a problem. In other words, he becomes able to structure experience. But as Bruner (1963) indicates, the child still cannot deal successfully with possibilities that are not actually before him. He cannot *systematically* go beyond the range of information at his disposal in order to describe or prophesy what else might occur (see Swain and Gregory, 1967, pp. 92–93). In the terminology of James Moffett (1968, p. 35), the child can *record* what is happening, *report* what happened, and *generalize* what happens, but he still cannot *theorize* what may happen.

3. FORMAL OPERATIONAL. In this stage (from 12–14 years onward, depending upon the rate of maturation) the child is at last able to *reason by hypothesis,* to *manipulate abstractions*—in short, able to engage fully in "displaced speech." In the terminology of Moffett (1968, p. 35), the child can now theorize what may happen (see also Swain and Gregory, 1967, p. 93).

As Piaget and others have indicated, the thought processes of the child in the pre–operational stage tend to be *syncretic,* whereas in the formal operational stage they tend to be *analytic* or a mixture of the two forms. Regardless of the method or methods underlying the thought processes of the child, these three stages in his conceptual development are so important that they demand further attention.

PRE–OPERATIONAL STAGE. The pre–operational stage of the child's conceptualization runs from birth to about 5–6 years. As Carroll (1961, p. 339) has indicated, in this stage the child tends to *communicate with one person at a time.* As Gesell and Ilz (1959), Van Riper (1954), and others have fully documented, the child begins expressing his attempts at conceptualization by vocalizing to his toys, in a kind of phatic communion, at the age of six months. Mediating all experience through his language, the child grows from having a vocabulary of about five words at one year to having a vocabulary of 50 to 300 words at the end of his second year. At the age of two, the child tends to verbalize his immediate experience, to refer to himself by name, and to soliloquize. His single–word communications *stand for a complete thought*—that is, his cognitive and interpretive ability outstrips his articulatory skill. Even though the two–year–old learns to place classes of words in grammatical sequence through imitating the performance of his elders, his sentences are nevertheless *condensed:* they consist primarily of words that carry full referential meaning (see Church, 1961), as in *Doggie* and *White* for *There is a doggie; the doggie is white.*

As Young (1941) has indicated, during the third year the child begins to *use structural markers* (e.g., articles, prepositions, inflectional forms) as a conceptual movement toward establishing syntactical and therefore logical relationships. By using faulty analogy and the principle of regularization, of course, the child commits such word–form errors as these: *mans* for *men, comed* for *came, funner* for *more fun,* and *he gots to* for *he's got to.* Such errors are really an indication of the child's innovative intelligence and not an indictment of his lack thereof.

As the child enters his fourth year and all during it, according to Erwin and Lee (1964), he increases his use of pronouns over nouns and further extends his mastery over verbs, adjectives, prepositions, and conjunctions. By the end of the fourth year the superior child, at least, has come to use almost all types of English sentences, and by four and a half he can use all the parts of speech and all the inflections of his immediate language environment. Between the age of four and five, this same superior child exhibits a *transmission* vocabulary of 1500 to 2500 words and a *reception* vocabulary of about twice that range. The child, that is, can decode far more meanings than he can encode. By the time he enters the first grade, the superior child has a transmission vocabulary of 5000 to 8000 words and a reception vocabulary of 10,000 to 16,000 words. In extremely rare instances, some exceptionally intelligent and culturally advantaged first–graders can understand, within properly prepared contexts, close to 20,000 words.

Yet despite the child's phenomenal growth in mastery of ' the English lexicon during the pre–operational stage of conceptual development, he still remains a captive of *egocentric,* as distinct from *socially–directed,* speech. The term *egocentric,* first coined by Piaget (1926), does not signify its "popular" or "moral" meaning—i.e., utter selfishness—but rather what Vigotsky (1961) has come to interpret as the *per-*

sonal point of view, or what Piaget and Inhelder (1969, p. 119) have characterized as "a total lack of differentiation between social behavior and concentration on individual action." In the words of Piaget and Inhelder (1969, pp. 120–121), *egocentricity* means that "the speech of subjects between four and six (observed in situations in which children work, play, and speak freely) is not intended to provide information, ask questions, etc. (that is, it is not socialized language), but consists rather of monologues or 'collective monologues' in the course of which everyone talks to himself without listening to the others (that is, egocentric language.)" As both Piaget (1926) and Vigotsky (1961) have demonstrated, so long as the child remains a captive of egocentric speech he tends to speak mainly in the present tense and primarily about things that are immediately present in his context situation. He also tends to confuse himself with his environment, the real with the unreal, and the animate with the inanimate. Dominated by "quasi–magical attitudes" (see Piaget and Inhelder, 1969, p. 111), the child cannot yet engage in true conversation, in the genuine give–and–take exchange of information. He operates, as Moffett (1968, p. 39) indicates, by means of *interior dialogue*, or the structures of "inner speech."

According to Moffett (1968, p. 40), "In interior dialogue we have subjective, spontaneous, inchoate beginnings of drama (what is happening), narrative (what happened), exposition (what happens), and argumentation (what may happen)." These beginnings, however, are usually full of frustration for the child, simply because, as recorded in Gregory and Tingle (1967, p. 101), the structures of inner speech are different from those of external speech: "greatly condensed, with subject omitted, only predication and words that carry meaning preserved. This inner speech, then, is thought itself—concerned with semantics, not with phonetics or syntax. Because the structure of inner speech is different from that of external speech, the [child] may experience great difficulty in expressing his thought, in translating his inner speech into external speech."

In summary, therefore, during the pre–operational stage

of his conceptual development the child is basically a recorder of what is happening and perhaps of what has happened, but at times unsteadily so, rather frustratedly so. He cannot as yet systematically report, generalize, or theorize.

CONCRETE OPERATIONS STAGE. Entering the concrete operations stage of conceptual development at about 5–6 years, depending upon the rate of maturation, the child has come to master the following statement hierarchy, as outlined in Bereiter and Englemann (1966, pp. 128–136):

> 1. *First–order statements.* These statements conform to this general pattern: This is a(n) _____ . In other words, the child's syntax is able to point out or designate some object in his context situation. The function of first–order statements is thus basically a *naming* one, as in: *This is an apple. This is a ball. This is a cat.*
>
> 2. *Second–order statements of polar concept.* These statements conform to this general pattern: This _____ is _____ , wherein the qualifier following *is* has an opposite, as in: *This dog is big. That dog is small. This noise is loud. That noise is soft.*
>
> 3. *Second–order statements of a nonpolar concept that is shared by only some of the members of the identity class.* These statements conform to this general pattern: This _____ is _____ , wherein the qualifier following *is* does not have an opposite shared by all the members of the identity class, as in: *This dog is white. That dog is brown. This dog is in the yard. That dog is on a leash.*
>
> 4. *Second–order statements of a nonpolar concept that is shared by all members of the identity class.* These statements conform to this general pattern: This _____ is _____ , wherein the qualifier not only does not have an opposite shared by all members of the identity class, but also does apply to all members of the class so designated, as in: *This dog is an animal. This dog is a mammal. This dog is four–legged.*

As the foregoing illustrations show, all second–order statements have the same basic structure, but not the same basic conceptualization—surely, a lesson in the danger of trying to causally relate form and meaning in any simplistic manner. Just as first–order statements *specify,* so second–order statements *qualify.* First–order statements, that is, are associated with the first major function of any English sentence—namely, *identification.* Second–order statements, on the other hand, are associated with the second major function of any English sentence—namely, *predication.*

As the child comes to master the syntactical processes of specifying and identifying, of qualifying and predicating, he deepens his control of the concrete operations stage of his conceptual development. How? By means of what Piaget (1926) has called *accommodation* and *assimilation*. As Hunt (1961, p. 258) has indicated, "In any given situation, the first response of the child is one of those behavioral structures (schemata) already present from past assimilation. What variations in the environment do is to force the child to cope with [these variations], and, in the coping, to modify the structures (schemata). This latter is accommodation, and the modifications are then assimilated. . . ." As the hierarchy of statements moves, for example, from first–order to second–order or from polar to nonpolar conceptualization, the child accommodates the stimuli of the new structures and/or concepts by means of the schemata of his past linguistic behavior, internalizes them, and eventually assimilates them so that what he understands in reception he can eventually make others understand in transmission. This organic–like relationship among the child, his environment, and his use of English may be called *conceptual growth* and can be schematized, much in the manner of language–learning (see p. 39), as shown in Diagram 2 below.

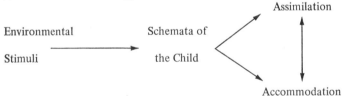

DIAGRAM 2. CONCEPTUAL GROWTH.

As illustrated in the foregoing diagram, environmental stimuli are fed into the schemata of the child, to be accommodated at one level and assimilated at another. In relating this diagram to the previous one on language–learning (Diagram 1), the psycholinguist can say that the environmental stimuli are to the modeled version of Modern American English as the schemata of the child are to his innate instinct (or capacity) for language–learning—that is, as accommodation is to his performance and as assimilation is to his competence. What this series of relationships means, of course, is that *as the child increases his capacity as a receiver and a transmitter of English, he also increases his capacity to abstract and therefore to conceptualize.* And as the child increases his capacity to conceptualize, he also increases his capacity to extend the rhetorical range of his discourse, both earlier in speaking and later in writing. It is in the stage of concrete operations, especially, that the child moves on from being a mere recorder of drama (what is happening) to becoming first a reporter of narrative (what happened) and then a generalizer of exposition (what happens).

According to Carroll (1961, p. 339), in the concrete operations stage of conceptual growth, which lasts until about 12 to 14 years, depending upon the rate of maturation, the child *learns to communicate with groups.* Learning to read, write, and compose in this stage of conceptual growth, the child gradually increases his ability to accurately express logic relationships and to make transformation variations within the basic sentence patterns of English (Loban, 1963). By the time the child is seven years old he should be able to relate an experience *in chronological order*—an act which moves him from mere recording to more elaborate reporting.

Through grades 1 to 6, or from about age 6 to 12 years, the child deepens his control of narration and completes the transition from *personal* writing (mainly narration of private experience gained at first hand) to *functional* writing (mainly exposition based on reading, or public experience gained at second hand). As McCarthy (1967, p. 130) has demonstrated, second–graders devote most of their attention to discussing their own activities or those which go on in their own homes. Fourth–graders, on the other hand, are about midway in their transition from the use of immediate experience to the use of vicariously acquired information. Sixth–graders, by way of contrast, spend most of their psychic energy on discussing information which has come to them vicariously, most often through their own reading.

Somewhere around the age of 12, about the beginning of the seventh grade, the child fully enters functional writing. When he does so, of course, he moves from being a reporter of what happened and becomes a generalizer of what happens. Having mastered the fundamentals, at least, of both drama and narration, he now comes to grips with exposition and relies heavily upon the reflection of others for his subject matter. Between the ages of 12 to 14, from grades 7 to 9, the child consolidates his gains in functional writing and in the expository method. Junior high school is thus the period of intense training in generalizing what happens. Most students in this age range still cannot theorize what may happen, nor can they think abstractly in a really systematic and thoroughly reliable way, nor can they outline the pros and the cons of an argument (see Gregory and Tingle, 1967, p. 99). By the time the child can theorize what may happen, think abstractly in a systematic and reliable way, and outline the pros and the cons of an argument, he is about fourteen years old and in the formal operational stage of conceptual development.

FORMAL OPERATIONAL STAGE. At about age fourteen, though earlier in some exceptional students, the child enters the formal operational stage of his conceptual growth and development. Throughout high school and college and into mature adulthood, the individual continues to deepen his mastery of the ability to reason by hypothesis, to manipulate abstractions, to theorize what may happen. Such ability, as distinct from the skills of encoding (transmitting) and decoding (receiving and interpreting) English structures, is *open–ended* rather than closed.

As childlike students of the semantic extensions of logic, rhetoric, and style, all adult speakers of Modern American English continue to grow beyond the time when they have functionally mastered the grammatical and phonological systems of their mother tongue. Continue, that is, unless they have been severely handicapped in the use of English, either by social disadvantage, cultural deprivation, emotional warping, or by destitution in language models. So long as they continue to grow in the capacity to conceptualize, these same adults continue to increase their mastery over abstraction. This mastery, of course, constitutes both a gain and a loss, for as Moffett (1968, p. 23) says, "Abstraction, by selecting and ranking elements of experience, reduces reality to manageable summaries. To abstract is to trade a loss of reality for a gain in control." Education, in other words, is a subtle form of death.

Such death is a necessary prerequisite to life—that is, man cannot make anything new without first passing through a phase of destroying the old. Michelangelo, for example, could not sculpt *Moses* without having first committed himself to the principle of destroying the block of marble in its original shape. Neither can a poet, playwright, or novelist give his articulate vision of reality without first agreeing to the principle of editing out all the nonessential details in the continuum of expression that he seeks to establish. Perhaps that is why student writing in the formal operational stage of conceptual development tends to be neither personal nor functional, but rather *creative*—i.e., tending toward the use of language as an esthetic end in itself.

THE IMPORTANCE OF LANGUAGE–MODELING

How well students in high school will perform—and even *if* they will perform—at the level of creative writing, depends in large measure upon the quality of their early training in some version of Modern American English. The term *quality*, of course, means the *extent* and the *intensity* of that early training. Now there can be no doubt that every child, unless he is suffering from some pathological speech disorder, has the *genotypical capacity* (see Lenneberg, 1967, Ch. 4) to learn any natural language on earth. Which language or languages he learns, however, depends on the *phenotypical modeling* he is exposed to, as was brought out earlier in this volume. In essence, then, all language–learning results from an organic–like union of the genotypical capacity of the child (or some surrogate equivalent) with the phenotypical modeling of the parent (or some surrogate equivalent), and may be schematized as follows:

Language–Learning = Genotypical Capacity + Phenotypical Modeling

What this formula does not indicate, however, is the extreme

importance of both the extent and the intensity of the modeling during the optimum time for learning a natural language, the optimum time known to linguistic science as the
period of *resonance.*

Resonance

As Lenneberg (1967, Ch. 4) demonstrates in meticulous
detail, certain features of physiological maturation occurring
between age two and age twelve years, like structural changes
in the brain, accompanied by crucial changes in both the
chemical composition and the electro–physical energy output
of the brain, result in the creation of the optimum time for
language acquisition—that is, the period of *resonance.* Between the ages of 2 and 12, therefore, the child is in a highly
plastic time for the learning of any natural language, which
he will tend to speak (depending on the extent and the intensity of the modeling and on the exact time when he begins
his learning) *with a native rather than a foreign accent.* The
child's resonant learning of his native language, then, is a
concomitant of his physiological maturation, and may be
summed up in the words of Lenneberg (1967, p. 158) as follows:

> Language cannot begin to develop until a certain level of physical
> maturation and growth has been attained. Between the ages of two
> and three years language emerges by an interaction of maturation
> and self–programmed learning. Between the ages of three and the
> early teens the possibility for primary language acquisition con-
> tinues to be good; the individual appears to be most sensitive to
> stimuli at this time and to preserve some innate flexibility for the
> organization of brain functions to carry out the complex integration
> of subprocesses necessary for the smooth elaboration of speech
> and language. After puberty, the ability for self–organization and
> adjustment to the physiological demands of verbal behavior quickly
> declines. The brain behaves as if it had become set in its ways
> and primary, basic language skills not acquired by that time, except
> for articulation, usually remain deficient for life.

Lenneberg's scientific observations mean that within the
period of resonance itself, the child acquires his
PREFERRED RESONANT LANGUAGE, both as a geographical dialect and as a social–class lect. This overwhelm-

ingly important and securely incontrovertible linguistic phenomenon must be taken into account in all analyses of the problem of handicapped English and in all suggestions for the solution of this problem.

Preferred Resonant Language

From the foregoing discussion it is apparent that the phenotypical modeling of a specific natural language within the child's period of resonance is more important for the achievement of the *preferred resonant language* than is the child's genotypical capacity for language acquisition *per se.* In other words, it is the phenotypical modeling which determines whether the child will speak English, French, or German, and not the child's innate instinct to learn English, French, or German—or any other natural language that may be modeled for him. It is just such phenotypical modeling, for example, which resulted in the German–American novelist Erich Maria Remarque's acquisition of German as his preferred resonant language. Remarque (1897–1970), that is, learned his native German during the period of resonance; he learned his adopted American English as an adult, or outside the period of resonance. Married in later life to the American film actress Paulette Goddard and eminently proficient in the language of his wife's fellow countrymen, Remarque nevertheless could not speak Modern American English without a heavy German accent. Why? Because Remarque learned his adopted language, in the terminology of Lenneberg (1967, p. 159), *after* the "loss of flexibility for cerebral reorganization." To be sure, Remarque was not a speaker of handicapped English. His segmentation of reality in Modern American English was more than adequate; his image of himself and the language roles he had to assume in his adopted tongue was perfectly appropriate. But whenever Remarque wrote a new novel, he did so in his native German, the preferred resonant language from his childhood.

The reasons why Remarque continued to write his novels in German, even after he had become an American citizen, are indeed not hard to find. As his preferred resonant language, German was much easier for Remarque "to be at home in" than was his adopted and heavily accented English. Remarque could think better in German, feel better in German, imagine better in German, structure empathetic experience better in German, express character and motivation better in German, achieve stylistic grace and esthetic beauty better in German. In short, he could create an artistic world of discourse better in German, because only in German could he fully capture "the living accents of men and women," German men and women, as they spoke their own geographical dialects and social–class lects. Only in German could he truly prove that literary art is the representational liar who tells a truth larger than mere fact—*verisimilitude,* or the illusion of reality that convinces the will of the reader of its own authenticity. To have asked Remarque to write his novels in Modern American English, no matter how proficient he had become in the language *as an adult,* would have been about as prudent as to have asked Dante to compose *La Commedia* in the language of Homer, or Shakespeare to cast the blank verse of *King Lear* in the Parisian French of Molière.

The literary experience of Remarque provides an excellent lesson in, and an eminent example of, this central fact: a truly *bilingual* person, one who is *completely* "at home" in two languages and hence prefers neither one to the other, is extremely rare. Why? Because even if the person learns two languages during the period of resonance itself, the chances are that the phenotypical modeling of each will not be the same in onset, extent, and intensity. Such reinforcing factors as preference of favorite parent, relative prestige, medium or register of school instruction, peer–group remodeling, mass–media influences, national linguistic goals, and preferred resonant language of mate will tend, furthermore, to enhance the resonant status of one of the languages and reduce the resonant status of the other. If bilingualism is achieved as an adult, as in the case of the British novelist Joseph Conrad (1857–1924), then specialization is bound to occur, so that Language A will function in Role I and Language B in Role II. Conrad himself, of course, is an excellent example of an *adult* and *literary* mastery of English that somehow fails to convince the reader that he is hearing "the living accents of men." A native speaker of Polish and an earlier master of French than of English, Conrad lacks the "resonant ear" to achieve perfect verisimilitude in the speech patterns of nineteenth–century British English. Vladimir Nabokov (b. 1899), on the other hand, learned his tutored English before he learned his native Russian; he therefore does have the "resonant ear" to achieve a perfect verisimilitude in the speech patterns of twentieth–century American English. Nabokov's self–styled "life–long love affair with the English language" demonstrates that in the real mastery of any language *resonance is all!*

Since onset, extent, intensity, and the reinforcing factors mentioned above also apply to the *speech varieties* within a language, it is obvious that the child who learns a preferred resonant language also learns at the same time a preferred resonant geographical dialect and a preferred resonant social–class lect. From the linguistic phenomenon of preferred resonant geographical dialect springs such regional speech varieties of Modern American English as Northern, Midland, and Southern (see Nist, 1973, Ch. 4). From the linguistic phenomenon of preferred resonant social–class lect springs such status versions of Modern American English as "standard," "vernacular," and "uneducated" (see Francis, 1963, 1965, pp. 244–253). Both of these linguistic phenomena—i.e., regional speech varieties and status versions—will be studied in detail in Chapter 3. In the meantime, Hawaii offers an excellent example of how three categories of language and therefore potentially three different languages compete for dominance in phenotypical modeling during the period of resonance for the child: (1) *ancestral,* or the language spoken by the child's relatives of more than two previous generations (that is, from great–grandparents back); (2) *native,* or the language modeled in the home by the child's parents; and (3) *national,* or the official language of the child's citizenship, the one used as the medium of instruction in the public schools.

Ancestral, Native, National

During the two centuries since their discovery in 1778, the Hawaiian Islands have become a linguistic mixing bowl in which the following *ancestral* tongues have vied with one another for both *native* and *national* status: Hawaiian (or Kanaka), Japanese, Chinese, Filipino, Portuguese, Puerto Rican Spanish, and Korean. That not one of them has fully succeeded in achieving either status *on a permanent basis*, of course, is due to the fact that Modern American English has exercised such an overwhelming influence on the cultural evolution of the political entity that was to become the fiftieth state in the Federal Union.

LINGUISTIC CONFLICT: AN EXAMPLE. The language indigenous to the Islands was at first ancestral, native, *and* national. Phonologically the simplest natural language on earth, Hawaiian has a total of only 13 segmental phonemes: the stops /p k/, the nasals /m n/, the lateral /l/, the aspirate /h/, the labial velar /w/, the glottal stop /ʔ/, and the five simple vowels /i u e o a/, which may combine to form the following three diphthongs: /oi ai au/. An extremely "musical" language, one in which every syllable ends upon a vowel, Hawaiian is also semantically able to express deep moral sentiments with poetic simplicity and ease. King Kamehameha III (d. 1854), for example, believed that *ua mau ke ea o ka aina i ka pono* ("The life of the land is perpetuated in righteousness.")

As the economic life of Hawaii became more and more dependent upon the United States, the need arose for the development of several different kinds of *pidgin* English, so that speakers of different ancestral, native, and national tongues could communicate with one another in the conduct of their business affairs. As Robert A. Hall, Jr. (1943, 1956, 1959) has indicated, a pidgin is designed precisely to let speakers of two or more different languages carry on their daily business in one simple language common to all. *Learned by adults as a second language*, then, a pidgin is of necessity highly redundant, phonemically loose, grammatically regular, lexically small, flexible in expression, and capable of borrowing from other languages. In Hawaii today there are six major kinds of pidgin English in use: Kanaka, Japanese, Chinese, Filipino, Portuguese, and mixed. The most difficult of these pidgins are the Filipino and the mixed; in general, the other four major pidgins are mutually intelligible.

Since a pidgin is learned by adults as a common medium in which to conduct their business affairs, it is *not* ancestral, nor native, nor national. When parents teach a pidgin to their children so that it becomes their children's *first* language, then the pidgin becomes a *creole.* A creole language is like a pidgin in that it is neither ancestral nor national; a creole language is unlike a pidgin in that it is native. Now since a creole is native, it competes within the child's period of resonance against the national language taught in school—competes, that is, for assumption of the role and status of preferred resonant language, both as geographical dialect and social–class lect.

Because the onset of learning a creole usually precedes that of learning a national language, and since the extent and the intensity of learning a creole usually exceed those of learning a national, it is apparent that any form of creole English employed as a phenotypical model within the child's period of resonance automatically becomes a primary candidate for the office of "linguistic handicapper." A brief study of Hawaiian creole, for example, will serve to illustrate something of the nature of this problem: *the interference of a native language with the learning of a national.*

HAWAIIAN CREOLE. Hawaiian creole deviates from the phonological and grammatical norms of so–called "standard" Modern American English in many demonstrable ways (see Reinecke, 1969). Hawaiian creole, in short, is "different"—a contemporary linguistic fact which can be illustrated in the following passage:

Some Nonstandard Features of Hawaiian Creole

1. Hawaiian creole regularly substitutes /t/ for /θ/ and /d/ for /ð/, as in *tink* for *think* and *doze* for *those.*

2. Hawaiian creole usually drops /r/ and /l/ in word–final positions, as in *cah* for *car* and *bawh* for *ball.*

3. Hawaiian creole generally does not use inflectional morphs to indicate the past tense of verbs, as in *Him no wuhk yestuhday. She wen walk out. My Grandma wen die.*

4. Hawaiian creole usually omits the verb *be,* both as main verb and as auxiliary, as in *Dis good. She goin home.*

5. Hawaiian creole generally uses *goin* or a zero morph as substitutes for *will* in the expression of future time, as in *I go stoah for you. Us goin play bawh tomorrow.*

6. Hawaiian creole regularly substitutes *can* for *could* and *will* for *would* so that nonimmediate aspect becomes immediate.

7. Hawaiian creole does not use *should* to express obligation, as in *Moah bettah you come. Us gotta go now.*

8. Hawaiian creole uses *stay* as a kind of omnipotent marker of progressive aspect in the present tense, as in *He stay try see where. Da baby stay put it on, da hat.*

9. Hawaiian creole does not make use of the passive voice. Thus *I goin pull my toot* means "I'm going to have my tooth pulled." And *Da cah wen hit da dog* means "The dog was hit by the car."

10. Hawaiian creole regularly substitutes *nevah* and *no* for *don't/doesn't* and *didn't.*

11. Hawaiian creole does not use *there* as an expletive or dummy subject. Thus *Get one stoah in Keaukaha* means "There is one store in Keaukaha."

12. Hawaiian creole makes no use of the regular possessive allomorphs /s∼z∼/ɨz/.

13. Hawaiian creole constantly confuses singulars and plurals, as in *He got one seestahs and no bradah. He bring da mails.* As a result of this confusion, Hawaiian creole frequently fails to distinguish count nouns from mass nouns and mass nouns from count.

14. Hawaiian creole regularly uses *dakine* as an omnipotent determiner, as in *You see dakine dog? He get dakine surfboard.*

15. Hawaiian creole frequently leaves prepositions out of constructions that call for them in so-called "standard" versions of Modern American English, as in *He goin stoah fo you.*

16. Hawaiian creole frequently substitutes *fo* for *to,* as in *Dis no time fo eat.*

17. Hawaiian creole does not use dependent–clause markers like *when* and *if.* The language is markedly deficient in its connective system and therefore does not readily show subordinate logical relationships by means of hypotactic constructions.

These seventeen nonstandard features of Hawaiian creole could be added to many times over. They do not, in short, even begin to fully delineate the "differentness" of this social–class lect. But they do establish the fact of that "differentness."

A Question of Differentness

The fact of that "differentness," in and of itself, is of extreme importance in any study of the child and his language. Why? Because it is precisely that very "differentness" which the child learns from the phenotypical modeling of Hawaiian creole during the *earliest* stages of his period of resonance.

Thus as Hawaiian creole becomes the preferred resonant lect of the child, so its "differentness" becomes his preferred resonant method of mediating all his experience with the world about him. The child, that is, segments reality and achieves an attendant image of himself and the language roles he must assume by means of the "differentness" of the code that is his Hawaiian creole. The crucial question inherent in the phenotypical modeling of that code, of course, is simply this: Is the "nonstandardness" of Hawaiian creole the equivalent of "substandardness" insofar as Modern American English is concerned? Or, to take this specific example and give it a universal application, does "different" equal "inferior"? So crucial is this question that it demands a chapter of discussion all to itself.

Chapter 3

DOES "DIFFERENT" = "INFERIOR"?

T HE VARIOUS VERSIONS of Modern American English spoken in Hawaii today illustrate the linguistic fact that within every geographical dialect area of the United States there are at least three different social–class lects in current use (see Nist, 1973, Ch. 4): the educated *acrolect*, the vernacular *mesilect*, and the uneducated *basilect* (see Stewart, 1964, 1967, Spring 1967, Spring 1968, and Spring/Summer 1969). In the Hawaiian Islands themselves, for example, college graduates of the younger generation generally tend to speak acrolect; with maximum prestige attached to the use of their code, these socially advantaged Americans are fashioning the so called "standard" English of Hawaii. By way of contrast, however, their middle–aged parents, usually native born, who grew up with Hawaiian creole as their preferred resonant lect and then moved on to partially master some form of mainland American English, generally tend to speak mesilect; with medium prestige attached to the use of their code, these somewhat socially advantaged Americans of high school education are lending their moral support to the fashioning of the so–called "standard." By way of further contrast, however, their old–aged parents, usually immigrants to the Islands, who were adult learners of one of the pidgins simply because they grew up with some foreign tongue as their preferred resonant language, generally tend to speak basilect; with minimum prestige attached to the use of their code, these socially disadvantaged Americans of no more than grade school education are little better than "innocent bystanders" on the linguistic scene. Simplistic as this analysis may be, it implies an important relationship between the term *different* and the term *inferior* as each applies to the linguistic phenomenon known as social–class lects—namely, the relationship of *prestige.*

AMERICAN SOCIAL–CLASS LECTS
The Problem of Prestige

When a linguist says that "everybody talks funny," he is merely making a popular assessment of the linguistic facts about the major speech varieties of every natural language on earth. These linguistic facts, in turn, mean that no living language is ever *completely uniform* in such formal characteristics as vocabulary and meaning, morphology and syntax, segmental phonology and intonation patterns (see Bloomfield, 1933, 1962, Ch. 19). Hence the characteristic differences among British English, American English, and the various kinds of Commonwealth English (see Nist, 1966, pp. 21–27). When the same linguist says that not everybody speaks some variety of his language with the same amount of prestige, however, then he is not making so much a linguistic assessment as he is a sociological one. But facts are facts, whether linguistic or sociological. And this is a fact: the same amount of prestige does *not* apply to all the speech varieties of a language.

Because of the vast amount of variety within its some thirty–eight geographical dialects, for example, present–day British English (see Nist, 1973, Ch. 4) has made a virtue of necessity by accepting the historical emergence of its *Received Pronunciation Standard* (known in acronym abbreviation as *RPS*) as the most prestigious of its current versions. Accepting both Scots and Irish English as regional standards to supplement its RPS (see Francis, 1963, 1965, p. 234), contemporary British English is nevertheless characterized by the enormous range of its dialect variants. Indeed as Nist (1966, p. 25) has said,

No version of the language in the United States [and Canada, or anywhere in the Commonwealth for that matter] can imitate the whine of Suffolk, the clipping of Yorkshire, the guttural throatiness of Northumberland, the glottal stopping of Lancashire, the bardic pitch patterns of Wales, or the Gaelic thickness of the Scottish Highlands. A simple question in South Staffordshire, for example, betrays ancient Germanic influence on syntax and Middle English control of pronunciation: *"Bist tha bi guwin' uwt?"* ("Are you to be going out?") A fundamental command by a Cockney, on the other hand, might run to such incomprehensible limits as these: *"Pu' th' 'ud i' th' o'!"* ("Put the wood in the hole!"—i.e., "Shut the door!")

As contrasted with RPS, the acrolect of the universities and the BBC, the geographical dialects of present–day British English exemplify the key lesson in Shaw's *Pygmalion*—namely, that failure to master the *RPS* places terrible social, educational, and financial limitations upon the individual. Why? For one reason, because since RPS exists as the educated version of British English, any departure from that code, except for Irish English and Scots, marks the speaker as confined to either the vernacular of mesilect or to the "folk speech" of basilect or to both these rather nonprestigious forms of the language. In other words, except for Irish English and Scots, *geographical dialects in present–day British English automatically become social–class lects*. Within the linguistically elitist system of Great Britain, therefore, the term *different*, with the two exceptions noted, does tend very markedly to mean "inferior."

But what of the seemingly egalitarian linguistic system of the United States? Here the equation of *different* with *inferior* is not so easy to make. Why? Because no equivalent of RPS has emerged as an ideal code form for Modern American English; *acrolect* versions of the various geographical dialects of the United States have never impeded communication. In other words, in direct contrast to British English, Modern American English continues to maintain a rather high level of uniformity among the *well-educated* speakers of its various geographical dialects or regionalisms. This relatively high level of uniformity in well–educated versions of American English has been inherited from colonial days, and was praised in 1791 by the British editor of David Ramsey's *History of the American Revolution* as follows (see Nist, 1966, p. 365):

> It is a curious fact that there is perhaps no one portion of the British Empire in which two or three millions of persons are to be found who speak their mother tongue with greater purity or a truer pronunciation than the white inhabitants of the United States. This was attributed, by a penetrating observer, to the number of British subjects assembled in America from various quarters, who, in consequence of their intercourse and intermarriages, soon dropped the peculiarities of their several provincial idioms, retaining only what was fundamental and common to all—a process which the frequency or rather the universality of school–learning in America must naturally have assisted.

The relatively high level of uniformity seen in educated American English by the British editor in 1791 has been increased in the past two centuries, of course, by means of population mobility (both geographical and social), rapid transportation, mass–media communication, and universal education, This relatively high level of uniformity among *acrolect* versions of Modern American English means, moreover, that insofar as geographical dialects or regionalisms are concerned, in the language of the United States *different* does not necessarily mean "inferior."

The qualifier *necessarily* in the preceding value judgment applies, however, only to *acrolect* versions of Modern American geographical dialects. Insofar as *mesilect* and *basilect* versions of these same dialects are concerned, *different* does indeed mean "inferior," if in no other attribute than that of prestige. This attribute of prestige, in turn, depends in large measure upon the *principle of correctness*, indeed one might say in the words of Donald J. Lloyd (1952) the "national mania for correctness," in Modern American English. This principle may be depicted as follows:

The Principle of Correctness in American English

Correctness = linguistic usage + social acceptability

The social–acceptability part of the equation means that in addition to the *horizontal* dimension of the language, known as regional speech varieties or geographical dialects, there is also the *vertical* dimension, known as social–class lects. And it is precisely in this vertical dimension that the problem of prestige obtains.

In the coined terminology of William A. Stewart (1964, etc.), Co–director of the Education Study Center in Washington, D.C., *acrolect* corresponds with the educated or so–called "standard" version of a dialect; *mesilect,* with the vernacular; and *basilect,* with the uneducated vulgar or "folk speech." Thus speakers of acrolect tend to fit the cultural patterns of Hans Kurath's (see Kurath *et al,* 1939–43; Kurath, 1949; Kurath and McDavid, 1961) Type III of informants (see Atwood, 1970, p. 183)—that is, these speakers tend to enjoy a superior education (usually college), together with a culturally enriched background that includes wide reading and/or extensive social contacts and travel. Speakers of mesilect, by way of contrast, tend to fit the cultural patterns of Kurath's Type II of informants (see Atwood, 1970, p. 183)—that is, they tend to enjoy a formal education (usually high school), together with the social advantages of some reading and/or travel. Speakers of basilect, finally, tend to fit the cultural patterns of Kurath's Type I of informants (see Atwood, 1970, p. 183)—that is, this last group tends to suffer from the social disadvantage of little formal education, little reading, and restricted travel and contact with other people.

Using Stewart's terms for their scientific accuracy and their general lack of unpleasant connotations and emotional overtones, a linguist may relate these three social–class lects of Modern American English with the amount of prestige which they confer upon their speakers as follows:

Prestige and the Social–Class Lects of Modern American English

Acrolect → *maximum* amount of prestige for its speakers.
Mesilect:→ *medium* amount of prestige for its speakers.
Basilect · → *minimum* amount of prestige for its speakers.

Above and beyond their relationship with the phenomenon of prestige, these three social–class lects are so important within the various geographical dialects of Modern American

English that they must be characterized in some measure of detail. Hopefully, from that characterization will come a firmer basis upon which to build an answer to the question, "Does *different = inferior?"*

Acrolect

First of all, there is the *acrolect,* or the most prestigious form of any speech variety within the language. Without fully defining the form, a linguist may nevertheless list some of the most outstanding characteristics of this present–day American social–class lect as follows (see Nist, June 1969, p. 20):

Characteristics of the *Acrolect* in Modern American English

~ 1. Speakers of acrolect American English tend to be well-educated, culturally advantaged, socially adroit, and highly competent in performance.

2. Acrolect American English has a very extensive vocabulary, fully responsive to the discourse demands placed on the cultural levels of usage (standard, nonstandard, substandard) and the functional varieties of the language (e.g., colloquial, commercial, technical, literary).

3. Acrolect American English operates skillfully in all the styles or keys of discourse (see Joos, 1961, 1962, 1967; Gleason, 1965, Ch. 15)—intimate, familiar/casual, consultative, deliberative, rhetorical/oratorical—and appears frequently in published formal writing.

4. Acrolect American English is generally free of so–called "grammatical errors" and of stylistic lapses that violate mood, tone, or attitude.

5. Acrolect American English shows an extreme sensitivity to the immediate context situation and tends to keep emotive function at a pleasant level, usually positive in mood, tone, and attitude.

6. Acrolect American English is recognized for the foregoing five reasons, among others, as the "standard" and therefore the most prestigious version of its speech variety, regionalism, or geographical dialect.

In the sociolinguistic theory of Basil Bernstein (1970, pp. 45–46), speakers of acrolect Modern American English almost _ always come from families that foster intrapersonal methods of learning, open systems of communication, personal–appeals modes of control, and hence elaborated codes . (i.e., rhetorical means of mastering the message, both in transmission and in reception).

Drawing upon the wealth of *belles lettres* available in the language, and thereby avoiding any embarrassment that may be attached to the use of any "real–life" models, a linguist may illustrate the acrolect in Modern American English by means of the following passage from Chapter 40 of Thomas Wolfe's *Look Homeward, Angel* (1929):

> "What happens, Ben? What really happens?" said Eugene. "Can you remember some of the same things that I do? I have forgotten the old faces. Where are they, Ben? What were their names? I forget the names of people I knew for years. I get their faces mixed. I get their heads stuck on other people's bodies. I think one man has said what another said. And I forget—forget. There is something I have lost and have forgotten. I can't remember, Ben."
>
> "What do you want to remember?" said Ben.
>
> A stone, a leaf, an unfound door. And the forgotten faces.
>
> "I have forgotten names. I have forgotten faces. And I remember little things," said Eugene. "I remember the fly I swallowed on the peach, and the little boys on tricycles at St. Louis, and the mole on Grover's neck, and the Lackawanna freight–car, number 16356, on a siding near Gulfport. Once, in Norfolk, an Australian soldier on his way to France asked me the way to a ship; I remember that man's face."
>
> He stared for an answer into the shadow of Ben's face, and then he turned his moon–bright eyes upon the Square.

Although the diction in the preceding passage remains fairly simple, the magnificient prose–poetry of its rhythm and the lack of any grammatical or stylistic blemish mark the language as unmistakably acrolect. The narrator and his characters achieve both an adequate segmentation of reality and an appropriate image of the self and the language roles which that self must assume.

Mesilect

Second, there is the *mesilect*, or the most pervasive version of any speech variety within the language. Again without fully defining this version of Modern American English, a linguist may nevertheless list some of the most outstanding characteristics of the mesilect as follows (see Nist, June 1969, pp. 20–21):

Characteristics of the Mesilect in Modern American English

1. Speakers of mesilect American English tend to have no more than a high school education, to be neither very culturally advan-

taged nor very socially adroit, and to be only fairly competent in performance.

2. Mesilect American English has a rather restricted vocabulary, only partially responsive to the discourse demands placed on the cultural levels of usage and the functional varieties of the language (see Kenyon, 1948).

3. Mesilect American English operates only fairly skillfully through the three lower or more informal styles or keys of discourse (i.e., intimate, familiar/casual, and consultative) and appears most frequently in the writing of personal letters and very seldom in published form, except in the dialogues and *dramatis-persona-mask* narrations of Modern fiction.

4. Mesilect American English is generally full of *hyperurbanisms* (mistakes by overcorrectness) like *to whomever stays* and *between you and I;* of stylistic lapses that violate mood, tone, or attitude; of hackneyed expressions, sententious clichés, and modish slang.

5. Mesilect American English is not very sensitive to the immediate context situation, is often inadequate in public gatherings, and frequently steps emotive function up to an unpleasant level, whether positive or negative in mood, tone, and attitude.

6. Mesilect American English is not recognized as the "standard" and prestigious version of its speech variety, regionalism, or geographical dialect, but rather for the foregoing five reasons, among others, as the most representative and "average" manifestation of it.

In the sociolinguistic theory of Bernstein (1970, pp. 45–46), speakers of mesilect Modern American English usually come from families that foster interpersonal methods of learning (with emphasis on role obligation and differentiation), prefer closed systems of communication to open (though permitting open), and emphasize positional modes of control over personal–appeals and restricted codes over elaborated.

The following passage from Chapter 5 of Sinclair Lewis's *Babbitt* (1922) offers an excellent example of the mesilect in Modern American English:

> During the game of duck–pins, a juvenile form of bowling, Paul was silent. As they came down the steps of the club, not more than half an hour after the time at which Babbitt had sternly told Miss McGoun he would be back, Paul sighed, "Look here, old man, oughtn't to talked about Zilla way I did."
>
> "Rats, old man, it lets off steam."
>
> "Oh, I know! After spending all noon sneering at the conventional

stuff, I'm conventional enough to be ashamed of saving my life by
busting out with my fool troubles!"

"Old Paul, your nerves are kind of on the bum. I'm going to
take you away. I'm going to rig this thing. I'm going to have an
important deal in New York and—and sure, of course!—I'll need
you to advise me on the roof of the building! And the ole deal
will fall through, and there'll be nothing for us but to go on ahead
to Maine. I——Paul, when it comes right down to it, I don't care
whether you bust loose or not. I do like having a rep for being
one of the Bunch, but if you ever needed me I'd chuck it and
come out for you every time! Not of course but what you're——
course I don't mean you'd ever do anything that would put——that
would put a decent position on the fritz but——See how I mean?
I'm kind of a clumsy old codger, and I need your fine Eyetalian
hand. We——Oh, hell, I can't stand here gassing all day! On the
job! S'long! Don't take any wooden money, Paulibus! See you soon!
S'long!"

In this passage, of course, Lewis as narrator uses acrolect,
while letting his characters speak in mesilect. Paul, for
example, steps emotive function up to a rather unpleasant
level with such unit tacts as *sneering at the conventional
stuff, ashamed of saving my life,* and *busting out with my
fool troubles.* His slangy use of *old man* as a vocative of
friendship is matched by his casual omission of *have* in the
unit tact *oughtn't to talked about.* Even more important, however, is the fact that Paul Riesling, unhappily married as he
is, has become a victim of his own interpersonal methods
of learning. His own moral emphasis on role obligation has
trapped him in an inadequate segmentation of reality—an
inadequacy which is reinforced by the inept and closed code
that will not permit him to achieve an appropriate image
of himself and of the language role he must assume, if possible, with Babbitt.

And what about Babbitt? Emotionally incapable of handling
intimate subject matter in familiar or casual key, Babbitt
embarrasses himself into breaking off the conversation with
his friend Paul Riesling, who has just "bared his soul" concerning his tragic marriage with Zilla. Babbitt's slangy use
of unit tacts like *kind of on the bum, rig this thing, bust
loose, the Bunch, chuck it, come out for you, on the fritz,
kind of a clumsy old codger, gassing all day,* and *on the
job* marks the language as unmistakably mesilect. As an

implicit note of warning to all purist sticklers for the importance of a so–called "grammatical correctness," Babbitt's
grammar is impeccable; it is his atrocious diction and his
stylistic lapses that violate mood, tone, and attitude which
are so reprehensible. Joining mild profanity *(Rats, Oh, hell)*
with syntactical ellipses *(See how I mean? On the job! See
you soon!)* and morphological clippings *(rep, S'long!)*, Babbitt
uses his brand of Modern American English like an irresponsible teen–ager sent out on an adult's mission. His ultimate
failure may be heard in the banally inappropriate *Don't take
any wooden money, Paulibus!* Babbitt, in short, is "cute"
without really being funny. As a matter of linguistic fact, he
is pathetic.

Pathetic because Babbitt, like his friend Paul Riesling, has
become a victim of his own interpersonal methods of learning.
Trapped in his own emphasis on role obligation, Babbitt is
even more handicapped in his mesilect than is Paul. Why?
Because Paul at least does not try to fool himself; Babbitt
does. The courage of his personal loyalty to Paul is constantly
being vitiated by his cowardice in the face of public opinion.
Thus the tension between "I don't care whether you bust
loose or not" at one pole of assertion and "I do like having
a rep for being one of the Bunch" at the other can find only
a partial release in this totally inept attempt at mixing explicit
exoneration and its attendant self-justification with implicit
exhortation and its attendant imperative mode of control: "Not
of course but what you're——course I don't mean you'd ever
do anything that would put——that would put a decent position on the fritz but——See how I mean?" Paul sees. Sees
that despite Babbitt's sterile attempt at humor, which merely
serves to betray his provincial prejudice in the insulting pronunciation of *Eyetalian* and his cultural insecurity in the
immature wit of Latinized *Paulibus,* Zenith's ace realtor is
fundamentally an arch-hypocrite who suffers unknowingly
from his own inadequate segmentation of reality and his own
inappropriate image of himself and the language role he
should assume, but has failed to assume, in mature compassion for his friend. What Paul sees, so eloquently indicated
by his silence, is what Lewis intends for the reader to
see—namely, this: *what Babbit cannot express he cannot*

experience. And so his mesilect has become for him a kind of pernicious anemia of the soul.

Basilect

Third, there is the *basilect.* As the generally recognized substandard form of any speech variety, regionalism, or geographical dialect, the basilect in Modern American English constitutes its own form of cultural deprivation and social disadvantage (see Evertts, 1967). Once again without fully defining this most nonprestigious version of the language, a linguist may nevertheless list some of the most outstanding characteristics of the basilect as follows (see Nist, June 1969, pp. 20–21):

Characteristics of the Basilect in Modern American English

1. Speakers of basilect American English tend to have no more than a grade school education, if that, to be both culturally disadvantaged and socially nonadroit, and to be very noticeably poor in both competence and performance.

2. Basilect American English suffers from an extremely restricted vocabulary, which is very inadequately responsive to the discourse demands placed on the cultural levels of usage and the functional varieties of the language.

3. Although no form of Modern American English is completely monostylistic (see Labov, 1970b, p. 19), the basilect does tend to operate most of the time by means of one key of discourse—a confusing blend of intimate, familiar/casual, and consultative—with the result that its speakers tend to look upon more sophisticated users of the language as outsiders and therefore as emotionally suspect. In its almost exclusively oral manifestation (except for its ubiquitous printed appearance in modern fiction), the basilect seldom appears even in personal letters, for the simple fact that at times it borders on illiteracy—indeed, at times it is illiteracy.

4. Basilect American English is generally full of such grammatical and stylistic lapses as these: faulty references, wrong verb forms, double or multiple negatives, pleonastic subjects *(My brother he)*, preference for the vulgar historical present tense, misuse of personal–pronoun forms and of *them* as a demonstrative, and an indiscriminate use of *ain't* and the so–called "flat" adverbs (see Mencken, 1963, Ch. IX). Shot through with malapropism, the basilect nevertheless varies grammatically from region to region, depending upon such factors as these: ethnic origin of its speakers, degree of their social isolation, amount of interference from *native* (as distinct form *national*) language, and relative prestige of *ancestral* tongue (i.e., that spoken by one's forebears of more than two previous generations).

5. Basilect American English is usually, though not always, insensitive to the immediate context situation, is generally inadequate in public gatherings, and has a strong tendency to step emotive function up to an unpleasant level, usually negative (though not always) in mood, tone, or attitude. Many black ghetto speakers of the basilect, understandably but unfortunately, tend to have a rather high and negative emotive function as addressers and a rather low and negative conative function as addressees.

6. Basilect American English is recognized, even stigmatized, precisely for the foregoing five reasons, among others, as the substandard and therefore the nonprestigious version of its speech variety, regionalism, or geographical dialect. Unless militantly alienated from the mainstream of present–day American culture, speakers of the basilect usually want their children to linguistically "get more out of life" than they have got.

In the sociolinguistic theory of Bernstein (1970, pp. 45–46), speakers of basilect Modern American English usually come from families that foster hierarchy methods of learning (with emphasis on authority and status), develop closed systems of communication rather than open, prefer imperative modes of control over both positional and personal–appeals modes, and produce, therefore, restricted codes instead of elaborated ones.

The following passage from Chapter 8 of John Steinbeck's *The Grapes of Wrath* (1939) serves as a splendid illustration of the basilect in Modern American English:

The preacher said, "I don't recollect that John had a fambly. Just a lone man, ain't he? I don't recollect much about him."

"Lonest goddamn man in the world," said Joad. "Crazy kind of son–of–a–bitch, too—somepin like Muley, on'y worse in some ways. Might see 'im anywheres—at Shawnee, drunk, or visitin' a widow twenty miles away, or workin' his place with a lantern. Crazy. Ever'body thought he wouldn't live long. A lone man like that don't live long. But Uncle John's older'n Pa. Jus' gets stringier an' meaner ever' year. Meaner'n Grampa."

"Look a the light comin'," said the preacher. "Silvery–like. Didn' John never have no fambly?"

"Well, yes, he did, an' that'll show you the kind of fella he is—set in his ways. Pa tells about it. Uncle John, he had a young wife. Married four months. She was in a family way, too, an' one night she gets a pain in her stomick, an' she says, 'You better go for a doctor.' Well, John, he's settin' there, an' he says, 'You just got stomickache. You et too much. Take a dose a pain killer. You crowd up ya stomick an' ya get a stomickache,' he says. Nex' noon she's outa her head, an' she dies at about four in the afternoon."

"What was it?" Casy asked. "Poisoned from somepin she et?"

"No, somepin jus' bust in her. Ap—appendick or somepin. Well, Uncle John, he's always been a easy–goin' fella, an' he takes it hard. Takes it for a sin. For a long time he won't have nothin' to say to nobody. Just walks aroun' like he don't see nothin' an' he prays some. . . ."

Several key features in the preceding passage from Steinbeck's great novel mark its two lower–class characters as speakers of basilect American English: the markedly "slurvian" patterns of their pronunciation, as in *fambly* for *family, on'y* for *only, ever'body* for *everybody, older'n* for *older than, meaner'n* for *meaner than, a* for *at, outa* for *out of, nex'* for *next, somepin* for *something, jus'* for *just, fella* for *fellow, nothin'* for *nothing, aroun'* for *around,* and *an'* for *and;* their use of wrong verb forms like *don't* with the third–person singular subject, *et* for *ate, settin'* for *sittin',* and *bust* for *burst;* Joad's preference for the vulgar historical present tense as the emotive function of his narrative rises; the use of double and triple negatives like *he don't see nothin'* and *he won't have nothin' to say to nobody;* the inability to articulate properly the learned word *appendix;* the use of *ain't;* the repetition of pleonastic *he* with *Uncle John* and *John;* and above all else, the unconscious saturating of the discourse with highly emotive unit tacts like *lonest goddamn man, crazy kind of son–of–a–bitch, stringier an' meaner, dose a pain killer, crowd up ya stomick, outa her head,* and *takes it for a sin.* Despite its lack of prestige, the basilect of this passage proves that Labov (1970b, p. 54) is right when he claims that nonstandard Modern American English is generally effective in its brevity and clarity. Indeed as many American writers have shown, because of the drama inherent in its high emotive function, basilect is often the linguistic stuff from which great literary art is made.

Great literary art not withstanding, the semantic deficiency inherent in basilect Modern American English clamors for attention in the passage quoted from Steinbeck's novel. Uncle John, the subject of Casy and Joad's discussion, is now a demented widower because of his own inadequate segmentation of reality and its attendant corollary: the inappropriate image which he once had of himself and of the language role he should have assumed with his then–pregnant but now-dead wife. Incapable of dealing with ambiguity (or plurisignificance) and multivalence, Uncle John diagnosed the cause of his young wife's sudden pain by means of an immature wishful–thinking pleasure principle, rather than by a mature fact–facing reality principle. More annoyed than alarmed by his wife's potentially dangerous indisposition, Uncle John resorted to his own hierarchy methods of learning, with their emphasis on authority and status, and came up with the wrong remedy—a remedy which treated merely a symptom rather than the illness. Abysmally ignorant of the exact location of the stomach in the human anatomy (a sign of his inadequate segmentation), Uncle John recommended his wrong remedy without the slightest trace of mitigation or politeness (a sign of his inappropriate image of himself) and in a very ugly and vulgar version of the imperative mode (a sign of his inappropriate image of the language role he should and must assume), a version which placed the unjust moral onus of gluttony and stupidity upon his young wife, who knew that her painful condition called for the professional care of a physician.

Implicit in Joad's account of the incident, of course, is the fact that such a physician's services will cost money. Reacting out of fear–boundedness rather than out of love–freedom, Uncle John covered his own insecurity with the mask of his position and therefore power within the family—i.e., the older and more experienced husband and head of the household. Behind that authoritarian mask of his status, Uncle John humiliated his young wife by reducing her role to that of a child, devoid of discretion, and permitted therefore only three possible external channels of expressive behavior (see Bernstein, 1970, p. 41): rebellion, withdrawal, or acceptance. From that reduction, death was inevitable. Although neither Joad nor Casy is fully aware of the dimension of the tragedy, their author most certainly is. And Steinbeck demonstrates, with an implicit vengeance, that the old saying "What a man doesn't know won't hurt him," is a lie. What a man doesn't know may *kill* him—or those about him. Truly "set in his ways," as Joad says, Uncle John is the tragic victim of his basilect American English and the terrible semantic deficiency which it entails. Dominated by the closed system of communication inherent in his painfully restricted code, Uncle John unintentionally lets his own avarice and stupidity kill his young wife and therefore destroy his own life. Insofar as his own basilect is concerned, the term *different* unquestionably *does* mean "inferior." The inferiority which springs from that "differentness" is the psychological murderer of Uncle John.

THE "DIFFERENT"

Inherent throughout the foregoing discussion of American social–class lects is the fact that they, rather than regional speech varieties *per se*, constitute the *true dialects* of the national language. The basis for calling any speech variety of any language a *true dialect*, of course, is simply this: Does the speech variety impede communication among the speakers of the national language? If it does, then it is a true dialect of that language. If it does not, then it is merely a *regional variant* of that language. In Modern British English, with the exception of Irish English and Scots, regional variants coincide with true dialects; in Modern American English, they do not. To be more specific, the acrolect and mesilect versions of Modern American English are the regional variants of the national language; the basilect versions, on the other hand, are its true dialects. Furthermore, these basilect versions constitute their own "differentness," as can be seen in any detailed study of what some linguists have called "Black English" (see, e.g., Dillard, 1972).

Any linguistic discussion of the "differentness" of so–called "Black English" must emphasize at the outset that this basilect version of Modern American English is *not* the only such version of the national language and therefore *not* the only source of social disadvantage in the current culture of the United States. Indeed, as the discussion on Hawaiian pidgin and creole (in Chapter 2) indicates, *wherever an ancestral and/or a native tongue interferes with the learning of the acrolect version of the national language in the local speech community, there the linguist will find the handicapped English of a basilect.*

Cantonese

Such interference may be seen, for example, among the Chinese immigrants of San Francisco (see Tucker, Spring/Summer 1969), who speak a native Cantonese which differs from Modern American English in such important features as these: (1) Cantonese operates in the written code by means of an *ideographic* system, as distinct from a *syllabic;* (2) Cantonese vowels occur in different tactic patterns with consonants, which seldom appear in syllable–final or word–final position; (3) Cantonese consonants do not occur in clusters; (4) Cantonese makes no singular/plural distinction among its nouns; (5) Cantonese does not discriminate between masculine and feminine gender among its pronouns; (6) Cantonese does not inflect its verb forms for number, tense, and aspect; (7) Cantonese does not manipulate its syntactical word order to produce changes in meaning based on transformation; and (8) Cantonese communicates by means of an entirely different form of prosody from that of Modern American English (Tucker, pp. 44–45). Since Cantonese is a *tonemic* language, its pitch heights are not only phonemic, but also morphemic and lexemic—that is, the same form spoken at different pitch levels takes on entirely different meanings. Hence the discrimination problem which the Chinese immigrant child has with the intonation patterns of his adopted language obtains, in the words of Tucker (p. 45), as follows:

> ... Every word that the Chinese child learns must be remembered in terms of a specific tone or pitch upon which that word depends largely for meaning. In listening to English words, he cannot help attending to their tone or pitch. Since pitch is a feature of stress which may vary on a particular word at different times, the Chinese student is predisposed to hear that word as several different words because of the several different stresses we have given it. For example the stressed, rising *mine* in "Is it mine?" sounds like a very different word from the low, even, weaker–stressed *mine* in "No, mine's at home."
>
> Because of the importance of syllabic tone in Cantonese, the student attends to the tone and stress of each word in a sentence and finds it difficult to learn to attend to the sentence intonation patterns. Consequently, our tendency to alter stress on words because of the requirements of a sentence intonation pattern is very confusing to him.

Tucker's analysis of the problem (Spring/Summer 1969) is a classic example of the difficulty encountered in learning a national language when the native language sets up a *code interference*.

In the case of Cantonese, of course, the code interference is that which an *intonational* language sets up with the learning of an *accentual* language (see Nist, Jan.-Feb. 1971, p. 22).

"Black English"

A similar code interference, though certainly with different local features, occurs when speakers of basilect Black English try to learn acrolect White English in the United States today. That code interference, in turn, is the historical outcome of the influence of West African languages upon the evolution of the creolized basilect spoken by the enslaved field hands on the plantations of the Old South (see Stewart, 1970; Dillard, 1972). In contradiction of earlier misguided linguistic views that present–day Black English is a descendant from archaic regional British dialects, William A. Stewart (1970, p. 357) makes the following well–substantiated claim for creolization:

> Of those Africans who fell victim to the Atlantic slave trade and were brought to the New World, many found it necessary to learn some kind of English. With very few exceptions the form of English which they acquired was a pidginized one, and this kind of English became so well established as the principal medium of communication between Negro slaves in the British colonies that it was passed on as a creole language to succeeding generations of the New World Negroes, for whom it was their native tongue.

That native tongue continued to offer code interference for the field hands, who had little access to the national language spoken by their masters in the "big house" and who were consequently "looked down upon" by the privileged domestic servants, who—by way of contrast—certainly did have access to the acrolect White English of their owners.

During the course of the eighteenth century, therefore, there occurred in the American South among the Negro slaves the following social cleavage, so eloquently described by Stewart (1970, p. 360):

Another change which took place in the New World Negro population primarily during the course of the eighteenth century was the
social cleavage of the New–World–born generations into underprivileged field hands (a continuation of the older, almost universal
lot of the Negro slave) and privileged domestic servants. The difference in privilege usually meant, not freedom instead of bondage,
but rather freedom from degrading kinds of labor, access to the
"big house" with its comforts and civilization and proximity to the
prestigious "quality" whites, with the opportunity to imitate their
behavior (including their speech) and to wear their clothes. In some
cases, privilege included the chance to get an education and, in
a very few, access to wealth and freedom. In both the British colonies
and the United States, Negroes belonging to the privileged group
were soon able to acquire a more standard variety of English than
the creole of the field hands, and those who managed to get a decent
education became speakers of fully standard and often elegant English.

The implicit cause of the social cleavage between field hands
and domestic servants, of course, was the opportunity for the
receipt, within the period of resonance, of the phenotypical
modeling of acrolect White English—an opportunity offered
to the children of the former and denied to the children of
the latter. And thus a vicious language circle perpetuated
a specialization of roles—and privileges—among the Negro
slaves.

Linguistically, the end result of such phenotypical modeling of acrolect White English for the children of the domestic
servants within the period of their resonance may be seen
and heard in the following quotation, made by Stewart (1970,
pp. 360–61), from a novel published in 1859 by *The Anglo–African Magazine;* the exchange is between Henry, an educated
Negro speaker of acrolect White English, and the wife of
Nathan, an uneducated Negro speaker of basilect Black English:

"Who was that old man who ran behind your master's horse?"
"Dat Nathan, my husban'."
"Do they treat him well, aunty?"
"No, chile, wus an' any dog, da beat 'im foh little an' nothin'."
"Is uncle Nathan religious?"
"Yes, chile, ole man an' I's been sahvin' God dis many day, fo
yeh baun! Wen any on 'em in de house git sick, den da sen foh
uncle Nathan' com pray foh dem; 'uncle Nathan' mighty good den!"

Quite obviously, the old "aunty" in the foregoing passage speaks the plantation creole of the field hands; Henry, on the other hand, speaks the acrolect "standard" Southern of the landed gentry. The fact that Henry is a Negro, of course, offers irrefutable evidence in support of this conclusion: THE PREFERRED RESONANT LANGUAGE THAT A PERSON SPEAKS DEPENDS UPON THE PHENOTYPICAL MODELING OF HIS CHILDHOOD AND NOT UPON HIS RACE. In other words, a socially advantaged Negro may speak an acrolect version of so–called "White English"; a socially disadvantaged white may speak a basilect version of so-called "Black English." In either phenomenon, resonance is all.

A product of generations of phenotypical modeling within the period of resonance, present–day Black English is the direct descendant of the plantation creole spoken by the illiterate field hands of the Old South. A notoriously nonprestigious basilect, Black English is the result of the interference of a native language with the national. That interference, in turn, has resulted in a social–class lect that is truly *different*, both in phonology and in grammar, from the so–called "standard" norms of any of the acrolect versions of Modern American English. Without trying to be exhaustive, a linguist may still list some of the most important differences of Black English as follows:

The *Different*: Some Important Divergences of "Black English"
I. In Phonology.

1. Basilect Black English has a higher degree of *r–lessness* than any other version of Modern American English (see Labov, 1969, p. 40). Thus in this speech variety such homonyms as the following may occur (see Labov, 1969, pp. 40–41): *Guard = god, par = pa, nor = gnaw, fort = fought, sore = saw, court = caught, Carol = Cal, Paris = pass*, and *terrace = test*.

2. In similar manner, basilect Black English has a higher degree of *l-lessness* than any other version of the national language (p. 41). This speech variety, therefore, produces such homonyms as these: *toll = toe, all = awe, help = hep, Saul = saw, tool = too,* and *fault = fought*.

3. Basilect Black English, more than any other version of Modern American English, simplifies final consonant clusters ending on /t/ and /d/ so that the stop drops out (see Labov, 1969, pp. 41–43). Thus in this social–class lect, the final consonant clusters /st ft nt nd ld zd md/ are reduced to /s f n n l z m/, respectively. Hence

past and *passed* sound like *pass* in the basilect that produces such other homonyms as these: *mend* = *men*, *rift* = *riff*, *wind* = *wine*, *meant* = *men*, *hold* = *hole*, and *tolled* = *toll* = *toe*.

4. In similar manner, basilect Black English, more than any other version of Modern American English, simplifies final consonant clusters ending on /s/ and /z/, so that the sibilant drops out in some clusters (e.g., *John's* = *John* and *its* = *it*) and remains in others (e.g., *let's* = *less*). Thus this social–class lect produces such homonyms as these: *six* = *sick*, *Max* = *Mack*, *box* = *bock*, and *mix* = *Mick* (see Labov, 1969, pp. 43–44).

5. Basilect Black English, more than any other version of Modern American English, weakens final consonants as a part of its general tendency *to produce less phonological information after stressed vowels* (see Labov, 1969, pp. 44–46). Hence this nonprestigious speech variety produces such homonyms as these: *Boot* = *Boo*, *seat* = *seed* = *see*, *road* = *row*, *poor* = *poke* = *pope*, *feed* = *feet*, *bit* = *bid* =*big*.

6. Basilect Black English, more than any other version of Modern American English, permits a confusing coalescence of *phonemic targets* (see Labov, 1969, pp. 46–47), among both the consonants and the vowels, so that the following wide range of homonyms may occur: *pin* = *pen*, *beer* = *bear*, *poor* = *pour*, *tin* = *ten*, *cheer* = *chair*, *sure* = *shore*, *since* = *cents*, *steer* = *stair*, *moor* = *more*, *peel* = *pail*, *find* = *found* = *fond*, *boil* = *ball*, *time* = *Tom*, *oil* = *all*, *pound* = *pond*, *Ruth* = *roof*, *stream* = *scream*, *death* = *deaf*, and *strap* = *scrap*.

II. In Grammar.

1. Basilect Black English is notorious for its failure to mark the possessive form of nouns and, in rapid speech, of such personal pronouns as *they* and *you* (see Labov, 1969, p. 51).

2. Basilect Black English frequently permits the coalescence of the colloquial future with the colloquial present (Labov, 1969, p. 51) so that the following homonyms may occur: *you'll* = *you*, *he'll* = *he*, *they'll* = *they*, and *she'll* = *she*.

3. Basilect Black English frequently leaves out the appropriate form of the copula *be* in sentences like *you tired* and *he in the way* (see Labov, 1969, pp. 51–52).

4. Basilect Black English regularly makes both grammatical and semantic distinctions, not present in sentences which leave out the appropriate form of the copula *be*, by using the unchanging infinitive form of the copula *be* (see Stewart, 1970, p. 361) in sentences like *he be busy* for "he is habitually busy" and *he be workin'* for "he is working steadily."

5. Basilect Black English usually fails to mark the past tense *of the regular verbs* by means of the appropriate inflectional ending (see Labov, 1969, p. 52), so that the following homonyms may occur:

pass = past = passed, pick = picked, miss= mist = missed, loan = loaned, fine = find = fined, and *raise = raised.*

6. Basilect Black English frequently negates verbs in the past tense with the use of *ain't* (see Stewart, 1970, p. 354), so that *Dey ain't like dat* really means "They didn't like that" rather than "They aren't like that."

7. Basilect Black English characteristically inverts the negative (see Labov, 1970a, p. 13), as in *Don't nobody know* for *Nobody knows.*

8. Basilect Black English characteristically achieves psychological emphasis by using the double negative, or what Labov (1970a, p. 13) calls "negative concord," as in *He ain't goin' to no heaven.*

9. Basilect Black English characteristically substitutes the dummy *it* for the dummy *there* in expletive constructions (see Labov, 1970a, p. 13), as in *It ain't no heaven.*

10. Basilect Black English characteristically employs a pleonastic subject (see Baratz, 1969, p. 99), as in *John he live in New York.*

11. Basilect Black English characteristically uses the past participle, unaccompanied, for the simple preterit in irregular verbs (see Baratz, 1969, p. 99), as in *seen* for *saw, drunk* for *drank,* and even *brung* for *brought.*

12. Basilect Black English characteristically fails to mark the agreement of subject and verb in the third–person singular of the present indicative (see Baratz, 1969, p. 100), as in *He run home* and *She have a bicycle.*

13. Basilect Black English characteristically either uses prepositions different from those of acrolect White English or leaves prepositions out altogether in its constructions (see Baratz, 1969, p. 100), as in *He over to his friend house* and *He work de city pool.*

In summary, these nineteen observations on the phonology and the grammar of basilect Black English reveal that this nonprestigious social–class lect is certainly *different* from any of the so–called "standard" versions of the national language. So different, in fact, that William Stewart himself (1970, pp. 355–356) admits that speakers of this form of the basilect are "speakers of the most radically nonstandard dialects of natively spoken English in the entire country."

Other Nonstandard Dialects

Stewart's admission, however, is also an implicit claim that there are other "radically nonstandard dialects of natively spoken English" in the United States today. Like basilect Black English, furthermore, these other "radically nonstandard dialects" are the result of generations of the interference of a native language with the national. More often than not, the native language in question is a creolized version of English. In Hawaii, for example, as the discussion in Chapter 2 has shown, the creole is based upon an Oriental or a European or a Kanaka or a mixed pidgin. Among Puerto Rican immigrants in the big city ghettos of the North, the Chicanos in Los Angeles and southern California, and the Mexican Americans along the Texas, New Mexico, and Arizona border, however, the creole is based upon a Spanish pidgin. On the Federal Government Reservations, by way of contrast, the creole is based upon some American Indian pidgin (e.g., Navaho in the Southwest and Sioux in the Dakotas). Among speakers of the Gullah dialect of the Carolina sea islands, the creole is based upon a Portuguese pidgin; among speakers of the Cajun dialect of Louisiana, upon a French pidgin; and, of course, among speakers of the "Pennsylvania Dutch" in and around Pittsburgh, upon a German pidgin. Wherever the interfering basilect is not based upon a creolized version of English, then the native language is probably a direct descendant of some archaic British dialect, with medieval and Renaissance features that diverge from the so–called "standard" norms of modern American usage (e.g., the "hillbilly English" that is vulgar Appalachian).

No matter what the local features of the interfering basilect may be, this much is linguistically certain: HANDICAPPED ENGLISH IS THE RESULT OF THE ATTEMPT OF A NATIVE LANGUAGE TO SUPPLANT THE NATIONAL LANGUAGE AS THE PREFERRED RESONANT MEDIUM OF COMMUNICATION. This attempt, of course, is successful in millions of cases of phenotypical modeling. It is precisely just such success on so large a scale that has resulted in the "differentness" observed by Stewart among "the radically nonstandard dialects" of Modern American English. The radical quality of the divergence from the norms of the so–called "standard" versions of the national language inherent in these "dialects" calls—by reason of the very nature of its radicality—for an answer to this question: "Does

*non*standard mean the same thing as *sub*standard?" In other
words, "Does *different* = *inferior?*" With regard to basilect
American English, of whatever form and history, the contention here is that the answer to both questions is *Yes!*

THE "INFERIOR"

Despite objections of some dialectologists to the contrary,
a linguist must—in all good conscience—arrive at a positive
reply to the foregoing question, if for no other reason than
the factor of prestige. "Different" here does *imply* some
inferiority. Actually, basilect versions of Modern American
English simply *do not* enjoy as wide a range of social acceptability as do acrolect versions, no matter who the speaker may
be and no matter what his race, religion, ethnic origin, age,
occupation, sex, or socio–economic status. Indeed, as William
Labov has demonstrated in his brilliant study *The Social
Stratification of English in New York City* (1966), speakers
of basilect American English are *stigmatized* as members
of the lower class and therefore as probably socially disadvantaged and as not well educated by reason of both their deviant
phonology and their deviant grammar.

Among speakers of basilect American English, the use of
such social–class markers as stops and affricates in place of
the *th–* sounds of the language, for example, are strong
indicators or predictors of the probability that they will also
pronounce the progressive aspect inflection–*ing* as though
it were –*in';* use double or multiple negatives, the demonstrative locatives *this here* and *that there,* and irregular preterits
and perfects erroneously; and, in the case of speakers of Black
English, substitute *do* for *if* and *whether* in the indirect
discourse that follows verbs of asking. Nor does it take very
long for the sensitive addressee to pick up and interpret the
stigmatizing features of the basilect that is being transmitted;
about eight to ten seconds of careful listening will do the
job. In the written code, as distinct from the spoken, on the
other hand, the addressee's reading of only one sentence will
often brand the addresser as a speaker of some form of basilect—as may be demonstrated in this gem from the recording

pen of Dillard (1972, p. 40): "An' so I comin' down an' she out there blabbin' her mouth told my sister I was playin' hookey from school." As *Newsweek* (August 14, 1972, p. 81) has observed, "The speaker is obviously black and poor. And to many white Americans his speech seems practically subversive—illogical, ungrammatical, unclear and, well, lazy."

Even if the stereotyped value judgment of the many white Americans stated by *Newsweek* is wrong—AND IT *IS* WRONG!—the fact remains that speakers of basilect are, more often than not, the victims of the prejudice of "linguistic superiority"— the type of linguistic superiority fostered by an immigrant–ancestor society that has been traditionally, from colonial days onward, the land of the culturally insecure and the home of the social–climbing snobbish. And it is truly ironic that much of the linguistic prejudice inflicted upon the speakers of basilect American English is inflicted either by themselves or by those people who have "graduated" from their own speech community into the mesilect of the lower middle class. Members of the lower middle class in the United States, no matter what their race or ethnic origin, are notoriously insecure in their command of the national language and at the same time linguistically ambitious to achieve social mobility in order to attain the privileges that go therewith. Hence Labov (1968, p. 248) is right with a vengeance when he makes the following claim:

> . . . A great deal of evidence shows that lower middle class speakers have the greatest tendency towards linguistic insecurity, and therefore tend to adopt, even in middle age, the prestige forms used by the youngest members of the highest ranking class. This linguistic insecurity is shown by the very wide range of stylistic variation used by lower middle class speakers; by their great fluctuation within a given stylistic context; by their conscious striving for correctness; and by their strongly negative attitudes towards their native speech pattern.

We say *right with a vengeance* because most of the English teachers in the public schools of America come from that same linguistically insecure lower middle class. These same English teachers are largely responsible for the phenomenon of "cumulative deficit" among the speakers of basilect once they enter the public schools—a source of further linguistic handicapping that will be discussed in detail in Chapter 6 ("Causes of Handicapped English").

The Problem of Grammaticality

In the meantime, the linguistic prejudice of the public schools against all forms of basilect Modern American English is not without some measure of justification. Why? Because speakers of the most nonprestigious social–class lect, no matter what their race or ethnic origin, do tend to *perform* in "inferior" fashion in the classrooms of the United States. Indeed as Labov himself (1970a, p. 35) has indicated, the reading performance of the speakers of basilect Black English whom he studied in his monumental work *The Social Stratification of English in New York City* (above referred to) was "more than two full years behind grade in the ninth grade." Handicapped even more severely than Negro children in the New York City ghettos in their classroom performance, are Indian children on Federal Government reservations, who, in the words of Hildegard Thompson (1967, p. 67), start their school careers "six years behind in English language development." These Indian children, in fact, emphasize two major areas—quite apart from prestige, prejudice, and stigma—in which all socially disadvantaged speakers of some form of the basilect or other will find their code tending to be "inferior": grammar and rhetoric.

In looking at the area of grammar first, a linguist discovers that *the problem of grammaticality* constantly besets the speakers of basilect Modern American English and makes their code "inferior" in its acceptability to more privileged speakers of the national, as distinct from a mere native, language. As Paul Roberts (1968, p. 3) has said, "There are at least seven different ways in which language can diverge from some specified grammar." These ways, therefore, constitute the seven types of ungrammaticality in present–day American English (see Roberts, 1968, pp. 3–8); they may be listed and illustrated as follows:

Seven Types of Ungrammaticality in Modern American English

1. Failure of a foreign learner. *Example:* "Because he have always earn good moneys at work, he go buy good suit at tailor shop."

2. Mistake of a child working by analogy. *Example:* "We saw some bad mans rob the bank on TV last night."

3. The archaic grammar of an earlier stage of the English language. *Example:* Shakespeare's query (*King Lear* IV,ii,92), "Knows he the wickedness?"

4. The divergent idioms of British (or Commonwealth) usage. *Example:* "Oh, I say, poor Chives looked rather a fool, you know."

5. The socially nonprestigious forms of American folk (basilect) speech. *Example:* "Me and George gone went and done it up real good."

6. The dangling–modifier constructions of careless writing. *Example: If thoroughly stewed, the patients will enjoy the prunes.*

7. The abnormal constructions of poetic license. *Example:* Gerard Manley Hopkins' lines (from "Spring and Fall: To a Young Child"),
Leaves, like the things of man, you
With your fresh thoughts care for, can you?

Most Americans, at one time or another, have confronted each of these seven types of ungrammaticality—either as speakers and writers or as listeners and readers. Though ungrammatical, the examples just heard (in quotation marks, to indicate spoken discourse) and read (in italics, to indicate written discourse) are not the linguistic equivalents of mortal sin. They are merely syntactic structures that deviate from the normal range of Modern American English sentences and are therefore considered as not being *conventionally* well made, according to the intuitive competence of the average sophisticated speaker of the national language (see Chomsky, 1970, pp. 108–112).

As the acknowledged leader of the *formal* linguists (see Bolinger, 1968, pp. 200–212), Noam Chomsky (1957; 1965) emphasizes the hierarchical precedence which the grammatical component takes over the phonological component in the act of encoding English sentences. Perhaps a proper interpretation of Chomsky's emphasis as it relates to all three components of English would read as follows:

Chomsky's Emphasis in the Three Components of English

1. The discourse needs of the sender of the message in the semantic component . . .

2. get their SYNTACTIC AND MORPHOLOGICAL MAPPING in the grammatical component . . .

3. and their ultimate expression in the phonological component (see Chomsky and Halle, 1968).

The three steps in the act of encoding a message, then, mean that a grammar is the interiorized system of competence rules, now become performance habits (see Twaddell, 1948, 1967), which allow the native speaker of some form of English to produce, hypothetically at least, all of the acceptable sentences of his language and none of the unacceptable ones.

Acceptable to whom? To another native speaker of English who shares the same, or at least an extremely similar, interiorized system of competence rules become performance habits—that is, to one who shares the same, or at least an extremely similar, grammar. An Elizabethan gentleman, for example, would have no trouble at all in accepting Shakespeare's "Knows he the wickedness?" as being completely grammatical. In Early Modern English a main verb could initiate a question; in Late Modern English a main verb does not normally initiate a question. And so Shakespeare's "Knows he the wickedness?" is the equivalent of the present-day "Does he know the wickedness?" in which the appropriate tense–carrying form of the omnipotent verb auxiliary *do,* initiates the question. Thus when the Duke of Albany asks, "Knows he the wickedness?" the modern auditor of *King Lear* interprets the question as being an example of archaic grammar, the product of an interiorized system of competence rules become performance habits that he no longer fully shares with the encoder of the message. Ungrammatical as the question is, however, it draws *distractive* attention to itself and in so doing foregrounds (see Mukarovský, 1964 the code rather than the message ONLY WHEN IT IS SPOKEN AS *CURRENT* USAGE. In the immediate context situation of *King Lear,* of course, the question is fully acceptable and therefore unimpeachably grammatical.

Here then, assuredly, is a major lesson in what constitutes ungrammaticality. *The phenomenon is a relative, not an absolute, thing*—and in essence amounts to this:

> **Ungrammaticality** = the unacceptability of a sentence as not being well made, simply because it draws a *distractive* attention to itself and consequently foregrounds the code rather than the message.

Germane to the problem of ungrammaticality in the various

forms of basilect Modern American English is this central fact: by the foregoing principle of linguistic relativity, the Appalachian farm boy who says, "Me and George gone went and done it up real good," may be extremely effective and hence completely grammatical when speaking to another Appalachian farm boy. But his sentence may draw laughter from others when he tries to pass it off as fully acceptable in town.

That potential laughter, of course, is a somewhat cruel reminder that not all forms of English grammar currently have the same amount of social acceptability. Looking at the problem of grammaticality from this sociological point of view, a linguist is forced—in all honesty—to make the following observation:

> **Grammaticality** = the widest possible social acceptance and therefore *credibility* for the code in which a person casts his messages.

The key term in the preceding definition of *grammaticality* is *credibility,* for it and it alone reveals why no would–be speaker of the national language of the United States today should want to sound like a foreign learner, or a child, or an Elizabethan, or a socially disadvantaged speaker of basilect, or a careless student in Freshman Composition, or an affected imitator of modern British usage: *his performance might violate approval in the conative function of his addressee.*

Underlying such a violation, quite obviously, is the conative function of the addressee himself, which operates by means of a *matrix of reception* (see Miller, 1964, 1967) through which the addressee interprets the meanings of new structures and expressions that are being transmitted to him in some form or other of the English language. Heavily influencing the role of the addressee and its attendant conative function, this matrix of reception operates by means of the following important factors (see esp. Miller, 1967, pp. 329–330):

Important Factors in the Matrix of Reception
1. Listening and hearing.
2. Matching of phonemic input with phonemic output.
3. Acceptance of the grammaticality of the code of the message.

4. Semantic interpretation.

5. Understanding of the contextual function of an utterance within the message.

6. Belief that the utterance and therefore the message within which it occurs are both valid in terms of one's own conduct.

So influential is factor number 3 (Acceptance of the grammaticality of the code) that it may interdict the other five factors in the matrix of reception and cause them to cease to function properly—or altogether. This factor, therefore, must be examined in some measure of detail.

Acceptance or nonacceptance of the grammaticality of the code means simply this: whether or not the addressee will conatively approve the sentences of the message as being well–formed ones. If the addressee does *not* accept the sentences as being well–formed according to the grammatical rules of the national, as distinct from any mere native, version of Modern American English, then he may very well dismiss the message itself as being unworthy of his serious attention. With this dismissal, of course, the addressee ceases to listen and hear, to try to match phonemic input with phonemic output (often a difficult task in itself when dealing with the radically deviant phonology of the basilect); he ceases to give the message a semantic interpretation, to try to understand the contextual function of any and every utterance within the message, and—finally and most importantly—he ceases to believe that the message as a whole is valid in terms of his own personal behavior. Because of this dismissal, the ungrammaticality of the basilect in question means that A MISMANAGED CODE HAS BECOME ITS OWN MISMANAGED MESSAGE.

As a result of this equation of distraction, the addressee will, more often than not, unfortunately dismiss the *sender* of the message as well for being something of an ignoramus. Why *unfortunately?* Because the ability to be thoroughly grammatical according to the norms of the national language is no guarantee of lofty intelligence or of high moral purpose. Neither is the inability to be thoroughly grammatical according to the norms of the national language a sure indication of illogicality, stupidity, laziness, or moral reprehensibility. But the receiver of the message may think this ungrammaticality stupid or lazy, or whatever, with such self–righteousness as to make its sender guilty of something almost as bad as original sin (see Lloyd, 1951, 1967; 1952, 1963). This self-righteous response, unfortunately again, is a social fact concerning the current use of basilect American English. And what this social fact means is simply this: THE UNGRAMMATICALITY OF THE BASILECT, MORE OFTEN THAN NOT, AUTOMATICALLY INFLICTS *A LOSS OF ETHOS* UPON ITS SPEAKERS. That loss of ethos, in turn, has direct bearing upon the second major area in which the "different" does equal the "inferior": mainly rhetoric.

The Problem of Rhetoric

The loss of ethos inflicted upon speakers of the basilect by reason of its ungrammaticality, usually results in a further intensification of the linguistic isolation and alienation of these speakers. Because their more socially advantaged addressees tend to "turn them off," speakers of basilect Modern American English frequently suffer from a distortion of their emotive function as transmitters and of their conative function as receivers of messages and this *in direct proportion to their degree of frustration!* As a consequence of such distortion, the socially disadvantaged speakers of handicapped English usually, though not always, have a negative and high emotive function as addressers and a negative and low conative function as addressees. That is, they tend not to believe in the validity of the messages which they receive, while at the same time (ironically enough!) rhetorically demanding, by means of vulgar and often downright profane or even obscene emotive tacts, that other people give more than normal credence to the messages which they themselves transmit (see Nist, June 1969).

The distortion in both the emotive and the conative function of the socially disadvantaged speakers of the basilect is immediately apparent in the rhetoric of their messages. In the following sample of basilect Black English supplied by Labov (1970a, pp. 12–13), the fundamental hostility of Larry, a fifteen-year-old member of a Negro street gang in New

York City, clamors for the attention of his adult interviewer
John Lewis:

JL: What happens to you after you die? Do you know?
LARRY: Yeah, I know.
JL: What?
LARRY: After they put you in the ground, your body turns
       into—ah—bones, an' shit.
JL: What happens to your spirit?
LARRY: Your spirit—soon as you die, your spirit leaves you.
JL: And where does the spirit go?
LARRY: Well, it all depends. . . .
JL: On what?
LARRY: You know, like some people say if you're good an' shit,
       your spirit goin' t'heaven . . . 'n' if you bad, your spirit
       goin' to hell. Well, bullshit! Your spirit goin' to hell
       anyway, good or bad.
JL: Why?
LARRY: Why? I'll tell you why. 'Cause, you see, doesn' nobody
       really know that it's a God, y'know, 'cause I mean I have
       seen black gods, pink gods, white gods, all color gods,
       and don't nobody know it's really a God. An' when they
       be sayin' if you good, you goin' t'heaven, tha's bullshit,
       'cause you ain't goin to no heaven, 'cause it ain't no heaven
       for you to go to.

In the opinion of Labov (1970a, p. 13), Larry's phil-
osophizing on heaven provides a quintessential example
of the rhetoric of basilect Black English, a rhetoric which
Labov commends: Larry "can sum up a complex argument
in a few words, and the full force of his opinions comes
through without qualification or reservation." Labov, of
course, ignores Larry's high and negative emotive function
as an addresser of his national culture and his low and negative
conative function as an addressee of that same culture. The
terrible distortion in both functions results in Larry's self-
victimization through the over-generalization of his categorical statements. As morally impatient as Steinbeck's Uncle
John and just as eager to remove every trace of ambiguity
or plurisignificance, Larry unwittingly commits a kind of
rhetorical suicide through the ironic under–emphasis of his
over–emphasis. Why? Because if everything is emphasized,

then nothing is emphasized; if all is "bullshit," then nothing is "bullshit." And so Larry robs himself of the full force and efficacy of even his profanity.

The rhetorical suicide which produces such ironic self-robbery is the almost inevitable by-product of the militant isolation and resentful alienation of Larry's basilect subculture, a subculture which the teen–age Negro gang member equates with *hell* itself (see Labov, 1970a, p. 14):

JL: Well, if there's no heaven, how could there be a hell?
LARRY: I mean—ye–eah. Well, let me tell you, it ain't no hell, 'cause this is hell right here, y'know!
JL: This is hell?
LARRY: Yeah, this is hell right here!

In the words of Labov (1970a, p. 14) concerning the hidden fallacy of going to a nonexistent hell, "Larry's answer is quick, ingenious and decisive." It is also flawed in its logic. Like an amateur chess player who allows one of his opponent's knights to place one of his own bishops and one of his own rooks under a forking attack that will surely capture one of them (probably the rook, since it is the more valuable piece), Larry permits his argument to lead his atheistic creed into a perpetual vicious circle of reincarnation, in which the released spirit is constantly being condemned to live again in the nonexistent hell of this world. Which world? Larry's world. The unjust world of the Negro ghetto, where the terrible distortion of both the emotive and the conative function in the rhetoric of a fifteen-year-old boy pleads for a too-often-unachieved credibility and its attendant ethos with the unconscious and yet pitiful formulaic tags *you know* and *you see.*

Larry's World

A world which Labov (1970a, p. 15), in an unguarded moment of specialist zeal, praises for the fact that so many of its basilect speakers "take great delight in exercising their wit and logic on the most improbable and problematical matters"—such is Larry's world. That exercise, sadly enough, is one of the central attributes of a subculture which is *not* actively engaged in either the dignifying work or the self-fulfilling decision-making that accompanies the mastery of some acrolect version of the national language. And just as love in its highest expression is deeds rather than words, action rather than sentiment, so the highest use of logic results in decisions rather than in mere idle conjecture, in mature work rather than in childish wordplay. Hence when Labov (1970a, p. 15) commends Larry for his "great 'verbal presence of mind,' " this eminent linguist is unintentionally misleading, for it is Larry's so–called "verbal presence of mind" that directs his thought into the crudest form of alienated and alienating anthropomorphism, in which God Himself becomes the ignominious ally (and creature) of "the average whitey," whom Larry considers as his exploiting enemy (see Labov, 1970a, p. 15):

JL:. . . But, just say that there is a God, what color is he? White or black?

LARRY: Well, if it is a God . . . I wouldn' know what color, I couldn' say——couldn' nobody say what color he is or really *would* be.

JL: But now, jus' suppose there was a God——

LARRY: Unless'n they say . . . .

JL: No, I was jus' sayin' jus' suppose there is a God, would he be white or black?

LARRY: . . . He'd be white, man.

JL: Why?

LARRY: Why? I'll tell you why. 'Cause the average whitey out here got everything, you dig? And the nigger ain't got shit, y'know? Y'understan'? So—um——for——in order for *that* to happen, you know it ain't no black God that's doin' that bullshit.

It is clear from Larry's argument, such as it is, that the moral universe of this socially disadvantaged teen-age Negro is like a mountain without a peak: the summit of Godhead has been usurped by his own fear and animosity, by the projection of his own hostile resentment. Larry's profanely insistent rhetoric, constantly begging for an understanding of the inchoate and inarticulate logic which it fails to make explicit, is the inept organizer of a handicapped English that continues to victimize its speaker in these two all-important and fundamental ways: (1) the inadequate segmentation of reality and

(2) the improper image of the self and of the language roles which that self must or should assume.

It is the inadequate segmentation of reality which leads Larry's argument into the categorical statements of his over-generalization. It is the improper image of himself and of the language role which he should assume with "John Lewis," which keeps Larry from applying forms of mitigation and politeness, from avoiding basilect profanity when discussing the Deity, from implicitly insulting his interviewer with constant appeals for him to acknowledge his understanding. Like Babbitt, Larry cannot experience what he cannot express; like Uncle John, Larry cannot express well even that which he does experience. Flawed like his logic, Larry's rhetoric shows that, in the organization of his messages, his basilect Black English is deficient in what Labov (1970a, p. 19) calls the "subtle and sophisticated mode of planning utterances, achieving structural variety, [and] taking the other person's knowledge into account." As Labov (1970a, pp. 11–12) himself admits, Larry's ghetto form of handicapped English is also deficient in "precision in spelling, practice in handling abstract symbols, the ability to state explicitly the meaning of words, and a richer knowledge of the Latinate vocabulary." In summary, then, Larry's own peculiar form of basilect is a microcosmic proof of this macrocosmic fact: IN ALL FORMS OF BASILECT MODERN AMERICAN ENGLISH, "DIFFERENT" DOES INDEED EQUAL "INFERIOR."

The following two chapters will illustrate this value judgement in detail.

Chapter 4

INADEQUATE SEGMENTATION OF REALITY

As the first great semantic deficiency among the speakers of basilect, the inadequate segmentation of reality involves them immediately in the problem of *meaning*. And the problem of meaning in Modern American English, or in any other national language for that matter, is the largest single problem facing the scientific and theoretical study of man's capacity (or incapacity) to communicate with his fellow man. Why? Because meaning is the one subject which many linguistics have deliberately stayed away from, while preferring to make their taxonomic studies of *form* and *function* first. Because meaning, together with its attendant *value*, is what the use of language is ultimately all about, and—as such—it is the *closest* thing to its users personally (see Chomsky, 1968, pp. 21–23). It is a truism of science, moreover, that man studies the things *furthest* away from his immediate consciousness *first* (see Bolinger, 1968, p. 184): that is why astronomy, for example, developed centuries ahead of psychology. Meaning, therefore, is the most complex and difficult-to-analyze factor in communication. Perhaps that is why meaning lies hidden in the very heart of the sociolinguistic phenomenon known as handicapped English.

104

THREE KINDS OF MEANING

Whenever one American communicates with another in some current form of the English language, three kinds of meaning are engaged in the encoding and the decoding of his message: (1) *designative* meaning, or the relationship of linguistic signs to items in the cultural context; (2) *implicative* meaning, or the relationship between linguistic signs and other linguistic signs; and (3) *expressive* meaning, or the behavioral relationship between the sender and the receiver of the message. If a linguist were to relate these three kinds of meaning with the terms *semantic, grammatical,* and *pragmatic* (see Landar, 1966, pp. 48–49), his correspondence would run as follows:

Three Different Kinds of Meaning in Modern American English

Designative or *semantic* meaning. This is the meaning of the relationship between linguistic signs and the objects which they refer to. The word *duck,* for example, designates a familiar feathered fowl that waddles and makes a noise that sounds like *quack.*

Implicative or *grammatical* meaning. This is the meaning of the structure of contrasts among the linguistic signs themselves. The grammatical system of selection in the language, for instance, is the means by which one word or word group dictates the choice of form in another word or word group; when any pronoun capable of showing so–called "case endings" is in the "objective," therefore, speakers of English conventionally give it the implicative meaning of "object of either a transitive verb/verbal or a preposition."

Expressive or *pragmatic* meaning. This is the meaning of the response elicited from the receiver of the message by the sender. Miss Jones, for example, asks her first–grade student Jimmy Brown to draw a picture of the animal which "waddles and says, *Quack!*" Because Jimmy has understood both the semantic and the grammatical meaning of his teacher's request, he responds with his own pragmatic meaning by drawing the picture of a duck.

From the foregoing discussion, then, it is apparent that the semantic component of Modern American English is the result of an organic–like union of three ranges of experience: (1) the relation of signs to referents, (2) the relation of signs to signs, and (3) the relation of signs to their users. These three ranges of experience involve man in the world about him and in the language he uses to apprehend and comprehend that world by means of segmenting its reality through *sign, referent*, and *reference* (see Bolinger, 1968, pp. 220–240). The organic–like union that produces these three ranges of experience may be schematized as in Diagram 3.

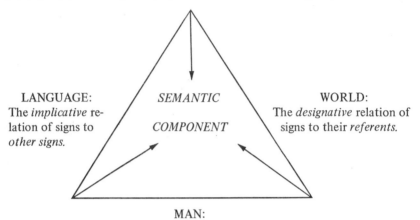

LANGUAGE:
The *implicative* relation of signs to *other signs.*

SEMANTIC

COMPONENT

WORLD:
The *designative* relation of signs to their *referents.*

MAN:
The *pragmatic* relation of signs
to the *references* of their users.

DIAGRAM 3. THREE RANGES OF EXPERIENCE IN
MODERN AMERICAN ENGLISH.

Metaphorically, the scheme itself may be called "The Brand of Meaning." Whenever a speaker of some form of Modern American English marks a segment of reality with this brand, he gives expression to the three kinds of meaning which constitute the semantic component of his language, his world, and himself (cf. Diagram 3). Just how effective that expression will be, however, depends in large measure upon just how well the language of the speaker relates him to the national language, to the world which produces that language, and to the people who inhabit that world.

SEMANTIC VARIABLES

It is the contention here that all forms of the basilect in the United States today are inadequate in their segmentation of reality, and hence are truly handicapped English, precisely because they are so deficient in their expression of the implicative, the designative, and the pragmatic ranges of experience. And perhaps there is no better place to begin a demonstration of this deficiency than in that area of the matrix of meaning which linguists have called the *semantic variables* (see Landar, 1966, pp. 58–63) of the language. These semantic variables, in turn, may be named, symbolized, and illustrated as follows (see Nist, 1971b, p. 328):

Eleven Factors in the Matrix of Meaning

1. SITUATIONAL STIMULI: S—Example. A school bus approaches a bus stop where several children are waiting.

2. BEHAVIORAL RESPONSES: R—Example. Mary Smith says, jumping up and down excitedly, "Here it comes!"

3. EXTERNAL EVENTS: E—Example. It has been snowing heavily, the children are cold, the bus is late, and there was a school bus accident only yesterday in which some other children were hurt.

4. INTERNAL EVENTS: I—Example. Mary Smith's high emotive function because of her relief from anxiety: the bus, though late, is safe, and she and the other children will soon be warm and on their way to school.

5. NONLINGUISTIC CONTEXTS: N—Example. The entire set of referential factors relating to the approach of the school bus.

6. LINGUISTIC CONTEXTS: L—Example. The worried conversation that the children waiting at the bus stop have been engaged in before Mary Smith sees the bus and says, jumping up and down excitedly, "Here it comes!"

7. LINGUISTIC TOKENS: T—Example. An individual word in an utterance, like *comes* in Mary Smith's statement, "Here it comes!"

8. LINGUISTIC TYPES: T—Example. A set of linguistic tokens and therefore of class structures and their membership, as in the linguistic type known as *intransitive verb*, from which *comes* is generated.

9. COMPONENTS: C—Example. The distinctive features or criterial attributes that distinguish one language structure from another, as in the emphatic word order of Mary Smith's "Here it comes!" as distinct from the normal declarative word order of "It comes here."

10. FREQUENCY FACTOR: F—Example. The literalness of logical convention in a statement, and therefore its high degree of predictability, as in the rather frequent and somewhat banal "We cashed a check."

11. NONFREQUENCY FACTOR: F—Example. The figurativeness of metaphoricality of psychological invention in a statement, and therefore its low degree of predictability, as in the highly infrequent and rather exciting homophonic pun "We cached a Czech," spoken by British Intelligence about an Iron Curtain defector from Prague.

So important are these eleven semantic variables in the determination of the three kinds of meaning or ranges of experience that they must be studied in some measure of detail, for they exercise an enormous influence on a person's segmentation of reality. Quite obviously, any student waiting for the school bus in the preceding series of illustrations who would say of Mary Smith's happy relief, "Why the hell is she flippin her lid over a damn bus?" is either ignorant of or insensitive to the total context situation of yesterday's tragedy and today's danger. Is, in short, the victim of "handicapped English."

The offensive language behavior of such a victim shows, of course, that in the measurement of psychological states such other factors as *intensity, speech habits, themata, overtness, covertness, suppression,* and *repression* have to be taken into account before any accurate interpretation of the total meaning of a message can be attempted (see Gottschalk and Gleser, 1969). That total meaning, in turn, depends to a large extent upon the relationship between internal events (i.e., those which occur *inside* man's own organismic being) as behavioral responses to external events (i.e., those which occur *outside* man's own organismic being) that act as situational stimuli. Both external and internal events can act, however, as either situational stimuli (i.e., anything in the cultural context that makes an impact on the consciousness of man) or as behavioral responses (i.e., man's reactions to the situational stimuli which enter his consciousness and are acknowledged or suppressed or repressed).

SOME DISTORTIONS OF REALITY

The meaningful relationship between external events as situational stimuli and internal events as behavioral responses may be illustrated by the following two dramatic scenes, which deal with the sale of a house:

1

MR. BUYER: How much did you say that Mr. Seller wants for that house?

MR. REALTOR: He says his asking price is thirty thousand dollars.

MR. BUYER: Thirty thousand dollars! Why, that little shack isn't worth more than twenty thousand, if it's worth a penny.

MR. REALTOR: Come now, Mr. Buyer, you must be reasonable. I said that thirty thousand dollars was Mr. Seller's *asking* price. I think we can get him to come down a bit. Say maybe to twenty–eight thousand.

MR. BUYER: Twenty–eight thousand! That's too much. My offer is twenty–four thousand, not a penny more. . . .

2

MR. SELLER: Twenty-four thousand! Why, the offer is ridiculous. Do you realize all the improvements my wife and I have put into that place to make it a real showpiece of the neighborhood?

MR. REALTOR: Yes, Mr. Seller, I realize that. In fact, I told Mr. Buyer that I didn't think you'd sell for less than twenty–six thousand.

MR. SELLER: Well, you can say that again! And add another thousand to it.

MR. REALTOR: You mean you'd consider an offer of twenty–seven thousand?

MR. SELLER: Not a penny less. Why, there's more than that amount in the place when you consider the interest we've paid and everything. . . .

In their segmentation of reality, it is apparent that all three men in the foregoing scenes have the same external event —namely, the house; but each man has a different internal event—namely, his vision of the house and the emotive function which that vision calls forth. Diagram 4 (p. 110) details these three viewpoints, or ways of looking at the same reality. From the drawings of these three visions, therefore, it is clear that the meaning of any external event or situational stimulus is very much "colored" or modified by the internal event or behavioral response.

The relationship between an item in *objective* reality and man's vision of that item in *subjective* reality is comparable

WHAT MR. BUYER SEES

WHAT MR. SELLER SEES

WHAT MR. REALTOR SEES

Diagram 4. THREE VIEWPOINTS.

to the drawing of three lines shown below in Diagram 5. As a person looks at the drawings, his first impression is that the line on the left is the longest, the line in the middle the next longest, and the line on the right the least long or the shortest. In reality, of course, each major line is exactly the same length, but the one on the left is *maximized* by two smaller lines at each end which appear to extend its length, whereas the major line on the right is *minimized* by two smaller lines at each end which appear to diminish its length. The line in the middle, however, is the exact length of the other two major lines: it is neither maximized nor minimized. In analogy with these lines, then—and comparing Diagram 5 with Diagram 4 above—what Mr. Seller sees is a maximized version of his house; what Mr. Buyer sees is

Diagram 5. THREE LINES: WHICH IS LONGEST?

a minimized version; what Mr. Realtor sees is the house as it actually is. Insofar as anyone can make subjective and objective reality coincide, Mr. Realtor's view is the closest to the truth.

OTHER BASILECT LIMITATIONS

As an applicable extension of the foregoing argument, it must be said here that most speakers of handicapped English tend to either maximize or minimize items in the cultural context that surrounds them. In other words, under the influence of a high emotive function, speakers of handicapped English tend to maximize external events like Mr. Seller; under the influence of a low conative function, these same speakers tend to minimize external events like Mr. Buyer. In either case, their segmentation of reality is distorted and therefore inadequate. Why? Because—ironically enough—if too little is insufficient, then so is too much.

Seldom able to turn on the proper current of feeling like Mr. Realtor, speakers of handicapped English are like unlit houses, the electricity in which is either too high or too low in voltage for their circuits. Hence Labov's Larry (see p. 102) stands in the night of his own emotive maximization when he overgeneralizes that "the average whitey out here got everything, you dig? And the nigger ain't got shit, y'know?" Thus Steinbeck's Uncle John (see p. 81) is imprisoned in the darkness of his own conative minimization when he dismisses his young wife's attack of appendicitis with this fatal advice: "You just got stomickache. You et too much. Take a dose a pain killer." Here, at least, is one "average whitey" who doesn't have everything.

Sensitivity to Content Rather Than Structure

As a result of their tendency to maximize and minimize and thus to distort the segmentation of reality, speakers of handicapped English are, in the words of Bernstein (1968, p. 224), sensitive "to the content rather than to the structure of objects." This sensitivity to content, rather than to structure, produces a perception (see Bernstein, 1968, p. 224) that "is of a qualitatively different order" from that of more advantaged speakers of the national language. In other words, speakers of basilect Modern American English are markedly inferior in their command over the semantic variables known as nonlinguistic contexts (i.e., any external or internal events or series of events or states of being that are *not* verbal in nature) and linguistic contexts (i.e., any external or internal events or series of events that *are* verbal in nature). The overgeneralization of Labov's Larry and the fatal diagnosis of Steinbeck's Uncle John are two examples of this markedly inferior command of nonlinguistic contexts. Bernstein (1968, pp. 226–227) himself offers the following extended example of and commentary on the failure of speakers of the basilect to achieve an effective control over linguistic contexts:

> When a middle-class mother says to her child, "I'd rather you made less noise, darling," the child will tend to obey because previous disobedience after this point has led to expression of disapproval or perhaps other punitive measures. The operative words in this sentence which the middle—class child responds to are "rather" and "less." The child has learned to become sensitive to this form of sentence and the many possible sentences in this universe of discourse. The words "rather" and "less" are understood, when used in this situation, as directly translatable cues for immediate response on the part of the middle—class child. However, if the same statement were made to a child from the family of an unskilled worker it would not be understood as containing the same imperative cues for response. "Shut up!" may contain a more appropriate set of cues. (Of course, the last statement is meaningful to a middle—class child, but what is important to stress is the fact that the middle—class child has learned to be able to respond to *both* statements, and *both* are differentially discriminated within a finely articulated world of meaning. We are discussing two modes of language and the working—class child has only learned to respond to one, and so although he may understand both, he will not differentiate effectually between the two.) Further, if the first statement is made by a middle—class person to a working—class child, the child will translate it into "Shut up" and will relate the difference between the statements to the different social levels. What he will not have, and what he cannot respond to *directly,* is the different language structure of the first sentence. The working—class child has to translate and thus *mediate* middle—class language structure through the logically simpler language structure of his own class to make it personally meaningful. Where he cannot make this translation he fails to understand and is left puzzled.

Although Bernstein's foregoing observation was originally made about British children, it is thoroughly applicable to American. And what the observation means in effect is this: socially disadvantaged speakers of basilect Modern American English suffer from an inadequate segmentation of reality in linguistic contexts to such a degree that if they fail to "translate" the message of a higher lect into the terms of their own, then they fail to understand the message at all. Adult Negroes in the Mississippi Delta, for example, generally cannot follow a spoken discourse if the average sentence runs to more than seven or eight words in length and if the level of abstraction is relatively high (personal observation). Most speakers of the basilect, young and old alike, would have great trouble in interpreting the following three "translations" of the nonlinguistic context of the house for sale, seen earlier in this chapter, into the linguistic context of what each man involved in the sale might say of the house in a holophrastic phrase:

MR. SELLER: Since a man's home is his castle, I have a right to call mine a *mansion.*

MR. BUYER: Since a man should get every last penny of value out of a dollar spent, I have a right to call Mr. Seller's house *a modest home.*

MR. REALTOR: Since I want to make my commission on the sale without giving offense to either Mr. Seller or Mr. Buyer, I have the duty to myself to see this piece of property for what it is: a middle–class home in fine repair in a respectable neighborhood and therefore *a good investment in family living.*

Each man in the foregoing paradigm of contrasts in the segmentation of reality has his own key term in the linguistic context of his final value judgment. Mr. Seller's key term is *home,* a warm word with strong emotional overtones; Mr. Buyer's key term is *house,* a cool word with weak emotional overtones; Mr. Realtor's key term is *piece of property,* a no–nonsense phrase of business. Thus Mr. Seller's *home* produces the maximized value judgment inherent in *mansion;* Mr. Buyer's *house* yields the minimized value judgment inherent in *modest home;* and Mr. Realtor's *piece of property* achieves the huckstering compromise between the other two value judgments: *a good investment in family living.*

Because speakers of the basilect are far more sensitive to content than they are to structure, most of them would have grave difficulty in perceiving the cause–and–effect relationship between the key terms of the foregoing set of illustrations and their resultant value judgments. These same speakers of the basilect, moreover, would probably fail to see the connection between both Mr. Seller and Mr. Buyer's term "right" and its somewhat self–centered distortion of reality, especially as that term is contrasted with Mr. Realtor's word "duty" and its paradoxically somewhat self–transcending faithful mirroring of reality. Such failure on the part of speakers of the basilect is due in large measure to their deficiency not only in linguistic contexts, but also in the semantic variables known as linguistic tokens, types, and components.

A Paucity of Vocabulary

Suffering from a "paucity of language" (Ponder, 1967, p. 27) and lacking in "verbal symbols for common objects and ideas" (Ponder, 1967, p. 23), speakers of handicapped English are notorious for the meagerness of their vocabulary. Since words are both linguistic tokens (i.e., individual items in the makeup of a distinctive language structure) and linguistic types (i.e., sets of linguistic tokens that constitute class structures and therefore class memberships like phonemes, morphemes, parts of speech, and sentence types), this impoverishment in the vocabulary of speakers of the basilect usually results in their failure to perceive how what is type at one level (e.g., the phoneme /k/) may become token at a higher level of linguistic structure—e.g., the phoneme /k/ as an ultimate constituent of the morpheme word *cat*. Such failure, of course, is the direct outgrowth of the faulty structuring of perception that is achieved by the constant use of an inferior lect that, in the words of Bernstein (1968, p. 228, n. 2), may be characterized as follows:

> . . . short, grammatically simple, often unfinished, sentences with a poor syntactical construction; simple and repetitive use of conjunctions (so, then, and), thus modifications, qualifications

and logical stress will tend to be indicated by non–verbal means; frequent use of short commands and questions; rigid and limited use of adjectives and adverbs; infrequent use of the impersonal pronoun (it, one) as subject of a conditional sentence; statements formulated as questions which set up a sympathetic circularity, e.g. "Just fancy?", "Isn't it terrible?", "Isn't it a shame?", "It's only natural, isn't it?" A statement of fact is often used as both a reason and a conclusion, e.g. "You're not going out," "I told you to hold on tight" (Mother to child on bus, as repeated answer to child's "Why?"). Individual selection from a group of traditional phrases plays a great part. The symbolism is of a low order of generality. *The personal qualification is left out of the structure of the sentence; therefore, it is a language of implicit meaning.*

The very implicitness inherent in basilect Modern American English, then, is a major direct cause of its inadequate segmentation of reality.

Attention to Surface Meanings

Such inadequacy in the basilect obtains in the semantic variable known as linguistic components, the distinctive features (see Jakobson, Fant, and Halle, 1963) or criterial attributes that distinguish one language structure from another. Because of their deficient control over linguistic components, most speakers of the basilect would fail to see the underlying *transformational* processes (see Jacobs and Rosenbaum, 1968, pp. 37–42) that produce the following two sentences with similar *surface* structures (see Chomsky, 1965, pp. 128–163):

> John is eager to please.
> John is easy to please.

Both these sentences appear to be identical in the components that make up their surface structures. Each one has a proper noun for subject, a form of the linking verb *be*, a predicate adjective, and an infinitive following that adjective. In fact, in all items except the adjectives, the very wording of these, two sentences is the same. But if a linguist looks at the *deep* structures of these two sentences, looks therefore at the structures that produce the different meanings of these two sentences, then he sees that they do not have the same *derivational* components:

John is eager to please everybody.
Reduced To: John is eager to please.
It is easy for anyone to please John.
Transformed To: John is easy to please.

As can be seen from the derivation components of these two sentences, in the deep structure of *John is eager to please, John* is the subject of the sentence. In the deep structure of *John is easy to please,* however, *John* is the object of the infinitive *to please.* Thus the components of the two sentences are ultimately neither identical nor similar.

Failure on the part of most speakers of the basilect to perceive the difference in the derivational components of the two sentences with similar surface structures, just previously discussed, is a direct result of the fact that such speakers live in a linguistic world of *static relationship* rather than of *dynamic process.* Terribly deficient in what Bernstein (1968, p. 227) calls the "process of individuation," the socially disadvantaged speakers of handicapped English in the United States today usually do not develop that sensitivity to structure which guarantees a maximum of growth in curiosity and receptiveness and hence in the capacity to segment reality. They tend to remain, therefore, as the literal–minded captives of the semantic variable known as the frequency factor, or the high probability that a construction will occur as a preferred utterance in the group solidarity of logical convention. That logical convention, in turn, dictates (see Bernstein, 1968, p. 228) that the high–frequency words used by the speakers of basilect Modern American English "are part of a language which contains a high proportion of short commands, simple statements and questions, where the symbolism is descriptive, tangible, concrete, visual and of a low order of generality. . . ." Such symbolism, moreover, is deficient in the semantic variable known as the nonfrequency factor, or the high probability that a construction will occur as a preferred utterance in the individual freedom of the figurativeness of psychological invention. Usually inept in the handling of instrumental metaphor, speakers of handicapped English do not restructure reality with the marked egocentricity, risk–taking, and flexibility of boundary (see Bernstein, 1970,

p. 46) that characterizes the creativity of more advantaged users of the language.

Reasons for Inadequate Segmentation

In summary, then, speakers of basilect Modern American English suffer from an inadequate segmentation of reality simply because they are deficient in their control over the semantic variables of the language and the world about them. Imprisoned in the insensitivity to structure which characterizes their overwhelmingly content–oriented methods of feeling and perceiving, these same speakers fail, more often than not, to comprehend the dynamic processes which underly the transformations of one linguistic structure into another and hence of one meaning into another. Just as their world tends to be one of static relationship, so their thinking about that world tends to be usually *iconic*, seldom *indexic*, and almost never *symbolic*. So important is this last characteristic of their inadequate segmentation of reality that it calls for a detailed study of both the nonlinguistic and the linguistic signs known as *icons*, *indexes*, and *symbols*.

ICONS, INDEXES, SYMBOLS

According to the great American philosopher, mathematician, and logician Charles Sanders Peirce (1839–1914), whenever one person sends a message to another in the English language, he resorts to the use of the following three kinds of signs (see Peirce, 1960, Vol. 2, pp. 156–173):

Peirce's Three Kinds of Signs

Icon: an image in the human mind, an appearance based on past experience.

Index: a real–thing sign related to an object in present experience.

Symbol: a conventional sign of an active law that makes both thought and conduct rational and thus helps to predict the future.

The following three dramatic scenes will serve to illustrate Peirce's definitions of icon, index, and symbol:

1

WIFE: Helen Smith called me yesterday.
HUSBAND: Oh. What did she want?

WIFE: Well, she and Bob wanted to know if we would like to join them for a picnic on Labor Day.

HUSBAND: A *picnic!* I should say not. Anything but that.

WIFE: Why, Tom dear, I've *never* seen you get so worked up about something as pleasant as a picnic.

HUSBAND: Who said a picnic was *pleasant?* All I can ever remember about a picnic was my old man getting drunk and making a fool of himself in public, and then picking on my mother until she'd cry, and all the time I'd be so scared he'd hit me that I'd feel like vomiting. No, thanks. No picnics for me.

2

FATHER: Now sit there steady and pose real pretty for me, honey.

DAUGHTER: Oh, Father. Do you have to keep on taking those instant pictures just to see if the Christmas present your office help gave you really works?

FATHER: Now, Marcia, you know your grandmother has been collecting candid snapshots of you ever since you were born. Now that you're turning twenty I want her to see how grownup and ladylike you look.

DAUGHTER: With the kind of line you toss out, who can resist?

FATHER: You got quite a line yourself. Now hold still. . . . That does it.

3

SON: Mom, you teach world literature at the junior college, so I wonder if you can tell me how it is that the grimy, sweaty, and crippled blacksmith of the gods could ever be the husband of the beautiful goddess of love.

MOTHER: You realize, of course, that Aphrodite is untrue to her husband.

SON: Yeah, with that musclebound god of war, Ares. You know, Mom, now that I think of it, Aphrodite's taste in boyfriends is strictly in her stomach.

MOTHER: And just what do you mean by that, Roger?

SON: Well, I mean that Hephaestus is a lot more cunning and clever and creative and mature than Ares.

MOTHER: Maybe you're beginning to solve your own problem.

SON: What do you mean?

MOTHER: I mean did it ever occur to you that perhaps Homer is trying to show something profound about the very act of creativity itself? Notice that Hephaestus, who makes the beautiful new armor for Achilles, carries psychological thorns in his soul which goad him into bringing order out of chaos through his artistic vision.

SON: You mean that since his personal life has so much of the ugly in it, he must make beautiful things as a kind of spiritual reward for the effort of creativity?

MOTHER: Yes, something like that. . . .

Quite obviously, the connotative image of a picnic, which so emotionally upsets the husband in scene 1, is an icon. By the same application of Peirce's thinking, the picture of Chris, which the father in scene 2 wants to send her grandmother, is an index. Similarly, the entire psychological complex of Hephaestus—including his disastrous marriage to Aphrodite, his ugly crippledness, and the grimy nature of his work—is, for Roger in scene 3, a symbol. As both a cause and an effect of their inadequate segmentation of reality, speakers of basilect Modern American English are involved in iconic scenes like scene 1 far more often than they are involved in indexic scenes like scene 2, and are involved in indexic scenes like scene 2 far more often than they are involved in symbolic scenes like scene 3. In fact, because of some terrible esthetic deficiency, a subject to be discussed in detail in Chapter 5 ("Inappropriate Image of Self and Linguistic Roles"), speakers of handicapped English are generally incapable of engaging in conversations like that between Roger and his mother in scene 3.

Because icon, index, and symbol are so important as *signs* in the segmentation of reality, they demand a study of their organic-like relationship with the two other major factors in the determination of meaning: *referents* and *references*. Insofar as Modern American English is concerned, of course, the term *signs* means "words considered as the linguistic designators of referents or objects in the cultural context, whether linguistic or nonlinguistic in nature." Thus *dog* is a sign for a nonlinguistic object; *it*, for a linguistic item. The term *referents* means "the objects in real life or within the language which are designated by the linguistic signs." Hence one and the same animal may be signified as the referent for both *dog* and *it*. The term *reference*, however, means "the semantic meaning of a word or expression; the mental content in the thought of the speaker using the word or expression or in the thought of the listener who hears the word or expression." That mental content for the sender of the message will have a foregrounded emotive function; for the receiver of the message, a foregrounded conative function. As has been stated several times in the course of this study, many speakers of handicapped English tend to have high and negative emotive functions as addressers and low and negative conative functions as addressees. The distortions within these functions, of course, are both a cause and an effect of their inadequate segmentation of reality.

Denotations and Connotations of Signs

From the foregoing discussion, then, it is apparent that a word or an expression as a sign in Modern American English may do two things: (1) it may *denote* the referent and (2) it may *connote* the reference. The term *picnic* in scene 1, for example, illustrates this dual role of a word very effectively. Both husband and wife in that earlier dialogue have the same *sign*—that is, they both are masters of the relationship between the phonemes /p/ and /i/ and /k/ and /n/ and /ɪ/ and /k/ and the morpheme word *picnic*. At the same time, both husband and wife have approximately the same *referent*—that is, they both know that the word *picnic* refers to some sort of outdoor social gathering at which food and beverages are served. But husband and wife most certainly do not have the same *reference*—that is, they do not agree on what the real semantic content or emotional meaning of the referent is. For the wife, a picnic is a pleasant social outing, made enjoyable by good food and drink and even better company. For the husband, however, a picnic is an ugly family affair at which parental drunkenness and attendant bullying make the food and drink unpalatable. And so a traumatic set of experiences from the husband's childhood has forced a serious breakdown in communication with his wife:

Breakdown in Communication
Same *sign:* /piknɨk/ = *picnic*
Same *referent:* outdoor social gathering at which food
and beverages are served
Different *references:*
Reference of wife: pleasant
Reference of husband: distasteful
Result: *Connotation noise* breaks down communication.

The connotation noise inherent in the wife's message is a microcosmic example of a macrocosmic sociolinguistic phenomenon—namely, that speakers of basilect Modern American English are constantly beset with the problem of a breakdown in communication due to their own inadequate segmentation of reality, both as the senders and as the receivers of messages. The connotation noise inherent in the wife's message, therefore, is instructive in miniature, for it is responsible for the wife's *partial* failure in the role of the addresser. Why *partial* failure? Because the wife succeeds in *informing* her husband about the telephone call from Helen Smith and of the stated desire which both Helen and Bob have concerning their all going out together for a picnic on Labor Day. But the wife fails to *influence* her husband into permitting her to accept the invitation. Here, then, are the two major roles of the addresser in his conveyance of the message: (1) *to inform* the consciousness of the addressee and (2) *to influence* the attitude and therefore ultimately the behavior of the addressee.

Now it is precisely because of their inadequate segmentation of reality that speakers of handicapped English often *fail* not only to inform but also *to influence* the speakers of superior lects. Surely this failure is one major reason for what Muriel Crosby (1967, p. 3) has called the "passivity and hopelessness" of so many of the socially disadvantaged in the United States today. Faced with the present challenge to achieve some control over future behavior in themselves and in their superiors, speakers of handicapped English resort to the past methods inherent in their social–class lect and find those methods lacking in efficacy. In other words, when presented with an indexic challenge to respond with symbolic strategy, speakers of basilect Modern American English too often *revert to iconic tactics,* the iconic tactics of their woefully restricted code. Such a reversion, according to Bernstein (1968, p. 234), "creates difficulties at many levels," because

> . . . The appropriate cues which enable a child to establish a personal relationship are absent; from the point of view of the working–class child the teacher's feeling is impersonalized through the language he uses. The public language is, in fact, a language to be used between equals (from a middle–class point of view) for it contains little reference to social status (i.e., a structured object) and the terms used to denote social status within the class environment are often judged unacceptable for use outside it. Thus the use of this language in a superior–inferior situation (to a doctor, teacher, etc.) may often be interpreted by the superior as a hostile or aggressive (rude) response. Because the working–class child can only use, only knows, a public language it is often used in situations which are inappropriate. The expressive behaviour and immediacy of response which accompany the use of this language may again be wrongly interpreted by the teacher. This may well lead to a situation where pupil and teacher each disvalues each other's world and communication becomes a means of asserting differences.

The breakdown in communication described by Bernstein in the preceding quotation often results in what Labov (1964, p. 94) has called the "conflict of value systems." Both phenomena are, however, primarily the outcome of *the conflict of signs* as they relate to referents and references. Such conflict, once again, is both a cause and an effect of the inadequate segmentation of reality associated with handicapped English.

As a microcosmic illustration of this conflict of signs, it is obvious that the wife's reference for the word *picnic* in scene 1 between wife and husband is a pleasant *index,* a real–thing sign related to an object in present experience, which leads her to adopt a pleasant *symbol*, a conventional sign of an active law that makes both thought and conduct rational and thus helps to predict the future. The wife's prediction, of course, is *positive:* A social outing with the Smiths on Labor Day will be great good fun. It is equally obvious, however, that her husband's reference for the word *picnic* is an ugly *icon*, an image in the human mind or an appearance based on past experience, which makes him adopt a very unpleasant symbol with which to predict the future in a *negative* manner: A social outing with the Smiths, or with any other family for that matter, on Labor Day or any other day, will be a little hell on earth. The conflict of signs inherent in this breakdown in communication is one of the major curses of an advanced civilization in this socially isolating and alienating twentieth century.

By way of artistic contrast, once the high school senior Roger, in scene 3 between son and mother, concentrates his mental energy on a proper interpretation of the meaning of the marriage of Hephaestus to Aphrodite, then he begins to really understand the symbolic intention of Homer in the *Iliad.* As Roger deepens his ability as linguist and literary critic, he will come to see that Homer succeeds in his role as the sender of a message, simply because Homer throws out more nets in which to catch the mind and will of his audience than do ordinary men in their normal conversation and writing of letters. And what are these nets? The very signs under discussion. Homer, that is, uses language to create an esthetic universe of discourse in which icon, index, and symbol all play a part in creating the myth of his story in the *Iliad.*

The great poem is an icon, just as a faded photograph of an ancestor is, because it is cast in a language no longer spoken, even in the somewhat archaic tradition of epic poetry, in present–day Greece. The great poem is an index, despite the iconic nature of its code, because its message is as up-to-date as today's X-ray of a human lung—even more so, because Homer is X–raying human nature itself, with all its sins and virtues, with all its demeaning weaknesses and ennobling strengths. The great poem is a symbol, because in the growth in compassion of both Zeus and Achilles there is the conventional sign of an active law that makes both thought and conduct rational and thus helps to predict the future: Through the exercise of profound love, after the endurance of much suffering in the evolution of the human conscience, both men and their gods will eventually become like the one true God and their rivalries and wars will ultimately give way to friendly cooperation and peace.

Relations of Signs to Rhetorical Modes

And so all unwittingly, Roger is on the threshold of discovering the real meaning of the *Iliad* as it relates to the three kinds of signs in the matrix of meaning: *As an epic poem, the* Iliad *is an iconic index of symbols that cohere in mythic relationship.* The rhetorical dominance of the *Iliad*, moreover, recapitulates in its resultant mythic microcosm the evolutionary emergence of the hierarchy of esthetic precedence in the literary macrocosm of the Western world. That hierarchy—in which narration takes rhetorical precedence over description and drama over narration and lyricism over drama (see Rockas, 1964)—calls for the application of a *crucial degree* to a mode of expression so that a *new kind* of expression can come into being (see Chardin, 1961).

When description, the eternal static mode, reaches a crucial degree, it undergoes a metamorphosis into narration, the temporal kinetic mode. When narration boils to a new identity, it becomes drama, the mimetic kinetic mode. When drama erupts beyond the point of crucial degree, it geysers upward into that most intense of all literary kinds: lyricism, the mental kinetic mode (see Rockas, 1964). Each kinetic mode, furthermore, has its own proper relationship with time and therefore its own proper function with tense. Narration deals mainly with the past and is concerned with history. Drama deals primarily with the illusion of the present and is concerned with the stage journalism of a direct account of "now." Lyricism draws upon both the past and the present in order to deal fundamentally with the future and is concerned with prophecy. Because description as individual texture may be dismissed as a minor mode of imaginative literature, subsumed into the hierarchy of the three major modes, the functions of these major modes constitute the following triad of values in an art object as a temporal "rage for order" (see Warren, 1959): icon, index, and symbol. In its historical emphasis, narration is *iconic;* in its contemporary emphasis, drama is *indexic;* in its prophetic emphasis, lyricism is *symbolic.*

Now it is precisely because socially disadvantaged speakers of basilect Modern American English are so deficient in their control over the rhetorical modes that they tend to *remain iconic* in their segmentation of reality. Sensitive to content rather than to structure, these same speakers of handicapped English fail to perceive that the three functional values of literature are not mutually exclusive, but rather mutually interpenetrative. The three functional values of literature, that is, combine into an organic–like union that constitutes description as universal structure, the total design of an art object in its eternal "order for rage" (see Warren, 1959): *myth.* Indeed, failure to achieve myth dooms a piece of writing to a partiality that maims it for the role of art.

Simply to recount the past is to turn the living body of human reality into stone tablets, the icon of a history which Aristotle, in the *Poetics,* saw as being less philosophical than poetry. Merely to record the present in all its dramatic confrontations of opposing wills gathered about a nonexistent point in ever–moving time, is to reduce that same living body to newsprint and video tapes—the never stable index of a journalism that almost immediately petrifies into icon. Solely to project a vision into the future, like captive Cassandra in a world of pragmatic and ill–fated Agamemnons, is to place that same living body in a strait jacket of quarantined madness, the symbol of a common incredulity that very quickly degenerates into the index of an uncommon insensitivity.

Speakers of handicapped English are the victims of the failure of all the foregoing isolated functional values. Why? Simply because they are, as we stressed above, oriented to the perception of *content* rather than of *structure.* Hence speakers of handicapped English constantly tend to give the metaphoric structuring of myth a literalist interpretation *according to its content.* If they believe in the Biblical story of Creation at all, these same speakers of handicapped English tend to see Adam and Eve as historical phenotypes, *iconic* in nature, rather than as poetic genotypes, indexic in nature, with symbolic extensions into universal prophecy. From such a misinterpretation, or partial interpretation—the result of an inadequate segmentation of reality—it is easy for speakers of basilect Modern American English to allow the Original Sin to degenerate from the disobedience of pride into the self-indulgence of gluttony, all too often *with little or no application to themselves and their own imperfections.* From such a misinterpretation, the "forbidden fruit" of God's command becomes an apple—the literalist icon of a faulty command of narration which cannot deal adequately with drama, simply because it cannot distinguish direct discourse from indirect. From that faulty command and that inadequate dealing, furthermore, emerges the resultant failure of speakers of handicapped English to achieve an appropriate lyric symbol—namely, the humble emotive admission that all men lose the Garden of Eden through their own perversion of will, a perversion which chooses the self, rather than God, as the highest good in the universe.

Ultimately, the victimization just described means that speakers of handicapped English do not have "a rage for order"; therefore, they do not have an order for their rage. "Psychologically deaf" to the splendid mythic music of great literature, especially as that music arises out of the organic–like union of the rhetorical modes, speakers of the basilect are trapped in their esthetic deficiency and cannot attain to that perfect balancing of willing and knowing which leads to creativity. Hence the following diagram of artistic achievement lies usually beyond their reach.

$$\text{KNOWING} \xrightarrow{} \downarrow \xleftarrow{} \text{WILLING}$$

$$\text{MAKING}$$

DIAGRAM 6. ARTISTIC ACHIEVEMENT.

Preferring to *have* rather than to *know about* and preferring to *know about* rather than to *know,* the socially disadvantaged in the United States today (as shown in Diagram 6) are scarcely capable of making anything of lasting beauty in the major modes of rhetoric. The disadvantaged are, in fact, much like the working–class child described by Bernstein (1968, p. 236), the child who is notorious for his inability to rise above the low level of curiosity and the short attention span of one enslaved by the descriptive processes of content orientation:

> . . . The working–class child has a preference for descriptive cognitive responses, and his response is an immediate one with only vague extensions in time and space; consequently his attention will be brief or difficult to sustain without punitive measures. Rather than pursuing the detailed implications and relations of an object or an idea, which at once create the problem of its structure and extensions, he is oriented towards the cursory examinations of a series of different items.

Such an enslavement to the *descriptive* processes of *content* orientation means that speakers of handicapped English are not only deficient in their transmission of narration, drama, and lyricism, but are also inadequate in their reception and interpretation of these three major rhetorical modes. Hence these same speakers are woefully handicapped in their dealings with esthetic discourse. For one thing, they do not understand that the communion of literary art, *as distinct from the communication of man's everyday use of the English language,* demands that *the message* act as an immediate *end* in itself by means of a code which is dominated by *formation* rather than by *information.* Neither do they realize that the way of *recursive pattern* is more important than the outcome of *discursive progression* in the literary art object, so that *structure* must take hierarchical precedence over *content.*

The result of such restrictive use of rhetorical modes is that speakers of basilect Modern American English generally fail to see other aspects of language communication. For example: an esthetic discourse in the national language constitutes its own interior universe and, as experience, is therefore infinitely repeatable by reason of the artistic merit inherent in its psychological invention. Rejecting the plurisignificance and the multivalence (often miscalled mere ambiguity) which obtain in *implicit structure* in preference for the certitude of *explicit content,* speakers of handicapped English, as both transmitters and receivers of messages, over-

whelmingly favor intellectual didacticism and moral pro-
paganda over literary art. This predilection on the part of
socially disadvantaged speakers, is, admittedly, both a cause
and an effect of their own iconic thinking—in short, of their
own inadequate segmentation of reality as it relates to the
organic–like union of the three major rhetorical modes in
the living body of myth.

Relation of Signs to English Words

The inadequate segmentation of reality among speakers
of handicapped English extends beyond their deficient control of the semantic variables and the major modes of rhetoric,
extends indeed right down into the very *words* that constitute
their individual vocabularies. Interestingly enough, moreover, those words are so structured within the lexicon
of Modern American English that they relate to the signs
known as *icon, index,* and *symbol* in the following manner:

Relation of Peirce's Signs to Modern American English Words

Icon = a summoner of imagery, as in the full lexical
words of the language: *dog, cat, snow, ice, bus, stop,
corner. . . .*

Index = an indicator of an item that stands as a substitute for an icon, as in the grammatical–lexical substitute
words of the language: *that, this, you, we, it, here, there,
then, now. . . .*

Symbol = a linguistic convention with no iconic or
indicative force, as in the empty grammatical or function
words of the language: *and, or, of, at, a, the, very, however. . . .*

As Nist (1971b, p. 336) has said,

> It is quite clear that full lexical words like *bus, stop,* and *corner*
> call forth images of items in past experience, so that when a native
> speaker of English hears the sentence *The bus stops at the corner*
> he gets a mental picture of a routine activity. Empty grammatical
> words, like *the* and *at,* are conventional symbols of the English
> language which allow its speakers to predict future thought and
> grammatical conduct in a sentence. Thus, the word *the* predicts
> a noun phrase or nominal structure, whereas *at* predicts a connec-
> tive word group known as a prepositional phrase. Finally, gram-

matical–lexical substitute words, like *there* and *it,* act with indicative force on objects that stand forth in present experience, as
in a child's cry *There it is!* when he sees that the bus is on time.

As a measure of the impoverishment of speakers of handicapped English within the vocabulary of their national language,
here also it must be said that their own segmentation of reality
at the level of the word tends to be *iconic* rather than either
indexic or symbolic. The following argument is offered in
support of this value judgment.

"SEGMENTATION" APPLIED TO LANGUAGE

In the sending and the receiving of messages in Modern
American English, certain conditions must prevail in order
that the limited signs of the language can deal successfully
with the items of an infinite reality in the world which surrounds the speakers of the language. These conditions occur,
of course, under the principle of the *segmentation of reality*
(see Bolinger 1968, pp. 220–240), as follows:

Conditions for Linguistic Segmentation of Reality

1. Linguistic signs must be *segmented.*
2. Linguistic signs must be *repeatable.*
3. Linguistic signs must have a built–in *ambiguity.*
4. Linguistic signs must be *storable* in human memory.

Whether native speakers of some form or another of Modern
American English realize it or not, as the senders and the
receivers of messages, they are all involved in the foregoing
linguistic segmentation. For all of them, whether they recognize it or not, *meaning* is simply *the contact that their language has with the outside world* as that outside world is
segmented by the human psyche. Otherwise they could not
cope with the continuum of reality at all. That is why Adam
had to name the animals before he could relate to them: naming is separating items from one another in the continuum,
which, without this process of separating, would remain the
"great blob" of an undifferentiated mass. In short, *naming
is segmenting reality.*

Effects of Code Limitations in "Handicapped English"

Now it is a well–known fact—fully documented in tons of recent research (see, e.g., Metz, 1967)—that speakers of handicapped English are markedly deficient in vocabulary. This deficiency is generally characterized by three failures in the segmentation of reality, as follows: (1) the sheer paucity of icons as names for items in the outside world (for example, black school children in Butler County, Alabama have no names for such familiar sewing items as scissors and thimbles); (2) the misuse of one index for another (e.g., *us* for *we, them* for *these* and *those, there* for *their,* and *hisself* for *himself*); and (3) the overwhelmingly insufficient control over the linguistic symbols that constitute the connective system of Modern American English (e.g., the substitution of *do* for *if,* the misuse of *to* for *at,* the zeroing of prepositions, the overemployment of simple and unspecialized conjunctions, and the anemic command of transitional words and phrases).

Furthermore, as Metz (1967, p. 14) has said, the acquisition of vocabulary itself is dependent upon the two mental processes known as *abstraction* and *symbolization:*

> . . . A child who calls a *ladder* a *get–up* is demonstrating inability in symbolization, or the knowledge of names or signs [icons] to stand for objects, acts, qualities, attitudes, and relationships. When a child calls a *horse* a *doggy,* he is failing in symbolization and also in abstraction, or the ability to generalize from nonidentical experiences to form concepts or classes such as *cars, fruits, animals.*

In the terminology of Metz, then, speakers of handicapped English are deficient in the *segmentation of reality* simply because they are deficient in the processes of *abstraction* and *symbolization* which would otherwise allow them to gain a full command over icons, indexes, and symbols in the acquisition of an adequate vocabulary.

This deficiency in abstraction and symbolization among speakers of the basilect is directly related to their *orientation to content* rather than to structure. In discussing the impoverishment of vocabulary among the socially disadvantaged, Bernstein (1968, p. 235) makes the following acute observation:

> The working–class boy is often genuinely puzzled by the need
> to acquire vocabulary or use words in a way that is, for him, pe-
> culiar. It is important to realize that his difficulties in ordering a
> sentence and connecting sentences—problems of qualifying an
> object, quality, idea, sensitivity to time and its extensions and modifi-
> cations, making sustained relationships—are alien to the way he
> perceives and reacts to his immediate environment. The total system
> of his perception, which results in a sensitivity to content rather
> than the structure of objects, applies equally to the structure of
> a sentence.

In the terminology of Bernstein, then, speakers of handicapped English are not only deficient in the *inventory* of their
vocabulary, but also in the *proper use* of that vocabulary,
simply because they are deficient in the total system
of their perception of and reaction to the immediate environment of the world about them. This deficiency, in turn, is
directly related to the fact that most speakers of handicapped
English are markedly ineffective in their handling of the processes of association and differentiation, especially as these
processes are involved in what B.F. Skinner (1957,
pp. 114–129) has called "the Problem of Reference."

Despite the enormous size and flexibility of its vocabulary,
the seemingly infinite resourcefulness of its syntax and
grammar, Modern American English is *not* an ideal code—that
is, not a code which demands that its every word should
always mean exactly the same thing, no matter what the
context situation, and that no two of its words should ever
mean even a similar thing, let alone the same thing, again
no matter what the context situation. If Modern American
English were an ideal code, then its vocabulary and inventory
of tacts (unit utterances) would have to be so immense as
to be unwieldy for the human memory. Just imagine how
large the lexicon of the national language would become if
a person could not call a house a "house" unless it met certain
rigid specifications as to size, location, and number of rooms;
or if he could not call a ship a "ship" unless it first traveled
at some designated speed and also displaced a precise number
of tons of water. Current difficulties with meaning, vast
enough as they are, would suddenly grow out of all proportion
to man's ability to cope with them, and human beings would

have to become walking dictionaries and grammatical ency-
clopedias.Why? Because on the scales of the linguistic signs
and their referents and references there would be no room
for *similarity,* but only for *sameness* and *difference.* And it
is precisely man's ability to recognize similarity that allows
him to segment reality into repeatable and memorable tacts
that carry with them their own built–in ambiguity, an
ambiguity which is a constant source of trouble for speakers
of handicapped English.

Because the national language does not furnish its speakers
with an ideal code, it has to operate by means of the following
scales for linguistic signs (or tacts) and their referents:

Scales for Linguistic Signs and Their Referents

Sameness → Similarity ← Difference

As the foregoing scheme shows, similarity is produced by
the union of the principle of sameness with the principle
of difference, and may be illustrated by the following seven
synonyms for the word *proverb: adage, saw, saying, maxim,
precept, aphorism, apothegm.* An *adage* is a proverb that has
been hallowed by a long tradition of acceptance, as in "A
man is known by the company he keeps." A *saw,* on the
other hand, is an adage that has been worn out by too much
use, as in the hackneyed "All that glitters is not gold." A
saying, however, is any memorable phrase, clause, or sentence that has been repeated over and over. A *saying* may
be a cliché, like *dead as a doornail* or *tight as a new boot;*
or it may be a rather recent metaphoric and slangy expression,
like "He really *flipped his wig,* as the saying goes." A *maxim*
is a saying that is concerned with a practical rule of conduct
or action, as in Polonius's advice to his son Laertes in the
play *Hamlet* (I, iv, 75): "Neither a borrower nor a lender
be." Despite the fact that Polonius calls his *maxim* a *precept,*
there is a difference: a *precept* is a *maxim* that deals with
personal ethics rather than with the mere practicality of one's
conduct, as in "A gentleman never offends unintentionally."
An *aphorism* differs from a saying and a proverb and all their
previously discussed synonyms in that its author is usually

known, as in George Bernard Shaw's memorable "If there's anything worse than not getting what you want, it's getting it!" An *apothegm* is like an aphorism in that its author is usually known, but an *apothegm* is different in that it startles by means of paradox, as in Christ's "He who seeks to save his life shall lose it."

Thus all seven synonyms share both in the principle of sameness and in the principle of difference. That double sharing, of course, constitutes their similarity, a fact that is attested by man's use of the words *proverb* and *proverbial* to cover these synonyms. Such use is exactly like a person's seeing a tanker, a naval destroyer, and a luxury liner and referring to all three of them with the single word *ship*. The principle of similarity in the use of Modern American English, then, is the very means through which the ideal and the real intersect. This intersection can be seen in the following diagram, which is a modification on one drawn by B.F. Skinner in his book *Verbal Behavior* (1957).

DIAGRAM 7. THE PROBLEM OF REFERENCE: SEMANTIC RANGE.

		STIMULUS		
		Same	Similar	Different
RESPONSE	Same	Ideal	Metaphor, Abstraction	Homonymy
	Similar	Metaphor, Abstraction	INTERSECTION OF IDEAL/REAL	Partial Homonymy
	Different	Synonymy	Partial Synonymy	Ideal

As Diagram 7 on semantic range indicates, when the same stimulus draws the same response or when a different stimulus draws a different response, then an ideal situation exists with regard to the verbal tact and its point of reference.

When a similar stimulus draws the same response or when the same stimulus draws a similar response, then metaphor and abstraction obtain, as when somebody says, "Mrs. Smith is a cat." The word *cat* in this statement is figurative and abstract; it does not mean a common household pet that purrs and drinks cream from a saucer. When a different stimulus draws the same response, then homonymy prevails—that is, there occurs an instance in which two words sound alike but mean entirely different things, as in *butter,* the dairy product a person spreads on his toast, and *butter,* or one who butts with his head. The antique riddle "What is black and white and /red/ all over?" is a good illustration of homonymy and its problem of reference, because the color *red* serves as the basis for a pun on *read,* the past tense of the verb to *read.*

When a different stimulus draws a similar response, however, then partial homonymy emerges. Tom, for example, says to his friend Jack, "Buzz me at eight," and Jack, thinking Tom has a cold in the head, drives up to *bus* his pal to the movie at eight—only to find that Tom is without a partner for the double date and merely wanted to be called on the phone at that hour. When the same stimulus draws a different response or set of responses, then there is a case of synonymy. The seven synonyms discussed above show that the word *proverb* can be interpreted as being any one of its different and specialized meanings. When a similar stimulus draws a different response, then a new realm in the problem of reference comes into being: that of partial synonymy. Two boys, for example, are eating breakfast together; the first boy gets a particularly lean piece of a familiar kind of meat, and the second boy gets a particularly fat piece. The first boy says, "Man! this is really good bacon." But the second boy disagrees: *"Bacon,* my eye. This is *sow belly."* The two verbal tacts, of course, are only partially synonymous.

Now the point of all this discussion is simply this: the socially disadvantaged speakers of basilect Modern American English are *deficient* in their control over all *the intersections of stimulus and response* which are represented on the diagram of semantic range. Because the inventory of their vocabularies is extremely limited (see Dale, 1967), speakers of handicapped English fall short of a complete mastery over the ideal, the synonymous, and the partially synonymous. Because the socially disadvantaged do not understand the fundamental principles of the national language and cannot generalize operations very well (see Bernstein, 1968, p. 235), they often fail miserably in their attempts to cope with metaphor and abstraction. Being victims of the perception patterns dictated by their own inferior social–class lect, speakers of handicapped English do not discriminate well among the phonological tacts of privileged speakers of the language, whose "foreign" dialect, lect, or language "accent" may seem "funny" and hard to understand. As a result of such difficulty with phonological discrimination, speakers of the basilect in the United States today frequently err in the areas of reference known as homonymy and partial homonymy; their malapropisms are consequently notorious.

Most important of all, however, is the fact that speakers of handicapped English fail so terribly in their understanding of the ideal, the real, and the intersection of the two. Why? Because the intersection of the ideal and the real is a symbol of the national language itself, the verbal means whereby speakers of Modern American English segment the world about them into repeatable signs that are memorable and somewhat ambiguous. In that segmentation, of course, they use their iconic lexical words to represent the real, their symbolic grammatical words to represent the ideal, and their indexic grammatical–lexical or substitute words to represent intersections of the ideal with the real. This use of English words may be schematized as in Diagram 8, which shows "Real" and "Ideal" intersecting in our word choices.

DIAGRAM 8. INTERSECTION OF IDEAL/REAL
IN ENGLISH WORDS.

IDEAL ⟶ *IDEAL/REAL* ⟵ *REAL*

| Grammatical Words | ⟶ Substitute Words ⟵ | Lexical Words |

As grammatical substitutes for the lexical words that they represent, grammatical–lexical words (e.g., pronouns, expletives, deictic adverbs) embody the principle of similarity as it rises out of the principles of sameness and difference. The intersection of similarity with grammatical words, on the one hand, and of similarity with lexical words, on the other, constitutes the union of the ideal and the real in the substitute words of the language.

But this principle of substitution, seen so clearly in the grammatical—lexical words, permeates the entire code of Modern American English as it relates to the semantic component. Ideal grammatical words (symbols) like *and* and *but* are ultimately substitutes for the abstract gestures of addition and subtraction, or of inclusion and exclusion, by which man sees the logical relationship between certain linguistic structures and their meanings. *And,* for example, is a substitute equivalent of some abstract gesture or sign of continuance and positive assertion, whereas *but* is a substitute equivalent of some abstract gesture or sign of reversal and negation. Similarly, real lexical words (icons) like *cat* and *dog* are ultimately substitutes for generic objects in the outside world, even as *Felix* and *Fido* are ultimately substitutes for individual expressions of the specific manifestations of those same generic objects. An *it,* by way of contrast, is an ideal/real grammatical–lexical word (index) or substitute for either an *and* or a *cat* or a *Felix.* Thus the very ontological nature of the words used in Modern American English is an indication of the *semantic range* that these same words and their referents inhabit.

Reactions to Semantic Grouping

As both a cause and an effect of their great deficiency in the semantic range of the vocabulary of Modern American English, speakers of the basilect encounter enormous difficulties with the *semantic groupings* of words. As Dwight Bolinger (1968, p. 237) has indicated, "There is probably no limit to the groupings that would make sense for one purpose or another" in a man's mastery of the national language. Without trying to limit these groupings, a linguist can nevertheless point to the following seven (see Bolinger, 1968, pp. 237–238) as examples of important areas where speakers of handicapped English often fail to extract adequate meaning from their code:

Seven Important Semantic Groupings for English Tacts

1. RECIPROCALS. Examples: We *come* and *go, buy* and *sell, read* and *write, speak* and *hear, give* and *receive.*

2. CHARACTERISTIC OBJECTS. Examples: We *eat food, hear sounds, see sights, spell words, wrap packages, drive nails, burn fuel,* and *steer courses.*

3. CHARACTERISTIC ACTION. Examples: Our *hearts beat, minds think, eyes see, ears hear, noses smell, tongues taste, legs run,* and *arms hold.*

4. CHARACTERISTIC SUBJECT–ACTION–OBJECT. Examples: *Criminals commit crimes, petty thieves pick pockets, priests hear confessions, judges hand down decisions,* and *inventors take out patents.*

5. CHARACTERISTIC QUALITY. Examples: *Ice* is *cold, sugar* is *sweet, vinegar* is *sour, water* is *wet, fire* is *hot, tacks* are *sharp.*

6. SYMPTON AND STATE. Examples: *Laughter* indicates *mirth, scream* indicates *terror, groan* indicates *pain, smoke* indicates *fire, dark clouds* indicate *rain.*

7. INCLUDED SEGMENTS. Examples: *Matter* includes *solid, liquid,* and *gas; gas* includes *hydrogen, oxygen,* and *nitrogen; occupation* includes *doctor, lawyer,* and *merchant; baseball scores* include *runs, hits,* and *errors.*

Speakers of handicapped English are deficient in their mastery of these foregoing seven semantic groupings precisely because they are culturally deprived and socially disadvantaged in relation to the mainstream of current American civilization. As a capsule summation of this deprivation and this disadvantage, Edgar Dale (1967, p. 32) makes the following value judgment:

> The deprived child, then, has actually been physically restricted in the number of things he has seen, heard, touched, and tasted. He lacks perceptual experience. There is also a lack of sequencing, the giving of order to these experiences. The child does not have a satisfactory filing system for storage or retrieval of experiences. This, after all, is what is meant by vocabulary and syntax—putting new and old ideas into new and varying patterns.
>
> But perceptual experience is not enough. Furthermore, perceptual experience is not guaranteed by the presence of things to be perceived, or we would all be able to name the trees, the flowers, the birds around us. Martin Deutsch has pointed out in *Education in Depressed Areas* that the child not only lacks perceptual experi-

ence but sustained attention as well, the perseverance necessary
to master these experiences.

This lack of perceptual experience and sustained attention
among the socially disadvantaged means that speakers of
handicapped English are semantically ill–equipped to deal
with arbitrariness and the context situation.

ARBITRARINESS AND THE CONTEXT SITUATION

Every tact (word or unit utterance) in Modern American
English has a dictionary nucleus of meaning and a context–
situation surrounding cell of meaning. Every tact in Modern
American English, that is, gains its full meaning only when
it takes part in some statement that is related to the context
situation at the moment when the addresser uses it. An American boy scout, for example, might say that he has sharpened
his knife to a *keen* edge; a young Britisher just home from
a date might say that he is rather *keen on* Constance, his
girlfriend. Both speakers use the word *keen,* but for the American boy scout the term is literal and descriptive, meaning
"sharp"; for the Britisher, however, the term is part of the
idiom *keen on,* which is figurative and emotive, meaning
"having taken a romantic fancy for." An idiom, then, is a
construction in English, or any other language for that matter,
the meaning of which cannot be deduced from a semantic
analysis of its component parts.

The British idiom *keen on* is an excellent example of the
arbitrariness of meaning within a national language. Such
arbitrariness, of course, is the very method by which words
and tacts can come to take on not only *different* but even
opposite meanings in the fullness of the union between their
immediate (or smaller) and their total (or larger) context situations and thereby keep the size of the vocabulary which they
inhabit within manageable limits. A few examples of such
arbitrariness in meaning run as follows:

The stars are *out* = the stars *are* shining.
The lights are *out* = the lights are *not* shining.
The horses are *off* = the race *is* underway.
All bets are *off* = the gambling is *not* underway.

Floyd *addressed* the crowd = Floyd *spoke* to the crowd.
Floyd *addressed* the golf ball = Floyd did *not* speak to
the golf ball.

Now it is precisely because speakers of basilect Modern
American English are so experientially deficient in both the
immediate context situations and the total context situations
within which words and tacts of the national language function, that they are frequently so very inept in their dealings
with the arbitrariness of meaning. That severe ineptitude is
but another mark of their inadequate segmentation of reality.

Their inadequate segmentation of reality, in turn, has a
corollary which rises out of their deficiency in both the
immediate and the total context situation of the message and
in the underlying categories of observation which inform the
organization of that message—namely, the inappropriate
image of themselves and of the linguistic roles which they
should or must assume for the achievement of effective communication. So large and important is this corollary, together
with its many psychological and sociological ramifications,
however, that it requires a chapter unto itself.

Chapter 5

INAPPROPRIATE IMAGE OF SELF
AND LINGUISTIC ROLES

SINCE MAN HAS AN INNATE mental capacity to recognize similarities among the items in segmented reality, he can organize the immense and indefinite world about him into repeatable and memorable signs. As Chapter 4 has demonstrated, it is precisely because speakers of handicapped English are deficient in their ability to recognize similarities (and differences) that they are also deficient in their capacity to segment reality through the national language, and therefore to organize the world about them into effective messages. The principle of the recognition of similarities, consequently, is a key factor in the relationship between man and his code. From their ability to recognize similarities (and differences), speakers of Modern American English organize both the transmission and the reception of a message into two *context situations* (see Bolinger, 1968, p. 229), one pertaining to the entire discourse itself and the other pertaining to the moment in a discourse when a particular word, phrase, clause, or sentence occurs. These two context situations may be named and characterized as follows:

The Two Context Situations of a Message

1. The *Total* Context Situation. This so–called "larger context" includes the entire discourse plus the total experience of the sender of the message plus the full resources of the national language.

140

2. The *Immediate* Context Situation. This so–called "smaller context" will foreground (see Mukarovský, 1964) one of the six dimensions of communication (see Jakobson, 1960, p. 353)—for example, the addresser when a doctor is speaking about an *operation* or the code when a criminal resorts to argot and calls a submachine gun a *typewriter.*

From an understanding of these two context situations, the receiver of the message interprets first the *primary* semantic elements that yield the "real meaning" of a statement, and then the *secondary* semantic elements that produce the "circumstances of the statement's use."

Speakers of handicapped English are markedly inferior in their control over both the total and the immediate context situation; hence they often fail to properly accommodate the primary semantic elements of a statement to the demands of the secondary. This lack of accommodation means, of course, that many times the real meaning of a statement in basilect is in conflict with the circumstances of its use. When such a conflict occurs, then the receiver of the message may interpret what he hears as being a violation of decorum or propriety—in other words, as not being suitable for its context situations. Such impropriety or lack of decorum is demonstrated by means of the inherent contrast between the following two dramatic scenes:

1

RECEPTIONIST: Hello. Dr. Smith's office. No, I'm sorry. The doctor isn't in at the moment. Will you please leave your name and telephone number? . . . I'll have the doctor call you as soon as he comes in. Thank you.

2

RECEPTIONIST: (*Obviously chewing gum*) 'Lo. Yeah, dis de doc's pad all right. Naw, he ain't to home raht now. Guess you hafta be callin' back.

From hearing the statements of these two receptionists, the addressee would normally have more faith in Dr. Smith, the employer of the first receptionist. Why? Because the first receptionist's use of Modern American English is far more in keeping with the total context situation. The addressee could be wrong in his interpretation, of course; the unnamed doctor who employs the second receptionist may very well be a much better physician than Dr. Smith. But if he is, he had better teach his receptionist how to answer a telephone properly—or get a new receptionist. The present conflict between the receptionist's real meaning and the circumstances of its use hurts the unnamed doctor's professional ethos.

CATEGORIES OF OBSERVATION

Socially disadvantaged speakers of the basilect are far more likely to sound like receptionist 2 than they are to sound like receptionist 1—that is, they are prone to violate linguistic decorum or propriety. Why? For one reason, because they are markedly deficient in their control over what Aristotle called in his *Rhetoric* the *categories of observation* (see Nist, 1969a, pp. 65-66). Despite disclaimers against the importance and the applicability of these categories (see Katz, 1966, pp. 224-239), they are nevertheless relevant to an understanding of Modern American English and many of its sister tongues in the Indo–European family of languages. As Nist (1971b) has indicated, how the speakers of a national language segment the world of reality about them is a key factor in determining the three components of their code: semantic, grammatical, and phonological.

As addressees, then, speakers of Modern American English share with their addressers the following ten categories of observation as they relate to the segmentation of reality and the national language:

1. SUBSTANCE. This category answers the question: "What?" Substance is the subject matter of sentences and generates the nouns, noun phrases, and nominal constructions in Modern American English.

2. QUANTITY. This category answers the question: "How large?" or "How many?" Quantity is thus the "muchness" or the "manyness" of things; it generates the cardinals and ordinals, the

adjectives and adverbs of size and amount, the morphology of singular and plural, and the class distinction between count nouns (e.g., *dollar*) and mass nouns (e.g., *money*) in Modern American English.

3. QUALITY. This category answers the question: "What sort of thing?" Quality is thus the kind that is posited upon a crucial degree; it generates much of the system of grammatical modification in Modern American English.

4. RELATION. This category answers the question: "What is the connection?" Relation occurs in comparisons and associations, including those of parts to wholes and means to ends. Relation generates figures of speech and the entire connective system (prepositions, coordinating and subordinating conjunctions, relative pronouns, and transitional words and phrases) in Modern American English.

5. PLACE. This category answers the question: "Where?" Place is the situation of a thing in space; it generates the demonstrative articles and pronouns, the deictic or pointer adverbs (e.g., *here* and *there*), and all the proper names and adverbial constructions of place in Modern American English.

6. TIME. This category answers the question: "When?" Time is the situation of a thing in relation to man's awareness of before and after, or during; it generates the verb systems of tense and aspect, and all the adverbial constructions of time, frequency, and duration in Modern American English.

7. POSTURE OR POSITION. This category answers the question: "In what attitude?" Posture or position is the expression of a thing through its own form—for example, upright or reclining, kneeling or sitting, in full-face or in profile. Posture or position generates the forms of restrictive and nonrestrictive modification of nouns, noun phrases, and nominals in Modern American English.

8. STATE OR CONDITION. This category answers the question: "How circumstances?" State or condition is the relative well-being of a thing—for example, healthy or sick, rested or tired, new or old. This category generates all predicates that are controlled either by the verb *be* or by the various kinds of so-called "linking" verbs in Modern American English.

9. ACTION. This category answers the question: "How is something *acting*?" or "What is something *doing*?" Action is the situation of a thing in relation to its own ability to move about, to play and work, to function and operate, to influence and make an impact on other things. Thus action generates all predicates that are controlled by the various kinds of transitive and intransitive verbs in Modern American English.

10. PASSIVITY OR AFFECTION. This category answers the question: "How is something being acted upon?" or "What is something

suffering?" Passivity or affection is the result of motion or behavior upon a thing—for example, unconscious and bloody, angry and weeping, or silent and ashamed. This category generates not only the prenominal and postnominal modifiers deleted from transformed kernel predicates, but also the entire transformational system of the passive voice in Modern American English.

So important are these categories of observation that it is no exaggeration to claim that the world itself speaks to man through them in his everyday experiences. Because they are woefully inadequate in their use of these categories of observation, socially disadvantaged speakers of the basilect do not hear the message of the world very clearly in the United States today. That failure to metaphorically "hear" well results in the "psychological deafness" of the speakers of handicapped English.

That "psychological deafness," in turn, is rooted in an impoverishment of perceptual experience within the categories of observation. It is a notorious linguistic fact that the socially disadvantaged speakers of basilect Modern American English are deficient in their command over the category known as substance, simply because they grow up in a cultural environment that deprives them of opportunities to taste and touch and smell, to see, feel, manipulate, and work on materials in the world about them. Such deprivation, of course, results in their failure to acquire names and labels for things—a terrible failure, for as Dale (1967, p. 33) observes: "The early vocabulary of children shows an emphasis on nouns." And yet, as a mark of their deficiency in the mastery of substance (Dale, 1967, p. 33), "Many children in a deprived area in Washington, D. C. [do] not know the word *pet*," simply because they have no direct active contact with such individual pets as dogs, cats, canaries, guinea pigs, white mice, lizards, and frogs. Hence a deprivation in concrete substance leads to a deprivation in abstraction.

In similar manner, speakers of handicapped English are deficient in their control over the categories of observation known as quantity, quality, and relation. Just as they tend to label items which they do not know as *a thing, do hickey,* or *somethin' out yonder* (see Ponder, 1967, p. 26), so they tend to accept too little as normal, and fail to see the relation between crucial degree (quantity) and new kind (quality). Indeed, as one Negro educator has said to Edgar Dale (1967, p. 32), deficiency in these three categories is a fundamental cause of poor readiness for reading on the part of the socially disadvantaged:

> . . . Here is a picture of a wagon with three wheels. What is wrong with it? The child sees nothing wrong with it. He often plays with a wagon with no wheels at all. Here is a table with three legs. This is not uncommon in his home. Why should he see anything wrong with it?

As further marks of their deficiency in the categories of quantity, quality, and relation, speakers of handicapped English tend to confuse plural with singular, violate noun and verb agreement, omit articles and other structure or function words, and generally fail to master the connective system of the national language. In his discussion of the difficulty which speakers of the basilect have with the conjunctions of Modern American English, Dale (1967, p. 36) illustrates their failure at relation:

> As long as they are the simple conjunctions such as *and,* there may be no problem. Difficulties arise, however, when conjunctions indicating pairing or causal relationship are developed. A time lag occurs before the meaning can be grasped, *e.g.,* "He was not only a scholar but also a gentleman." The idea must be held in mind to the end of the sentence. There are conjunctions of alternates such as *neither . . . nor,* and there are the conjunctions of inference. Some conjunctions are confusingly abstract little words such as *for, or,* and *so.* Some are not usually heard in conversation, such as *consequently, hence, therefore, as a result.* The conjunction often introduces a high level of abstraction, something for which the limited reading and perhaps the limited attention span of the deprived child is a serious handicap.

This serious handicap in the category of relation extends into the categories of place and time, insofar as speakers of the basilect are concerned. Restricted to a very narrow stage on which to enact their lives, most of the socially disadvantaged in the United States today seldom leave the confines of their native city or county, let alone state. Terribly impoverished in the geography of *where,* these socially disadvantaged speakers of handicapped English have little or no awareness of the importance of such political and cultural centers as London, Paris, Rome, Berlin, and Moscow. If they live in New York, Chicago is "a big dump" somewhere out West. But no matter where they live, it is precisely because they are so deprived in place that they become so deprived in time, a fact which their small variety of verb tenses (see Dale, 1967, p. 35) bears witness to. Indeed, as Bernstein (1968, p. 232) has remarked, both the deprivation in place and the deprivation in time are directly traceable to the family structure of the socially disadvantaged:

> The working–class family structure is less formally organized than the middle–class in relation to the development of the child. Although the authority within the family is explicit, the values which it expresses do not give rise to the carefully ordered universe spatially and temporally of the middle–class child. The exercise of authority will not be related to a stable system of rewards and punishments but may often appear arbitrary. The specific character of long–term goals tends to be replaced by more general notions of the future, in which chance, a friend or a relative plays a greater part than the rigorous working out of connections. Thus present, or near present, activities have greater value than the relation of the present activity to the attainment of a distant goal. The system of expectancies, or the time–span of anticipation, is shortened and this creates different sets of preferences, goals and dissatisfactions. This environment limits the perception of the developing child of and in time. Present gratifications or present deprivations become absolute gratifications or absolute deprivations for there exists no developed time continuum upon which present activity can be ranged. Relative to the middle–classes, the postponement of present pleasure for future gratifications will be found difficult. By implication a more volatile patterning of affectual and expressive behavior will be found in the working–classes.

The profound truth in Bernstein's observation means that socially disadvantaged speakers of handicapped English are woefully inadequate in abstract systems of thought, cause–and–effect relationships, moral patience, and time–oriented conscience. With a "chicken–today–and–feathers–tomorrow" philosophy of life, they generally tend not to plan ahead; consequently, they are frequently the victims of their own immature and piecemeal improvisation. Welfare recipients in the big city ghettos of America, for example, usually spend their allotments by mid–month and hence have to go privately begging before the next check arrives. Speakers of handicapped English, moreover, tend to react *automatically and compulsively* within a very narrow range of language structures. Their verbal activity, therefore, is *more like the genetic behavior of animals than like the socially conditioned and responsible and limitedly free behavior of men* (see Nist, June 1969, p. 16), a value judgment that will be sustantiated in detail later on in this chapter.

As with place and time, so with the categories of observation known as posture or position, state or condition, action, and passivity or affection: speakers of basilect Modern American English are markedly deficient in their control over them. Usually reared in *status*–oriented, as distinct from *person*–oriented, families, the socially disadvantaged in the United States today see adults treated like children, hear Negro men called "Boy," watch property rights take precedence over human rights, observe courtesy degenerating into shameful groveling, and sense everywhere the inferiority of their own position within the national culture as a whole. As a result of this impoverishment in position, many speakers of handicapped English adopt either a defensive posture of hopeless resignation or an offensive posture of hostile belligerence. In either case, the posture is strengthened by the fact that the state or condition of things around the speakers of handicapped English is usually one of going from bad to worse. Socially disadvantaged children are frequently abandoned by at least one of their parents. These same parents, in turn, live in a world where watches don't run, cars won't start, and sofas can't keep from sagging; where TV is a drug against boredom and liquor an anodyne for the usury of finance charges; where education is merely an escape from unemployment; where patriotism is an obscene gesture and religion the ultimate absurdity.

In either case, the posture results in an inappropriate image of the self—an image that is supported by the rather constant failure of speakers of basilect Modern American English to influence other more privileged speakers of the national language within the category of action, while at the same time enduring a great many social afflictions within the category of passivity or affection. As a consequence of such negative support, these same speakers of the basilect *unconsciously* see themselves as being either masochistic martyrs or sadistic avengers. In either case, the image—like the posture—is wrong. It leads, furthermore, directly into an inappropriate image of the linguistic roles which the self should assume if it would communicate effectively with others. As overall effects of their terrible impoverishment within Aristotle's categories of observation, then, speakers of the basilect in the United States today suffer from these two major extensions of an inadequate segmentation of reality: (1) an inappropriate image of themselves and (2) an inappropriate image of the linguistic roles which they should assume. These inappropriate images are the subject of the remainder of this chapter.

IMAGE OF THE SELF

It is a well-known fact in linguistic science that *kinesics* (body gesture and facial expression), *paralanguage* (voice qualities and vocalizations), *proxemics* (communicative use of space), and *haptics* (who may touch whom and under what circumstances) are all part of what Bernstein has called, throughout much of his writing, "expressive symbolism." It is an equally well–known fact in linguistic science that speakers of basilect Modern American English are more "hip" to expressive symbolism than they are to any rhetorical mastery of acrolect versions of the national language. Indeed, as Bernstein (1968, p. 235) himself has said,

> The fact that the working–class child attaches significance to a different aspect of language from that required by the learning situation is responsible for his resistance to extensions of vocabulary, the manipulation of words and the construction of ordered sentences. Because he has previously learned to make personal qualifications through expressive symbolism he has little desire to acquire new words or order his existing vocabulary in a way which expresses this qualification. There is, in fact, from his own standpoint, no *need* to do this. The "I" of the child is adequately communicated by tone–volume–physical set, not in the language he uses. Unfortunately, within a formal learning situation, this means of communication is not recognized and must necessarily be disvalued.

This disvaluation of the basilect's emphasis on expressive symbolism within situations of formal learning in the United States today means that there exists—and rightly so—a cultural war in the public schools of America between the mature demands of verbal orientation and the immature reliance upon the somewhat meager resources of nonverbal orientation. Consequently the nonverbal orientation of the socially disadvantaged is both a major cause and a major effect of their inappropriate image of the self.

Nonverbal Orientation

Like all other languages on earth, Modern American English accompanies the organic–like engagement of its three major components (semantics, grammar, phonology) with a highly specialized system of facial expressions and body gestures. As Ray L. Birdwhistell (1952, 1954) and others have demonstrated, in communicating with one another, human beings resort to a body language in order to "flesh out" the meaning contained only potentially in their words and their vocal performance. As Flora Davis (Dec. 1969, pp. 127–128) has said,

> Every culture has its own body language, and children absorb its nuances along with spoken language. A Frenchman talks and moves in French. The way an Englishman crosses his legs is nothing like the way a male American does it. In talking, Americans are apt to end a statement with a droop of the head or hand, a lowering of the eyelids. They wind up a question with a lift of the hand, a tilt of the chin or a widening of the eyes. With a future–tense verb they often gesture with a forward movement. . . .
>
> The person who is truly bilingual is also bilingual in body language. New York's famous mayor, Fiorello LaGuardia, politicked in English, Italian and Yiddish. When films of his speeches are run without sound, it's not too difficult to identify from his gestures the language he was speaking. One of the reasons English-dubbed foreign films often seem flat is that the gestures don't match the language.

Of utmost importance in any study of the kinesics of the basilect is the fact that gestures tend not only to match the language *but also to replace it.* Why? Because as Martin

Deutsch (1963) claims and Ponder (1967, p. 27) reaffirms, "the lower–class home is not a verbally oriented environment."

Accompanying facial expressions and body gestures in the actual speaking of any language are certain paralinguistic signals which convey the emotive function of the addresser in what the average layman thinks of as "tone of voice." Such paralinguistic signals, then, constitute the *paralanguage* of Modern American English. According to George L. Trager (1958, 1964), Henry Lee Smith, Jr. (1969), and their structural–linguistics adherents, the paralanguage (a term coined by A. A. Hill) of the national language consists of two major sets of performance features: (1) *voice qualities* and (2) *vocalizations*. By voice qualities, Trager (1964, p. 276) means such items as the following:

> . . . *pitch range, vocal lip control, glottis control, pitch control, articulation control, rhythm control, resonance, tempo.* Pitch range may be identified as *spread* upward or downward, or *narrowed* from above or below. Vocal lip control ranges from heavy *rasp* or hoarseness through slight rasp to various degrees of *openness.* Glottis control deals with *sharp* and *smooth* transitions in pitch. Articulation control covers *forceful* (precise) and *relaxed* (slurred) speech. Rhythm control involves *smooth* and *jerky* setting off of positions of vocal activity. Resonance ranges from *resonant* to *thin.* Tempo is described as *increased* or *decreased* from a norm.

Now insofar as these voice qualities tend to convey the high and negative emotive function of speakers of handicapped English, they will tend to occur among these same speakers as follows (personal observation): the pitch range will be spread upward, narrowed from below, and thus made harsh and shrill; the vocal lip control will usually produce rasp rather than openness; the glottis control will be marked by sharp, instead of smooth, transitions in pitch; the articulation will generally be slurred rather than precise; the rhythm control will be jerky, the resonance range thin, and the tempo increased from the norm.

Image Projection

In supporting Trager's position with regard to the voice qualities previously discussed, Smith (1969, pp. 95–96) makes the following claim:

The *voice qualities* of paralanguage are actual and recognizable speech events, phenomena separable and distinct from language proper and from other paralinguistic events. Voice qualities are part of culture, are learned and shared and systematized, and are used by the individual as over-all signals of his perception of the *culturally determined image* of himself in relation to his total environment. Thus he has an image of his body, his health, his status, his gender, his mood, his human rhythm, his toxic status, his locale.

In addition to the eight items listed as voice qualities by Trager, Smith includes *intensity range,* which may be either *increased* or *decreased* from the culturally induced norm. Among the socially disadvantaged in the United States today, this intensity range will tend to be decreased when the addresser is speaking with a superior and increased when he is speaking with an inferior. Of even more importance, however, is the fact that these voice qualities communicate the *culturally determined image* that the speaker has of himself, for as Smith (1969, pp. 96–97) says, the speaker may project an image far removed from reality:

A little man may compensate—or overcompensate—by cultivating a voice operating below the norm of his true pitch range and with an increased level of intensity and a booming resonance. On the other hand, a six foot four inch male hypochondriac with an ordinary cold might squeeze his pitch range and decrease his level of intensity to what might be expected in a preadolescent female in order to impress his wife with the seriousness of his condition. A man unused to alcohol might be convinced he is intoxicated after a single weak highball and project the culturally accepted image of the inebriate complex with slurred articulation, slowed tempo, and so on.

Within the context of these observations by Smith, the voice qualities of every speaker of Modern American English open an auditory window upon the psyche. For speakers of the basilect, that auditory window usually reveals a negative image of the self—a point to be taken up a little later on in this chapter.

Meanwhile, the second major set of performance features in paralanguage are vocalizations. According to Trager (1964, p. 276), these vocalizations occur in three kinds: (1) *vocal characterizers,* (2) *vocal qualifiers,* and (3) *vocal segregates.* As Smith (1969, p. 97) has indicated, vocal characterizers occur over the span of a single sentence, but are repeatable. They include such emotive–function manifestations as these: *laughing, giggling, snickering, crying, whimpering, sobbing, yelling, muffling, whispering, muttering, moaning, groaning, whining, breaking, belching, yawning.* Vocal qualifiers, by way of contrast, occur over one intonation pattern (Smith, 1969, p. 97), but are also repeatable. These vocal qualifiers exist in three dimensions (Trager, 1964, p. 277): *intensity, pitch height,* and *extent.* In its deviations from the culturally induced norm, intensity may occur in varying degrees of *overloudness* or *oversoftness;* pitch height, in varying degrees of *overhighness* or *overlowness;* and extent, in varying degrees of *drawling* or *clipping.* As for vocal segregates, they occur on single segments of speech (Smith, 1969, p. 98), are also repeatable, and include (Trager, 1964, pp. 277, 279) such things as hesitation noises, glottalized assent and dissent (*uh–huh* and *uh–uh*), dental continuants with either expiration or inspiration, alveolar aspirated clicks (*tsk–tsk, tut–tut*), closed– and open–lipped nasalizing, lateraling, trilling, and "raspberrying" in an almost spitting kind of Bronx cheer.

It is well known, of course, that socially disadvantaged speakers of basilect Modern American English rely heavily upon vocalizations to convey their exact meaning under the dominance of emotive function. Emotionally embarrassed in the context of mature verbalization, they usually relieve their own sense of inadequacy through some form of laughing, giggling, or snickering. These same speakers of handicapped English are notorious for their general lack of dignified reserve with regard to the expressiveness of their vocalizations. In the eyes of more advantaged speakers of the national language, from yawn to belch the speakers of basilect are "downright crude, rude, and vulgar." Addicted to the making of sheer noise, speakers of handicapped English are frequently overloud in intensity and overhigh in pitch. Whether they drawl or clip, they usually punctuate their messages with an excess of vocal segregates. And thus through the very expressive symbolism of their performance, speakers of basilect Modern American English become the ironic victims of their own emphasis on content rather than upon structure:

the content of their message is frequently merely its expression.

Why? Because verbalism is held to a minimum, while kinesics and paralanguage are relied upon to the maximum. Hence meaning is implicit rather than explicit, and feelings tend to become as undifferentiated as the language itself. In fact, as Bernstein (1968, pp. 232–233) has indicated, speakers of handicapped English are almost invariably involved in a vicious circle of emotive emphasis and nonverbal orientation:

> The language between mother and child is public: one which contains few personal qualifications, or it is essentially a language where the stress is on emotive terms employing concrete, descriptive, tangible and visual symbolism. The nature of the language tends to limit the verbal expression of feeling. The child learns only a public language from his mother and feeling is communicated by non–verbal means. It must be emphasized that with the use of a public language the child will tend to make and respond to personal qualifications which are expressed by an immediacy of communication. . . .
>
> As the nature of the language–use limits the verbal communications of feelings the latter tend to be as undifferentiated as the language. Consequently the emotional and cognitive differentiation of the working–class child is comparatively less developed, and the cues responded to in the environment will be primarily of a qualitatively different order. He is sensitive to the content of objects. Because the language is public, with a corresponding emphasis on emotive content, the very vehicle of communication precludes the structure of objects as major referent points. Of critical importance is the type of language–use upon which value is placed, for once a value is so placed, then that language–use will reinforce the emotional disposition which resulted in the initial preference.

Content-Oriented Language

From this vicious circle, of course, emerges slang, or the highly emotive and rather immature use of content–oriented language. Thus in a world where *weed* means "cigarette," *sad sack* "teacher," *snags* "teeth," *soft stuff* "skin," *winter heat* "overcoat," *pearl pusher* "toothbrush," *sweat job* "work," *chicken–picker* "thief," *wet stuff* "water," *hole in the wall* "house," *white stuff* "snow," *jingle* "coins," *shut–eye* "sleep," *ace* "good friend," *grays* "white people," *happy shop* "liquor store," *bread ain't done* "not very smart," *pull his coat* "bring to someone's attention," *juiced up* "drunk," *walking on the wall* "nervous," and *pounding brick* "looking for a job" (see Dale, 1967, p. 34)—it is no wonder that, in the words of David R. Heise (1969, p. 102), "the referent category for lawmen is linked not to 'policeman' or 'officer' but to synonyms such as 'cop,' 'the Man,' or 'fuzz,' whose connotations are more in line with . . . personal feelings." Indeed, as Heise (1969) has indicated, both the basilect and its expressive symbolism seek to minimize *dissonance* and *punishment* within the culturally deprived world of the socially disadvantaged.

As for the expressive symbolism associated with the basilect, it is rather difficult to assess just how important kinesics and paralanguage are to the exact conveyance of meaning among the speakers of handicapped English. But psychologist Albert Mehrabian (see Davis, December 1969, p. 128) has devised the following formula for the speakers of the national language as a whole:

$$\text{Total impact of a message} = 7 \text{ percent } verbal +$$
$$38 \text{ percent } paralanguage +$$
$$55 \text{ percent } kinesics.$$

Other Signals

If the percentage for kinesics seems inordinately high, it should be remembered that the eyebrows alone have a repertoire of about 23 possible positions and meanings, that a shrug of the shoulders may speak volumes about one's own admittedly unconcerned ignorance, that the kissing of a lady's hand may be merely a conventional gesture of Continental courtesy or the passionate outpouring of a grateful heart, that the winking of an eye may indicate the start of a joke or the beginning of a love affair, and that slouching in a chair may signal teenage boredom or adult relaxation. In other words, words themselves are frequently poor instruments of communication in a universe of discourse in which the code can seldom be separated from the encoder. This observation is especially true for the nonverbally oriented speakers of handicapped English.

Even though paralinguistic signals are analogous to facial expressions and body gestures and run parallel to action modifiers and motion qualifiers, neither the signals nor the expressions and gestures share in these universal attributes of language itself: *duality* (the relationship between "empty" structure and "full" meaning), *displacement* (the removability of the antecedents and the consequences of a message), and *productivity* or *innovativeness* (the infinite resourcefulness of finite resources). Lacking these key attributes of every natural language, then, both paralanguage and kinesics remain *closed* systems of communication, like those of the bee dance or the gibbon calls (see Hockett, 1958, pp. 571–573). Thus it is precisely because language itself is an *open* system of communication that it is so infinitely expressive and worthy of study—and of mastery in the formal learning situation of the public schools of the United States. If Romeo had had to rely upon paralanguage and kinesics alone, he never would have won the admiration, respect, and love of Juliet. Yet that is precisely what the speakers of basilect Modern American English metaphorically seek to do—win Juliet by means of their nonverbal orientation. Their failure, moreover, is inevitable. It is also a major cause for their negative image of the self, for their terrible sense of inferiority.

Sense of Inferiority

A fifteen-year-old Appalachian white boy, working to help support his destitute mining family, cries on national television and says, "I'm no good. I guess I'm just a bum." This same boy represents a basilect Modern American English which generates such deviant verb forms (see Ponder, 1967, p. 25) as these: *axt* for *asked, brung* for *brought, busted* for *burst, driv* for *drove* and *driven, fit* for *fought, heared* for *heard, rech* for *reached, seed* for *saw* and *seen, snuck* for *sneaked, takened* for *took* and *taken,* and *teached* for *taught.* The boy and his basilect are a microcosmic example of this macrocosmic fact: *speakers of handicapped English usually suffer from lack of confidence,* from atrophy of ambition,

from vitiated self–esteem. They are, in short, constantly
nagged by a sense of their inferiority in relation to more advantaged speakers of the national language. This sense of inferiority on the part of the socially disadvantaged is acutely
described by Allison Davis (1967, p. 57):

> In spite of his emotional spontaneity and expressiveness, the
> Negro child from the low socioeconomic groups is likely to lack
> confidence in his ability and in his future. His parents usually do
> not encourage him to compete in school, so that he usually lacks
> the *drive to achievement,* the prime incentive which middle–class
> parents seek to teach their children.
>
> Moreover, the school program itself (including the so–called
> but incorrectly termed) reading–readiness tests, the edu-
> cational–aptitude tests, the primers, readers, and the curriculum
> as a whole soon damage severely the confidence and the basic self-
> esteem of the Negro or white child from low socioeconomic groups.
> Finally, his low place in society and that of his parents, friends,
> and neighbors tend to weaken his self–esteem. This self–
> depreciation is typical of all low–status groups, and is the result
> of their having been severely stigmatized in most relationships with
> dominant groups. It results in a poor self–image for the Negro child
> and adolescent and in hidden self–contempt beneath the facade
> of stupidity and resentment.

The "hidden self–contempt," so clearly seen by Davis, is
not restricted solely to the basilect speakers of Black English.
Indeed this most powerful attribute of the sense of inferiority
extends to all speakers of any form of a native language which
interferes with their mastery of some prestigious version of
the national language known as Modern American English.

This sense of inferiority among speakers of handicapped
English, as many research studies show, is intensified by
the cultural warfare in the public schools of the United States,
the cultural warfare which demands that an immature nonverbal expressive symbolism give way to a mature verbalism
dominated by a sure control of grammar, rhetoric, and logic.
Intensified because, as Bernstein (1968, pp. 237–238) so
penetratingly observes, the socially deprived have a restricted
educational (and therefore social) mobility:

> The dynamics of sensitivity to structure "underlies the complex
> of attitudes favourable to educational and social mobility," whereas
> sensitivity to content, it would seem, is responsible for the poor

showing in formal educational subjects by working–class children even if they have a high I.Q. This mode of perception (sensitivity to content) would explain some of the discrepancies between verbal and non–verbal tests . . . and why working–class children tend to do less well on purely verbal tests. Although it has been found that working–class children do not become part of the social and cultural life of the grammar school . . . this fact in itself is not explanatory nor need it necessarily lead to poorer educational perfor- mance. In fact it has been shown that often working–class children in grammar schools come from homes where there is little diver- gence between the aims of the school and those of the home. . . . The fact that many working–class parents apparently hold middle–class attitudes does not imply that the children are equipped affectually and cognitively to respond to the grammar school opportunity, despite the level of their measured intellectual potential. . . . In order to equate ability with opportunity it is necessary to understand precisely the variables which determine the *expression* of ability. This is necessary at the present moment, when the society in order to survive must be able to profit by the expressed potential of all its members.

At the heart of Bernstein's argument, of course, is this implicit accusation: When *potential ability* does not equal *measured attainment*, then "psychological murder" is the result.

Such "psychological murder," tragically enough, is respon- sible for the fact that much of the sense of inferiority among speakers of the basilect in the United States today is *not* without foundation. Indeed, as Allison Davis (1967, p. 58) has indicated,

We know, for instance, that a third of the white children of unskill- ed and semiskilled families in a midwestern city already are retarded in grade placement by the time they are nine and ten years old. . . . By the time white children from these lowest occu- pational groups are in their tenth year, they are about one year behind the children from the top occupational families in reading, and ten points lower in I.Q. ratings. Negro children of the lowest economic group are about a year behind the white lowest economic group in reading, and six points lower in I.Q. at age ten.

The deficiency in measured attainment, so carefully observed by Davis among culturally deprived black and white children, is even further intensified among Indian children on Govern- ment reservations. As speakers of a basilect that is the result of the interference of some *foreign* native language, these same Indian children—according to Hildegard Thompson

(1967, p. 69)—usually start falling drastically behind their acrolect peers in formal learning when "English becomes the primary tool" for education, "usually about fourth grade," and the gap "becomes progressively wider until by the time they reach the upper elementary and high school grades they are two to four grades behind national norms." Analogously, Spanish–speaking Americans throughout the desert Southwest and the Far West fall behind the national norms at an alarming rate and usually climax their formal education by "dropping out" of school somewhere between the sixth and the ninth grade (see John and Horner, 1970, p. 145). As C.S. Knowlton (1966, p. 4) has said,

> The Spanish–Americans have been cut off from their own history and culture by the public school systems. . . . Spanish–American students coming out of the public schools . . . are completely ignorant of the cultural developments of Spain, Portugal, and Latin America. As a result they are filled with feelings of inferiority and suffer from self–hatred. They look down upon their own families and their own people.

When such failure in educational performance joins with such self–hatred, it is easy to understand why many speakers of handicapped English often think of themselves and of their basilect peers as "sons of bitches" rather than as sons of God: they are the victims of their own vulgar and profanely inappropriate image of the self.

Mitigation and Politeness

Such self–victimization on the part of speakers of handicapped English is a direct outgrowth of their high and negative emotive function as senders of messages and of their low and negative conative function as receivers of messages. The distortion within these functions, furthermore, produces an inability to deal with what Labov (1970b, p. 51) calls the "modes of mitigation and politeness." Because they have been reared in an authoritarian status–oriented environment which makes them deficient in their awareness of cause–and–effect relationship, many speakers of basilect Modern American English are dense to the use of polite periphrasis as a means of exhortation and command (see Dale, 1967, p. 35). If they can "translate" courteous statements in the acrolect of the school register into the basilect of the home and/or street register, they may very well be offended by their own misinterpretation of the emotive function of the teacher. Why? Because, as Dale (1967, p. 35) has indicated, inoffensively polite questions like "Are we all paying attention?" are usually heard as rude commands like "Get with it!" By the same token, when they are the addresser, rather than the addressee, speakers of handicapped English are frequently liable to fail in conveying their own emotive function. As Labov (1970b, p. 51) himself has said,

> The nonstandard speaker is undoubtedly handicapped in many ways by his lack of control over mitigating forms which are more highly developed in middle class and school language. These forms are used to avoid conflict between individuals who meet in some kind of face–to–face encounter. The child may not know the mitigating ways of disagreeing with the teacher which make such disagreement acceptable in the school situation. It is not uncommon for Negro children to simply accuse the teacher of lying where middle class white children might say, "There's another way of looking at it." Faced with the statement "You a lie!" most teachers find it necessary to react forcefully. After one or two such confrontations, most students learn to say nothing. But some students continue to object without learning the means of doing so without conflict. In the school records of boys we have studied, we find many cases where they have been reprimanded, even demoted, for their failure to use mitigating forms of politeness. . . .

The failure in forms of mitigation and politeness among many speakers of handicapped English is a failure to achieve an appropriate image of the self. The Negro boys whom Labov found either reprimanded or demoted for their discourteous modes of address were merely trying to be "honest" in their own eyes; instead, they were "boorish" and "uncouth" and "vulgar" and "impolite" and "offensive" in the eyes of others. When a highly emotive Negro boy "speaks his mind" about his school and its relation to the dominant national culture as a whole, the basilect result is liable to be this (see Labov, 1970b, p. 52):

> JUNIOR: Like I'ma tell you the truth. They jus' want everythin' taken away from us. . . . Who do we work for? Whities Who do we go to school for? Whities! Who's our teachers? Whities!

Eaten up with resentment, as Labov (1970b, p. 52) says, Junior
"may be unable to compete with the smart kids and finds
a way out in being 'bad.' " But whether he is unable to compete or not, this much is certain about Junior's discourse:
in the terminology of Martin Joos (1961, 1962, 1967; Oct.
1962, 1969), it is *exoteric, childish, intimate, popular* (vulgar),
bad, and therefore "incorrect." Junior's discourse is, in short,
the product of an inadequate segmentation of reality. That
inadequate segmentation, in turn, results in an inappropriate
image of the self—*and* an inappropriate image of the linguistic roles which the self should assume in order to communicate with others effectively.

IMAGE OF THE LINGUISTIC ROLES

In his extremely influential monograph *The Five Clocks*
(1967), Martin Joos demonstrates that according to his *age*
every speaker of Modern American English has his own peculiar *style* (method or manner), *breadth* (reflection of the *cultural* discipline underlying the code), and *responsibility* (reflection of the *personal* discipline underlying the use of the
code) in the organization and transmission of his message.
Drawing from a modification made upon Joos's terminology
by H.A. Gleason, Jr. (1965, Ch. 15), a linguist may schematize
the various relationships among age, style, breadth, and
responsibility as follows (see Nist, 1969a, p. 126):

Age	*Style*	*Breadth*	*Responsibility*
senile	rhetorical	genteel	best
mature	deliberative	puristic	better
adult	consultative	standard	good
teen–age	casual	provincial	fair
child	intimate	popular	bad

As Nist (1969a, p. 126) has said, "In the reporting of a preg-
nancy in the family, for example, each member of that family
will use a functional variety in keeping with his age, breadth,
and responsibility." Such reporting, furthermore, may be
illustrated as follows (see Nist, 1969a, p. 126):

Age	Person	Expression
senile	grandfather	*She's in the family way.*
mature	father	*She's an expectant mother.*
adult	big brother	*She's pregnant.*
teen–age	little sister	*She's going to have a baby.*
child	malicious uncle	*She's "knocked up" again!*

From this paradigm of contrasts it is apparent that each member of the family uses an expression in keeping with both his cultural and his personal discipline. Grandfather's breadth, for example, is genteel; his responsibility, the best. At the other end of the scale, however, is the malicious uncle, whose breadth is not only popular but downright vulgar and whose responsibility is therefore bad. Obviously immature, the malicious uncle is childish in his desire to draw negative attention to himself. Such childishness is a mark of the bad responsibility which characterizes the inappropriate image which speakers of handicapped English have concerning their linguistic roles.

Bad Responsibility

In his brilliant essay "Stages in the Acquisition of Standard English" (1964), William Labov shows that linguistic maturation is a growth in conformity with the adult norms of the national language. That linguistic maturation, according to Labov (1964, pp. 91–92), occurs in the following six stages:

1. THE BASIC GRAMMAR. During this stage, from birth to about five years of age, the child is under the influence of the phenotypical modeling of his parents. With emphasis on listening and speaking, the child comes to master "the main body of grammatical rules and the lexicon of spoken English" in order to "communicate his basic needs and experiences to his parents."

2. THE VERNACULAR. During this stage, from about five to twelve years of age, the child comes under the influence of the peer group and "learns the use of the local dialect in a form consistent with that of his immediate group of friends and associates" and "begins to learn to read in school." In the opinion of Labov, the vernacular stage "is the most important one from the point of view of the evolution of the language."

3. SOCIAL PERCEPTION. During this stage, from about twelve to fifteen years of age, the adolescent comes "into wider contact with the adult world," begins to learn the "social significance of the

dialect characteristics of his friends," and finally responds "to the subjective reaction test with patterns that resemble the adult pattern." More often than not, however, the adolescent speaker "is still confined to the single style of his own vernacular."

4. STYLISTIC VARIATION. During this stage, from about fifteen years of age onward (if at all), the speaker learns to modify his code in the direction of the regional acrolect "in formal situations, or even to some extent in casual speech."

5. THE CONSISTENT STANDARD. If the speaker is a member of the educationally and socially mobile middle class, during this stage—from young adulthood onward—he will achieve a new and consistent style of speech. Among the socially disadvantaged members of the lower class, however, the "ability to maintain standard styles of speech for any length of time is often not acquired at all."

6. THE FULL RANGE. During this stage, the mature speaker attains "complete consistency" in a "range of styles appropriate for a wide range of occasions" and does "not depart at all from standard syntax and word morphology" in his "mastery of the prestige forms" of acrolect Modern American English.

From an application of these stages of acquisition to the phenomenon of handicapped English, a linguist may say that most socially disadvantaged speakers of the basilect do not grow beyond the vernacular; hence they are markedly deficient in social perception and stylistic variation, cannot claim a consistent standard for their own, and are therefore utterly incapable of communicating through the full range of the national language. As a result of their linguistic handicapping, most speakers of the basilect suffer from a poor or even bad responsibility as senders of the message.

The characteristics of such poor or even bad responsibility on the part of most speakers of the basilect has been discussed by Bernstein in his seminal essay "Elaborated and Restricted Codes: An Outline" (1966, 1967, 1969). According to Bernstein, speakers of handicapped English operate by means of a restricted code that is notorious for its heavy reliance on extraverbal channels, for the narrow range of its lexicon, for the *communalized* symbols of its verbal *implicitness* (as distinct from verbal *explicitness*), for its general lack of "planning procedures," for the relatively low level of its syntactic organization, and for its general inability to switch linguistic roles with ease and efficiency. Indeed, as Bernstein (1969,

p. 131) has said, "The rigid range of synthetic possibilities" among speakers of basilect Modern American English

> . . . leads to difficulty in conveying linguistically logical sequence and stress. The verbal planning function is shortened, and in sustained speech sequences this often creates a large measure of dislocation or disjunction. The thoughts are often strung together like beads on a frame rather than following a planned sequence. A restriction in planning often creates a high degree of redundancy. This means that there may well be a great deal of repetition of information through sequences which add little to what has already been given. Role relations may be limited and code switching may be hampered by the regulative consequences of a restricted code. An individual limited to a restricted code will tend to mediate an elaborated code through his own regulation.

These characteristics of poor or even bad responsibility among most speakers of the basilect, so penetratingly observed by Bernstein, have been amply illustrated by Labov in the monumental study often referred to in these pages, *The Social Stratification of English in New York City* (1966).

In his attempt to isolate contextual styles, Labov (1966, Ch. 4) asks the following question (p. 107) of his informants: "Have you ever been in a situation where you thought you were in serious danger of being killed—where you thought to yourself, 'This is it'?" The answer which Labov seems to think was among the best belongs to a Mrs. Rose B., a woman in her late thirties, of Italian parentage, who was reared on the Lower East Side. Here, then, is the discourse of that sewing machine operator, hereafter referred to as "Mrs. B," as recorded by Labov (1966, pp. 108–109):

> . . . And another time—that was three times, and I hope it never happens to me again—I was a little girl, we all went to my aunt's farm right near by, where Five Points is . . . and we were thirteen to a car. And at that time, if you remember, about 20 or 25 years ago, there wasn't roads like this to go to Jersey—there was all dirt roads. Well, anyway, I don't know how far we are—I don't remember what part we were—one of the wheels of the car came off—and the whole car turned, and they took us all out. They hadda break the door off. And they took us out one by one. And I got a scar on my leg here . . . 'ats the on'y thing. . . . [When the car turned over, what did you think?]
> . . . it was upside down— you know what happened, do you know how I felt? I don't remember anything. This is really the

truth—till today, I could tell that to anybody, 'n' they don't believe
me, they think I'm kiddin 'em. All I remember is—I thought I fell
asleep, and I was in a dream. . . . I actually saw stars . . . you
know, stars in the sky—y'know, when you look up there . . . and
I was seein' stars. And then after a while, I felt somebody pushing
and pulling—you know, they were all on top of each other—and
they were pulling us out from the bottom of the car, and I was
goin' "Ooooh."

And when I came—you know—to, I says to myself, "Ooooh, we're
in a car accident"—and that's all I remember—as clear as day—I
don't remember the car turning or anything. All I know is I thought
I went to sleep. I actually felt I went to sleep.

No doubt Mrs. B's delivery of this discourse was accompanied
by what Labov (1966, p. 108) has called "a remarkable command of pitch, volume and tempo for expressive purposes."
In the terminology of Bernstein, Mrs. B's discourse undoubtedly relied heavily on the expressive symbolism of
its extraverbal channels. It had to so rely.

Implicit rather than explicit in the context–bounded
development of its story, Mrs. B's discourse furnishes an
excellent example of the poor or even bad responsibility
inherent in the grammar, rhetoric, and logic of basilect
Modern American English. Terribly deficient in Aristotle's
categories of observation, this narration of a car accident violates substance in its overwhelming use of vague pronouns
instead of specific nouns (e.g., just who are *they* and *we*?)
and is therefore immature and deficient in its quantity,
quality, and relation modifications. Place and time, furthermore, suffer from such an imprecision that the reader of this
discourse cannot be sure as to exactly when and where the
wheel came off and thus caused the car to turn *over*. In fact,
because Mrs. B leaves out this italicized directive particle
of the idiomatic verb phrase, the reader has to infer that the
car did not merely "turn" but actually did capsize. This deficiency in the category of posture or position is matched by
a similar deficiency in that of state or condition: nowhere
in the story does Mrs. B describe the car or tell which wheel
it was that "came off" or narrate the sensation of capsizing.
Instead, she jumps disconnectedly to an inadequate statement
about the action of some vague other people: "and they took

us all out." This inadequacy in the category of action, moreover, is repeated in that of passivity or affection. The inept observation that "I got a scar on my leg here," prompts Labov himself to imply that the scar indeed was *not* "the on'y thing"; hence he asks the question, "When the car turned over, what did you think?"

The answer to Labov's question, in turn, reconfirms the fact that speakers of handicapped English are rather irresponsible in their organization and transmission of the message. Mrs. B's relative irresponsibility is apparent in her childish reliance on a conjunctional parataxis which brings the rhetoric of her message into too close a coincidence with the grammar of her code. Her style suffers from what Chomskyan transformational–generative grammarians would call a terrible deficiency in the creative and economical transformations of "deep" structures into "surface" structures—in other words, simple sentences are strung together like beads in a necklace. And with just about as much organicity of relationship. This coldly mechanical and often irrelevant kind of rhetorical unity results in wasteful repetition of phrases and redundancy of ideas. Expressive verbosity acts as a kind of excelsior in which to pack away such clichés as these: "This is really the truth," "I actually saw stars," "as clear as day." Ironically enough, the Mrs. B who actually felt that she "went to sleep" does indeed go to sleep metaphorically in the telling of her story. She takes too much for granted on the part of her auditor and fails to convince her later readers that *she herself* was truly close to death. Why? Because HER CONCEPT OF THE SELF IS *VERBALLY UNDIFFERENTIATED*. The *they* who were "all on top of each other" are really the *us* whom *they* were pulling "out from the bottom of the car." In the immediacy of a recalled experience that has no room for mature adult reflection, the real metaphysical *I* is reduced to the lyric "Ooooh" of high emotive function. Or in the words of Bernstein (1969, p. 129):

> . . . In the case of a speaker limited to a restricted code, the concept of self will tend to be refracted through the implications of the status arrangements. Here there is no problem of self, *because the problem is not relevant.*

As the ultimate effect of linguistic irresponsibility, then, Mrs. B robs herself of her own identity.

Such linguistic irresponsibility is apparent in Mrs. B's failure to handle pronoun references correctly, in her inability to make her subjects and verbs to agree in number, in her constant shifting from the simple preterit to the vulgar historical present and back to the simple preterit, in her "tennis–match" switching of point of view, in her inability to handle the rhetorical modes of drama and lyricism in order to enliven her narration, and in her incapacity to create a true feeling of suspense that marks the crescendoing of interest in a discourse with a real beginning, middle, and end. Her own robbery of self–identity clamors for attention in Mrs. B's continual pleas for a high and positive conative function on the part of her auditor. Her story, therefore, is heavily punctuated with such "please grant me ethos" tags as these: "if you remember," "do you know what happened?" "do you know how I felt?" and "you know" time and again. Mrs. B, in short, fails to be explicit, and she knows it.

This failure to be explicit, symbolized by the fact that Mrs. B's car "turns" rather than "turns *over*," is a key attribute in the grammar, rhetoric, and logic of basilect Modern American English. Such failure, moreover, means that the socially disadvantaged in the United States today tend to create discourses that are much more context–bound than those of more advantaged speakers of the national language. This relationship between inexplicitness and context–boundedness may be demonstrated in the following two discourses employed by Bernstein (1970, p. 26):

[EXPLICIT]

A. Three boys are playing football and one boy kicks the ball—and it goes through the window—the ball breaks the window—and the boys are looking at it—and a man comes out and shouts at them—because they've broken the window—so they ran away—and then that lady looks out of her window—and she tells the boys off.

[INEXPLICIT]

B. They're playing football—and he kicks it and it goes through there—it breaks the window and they're looking at it—and he comes out and shouts at them—because they've broken it—so they run away—and then she looks out and she tells them off.

Based on two stories constructed by P.R. Hawkins (1969), these two discourses relate, in the words of Bernstein (1970, p. 26) to the following series of four pictures: "The first picture shows some boys playing football near a house; the second shows the ball breaking a window; the third shows a man making a threatening gesture; in the fourth, the children are moving away, while watched by a woman peering out of the window." As Bernstein (1970, p. 27) has said, insofar as the foregoing two discourses tell the story of the series of four pictures, they relate to the context as follows:

> With the first story the reader does not have to have the four pictures which were used as the basis for the story, whereas in the second story, the reader would require the initial pictures in order to make sense of the story. The first story is free of the context which generated it, whereas the second story is much more closely tied to its context. As a result the meanings of the second story are implicit, whereas the meanings of the first story are explicit.

By *implicit*, of course, Bernstein does not mean the plurisignificant indirection of art, but rather the vague and ambiguous taking–for–granted of non–art. The *implicitness* of art is the result of careful verbal planning; the *inexplicitness* (a much better term with which to describe the phenomenon) of non–art is the result of careless verbal planning or no verbal planning at all. Inexplicitness and context–boundedness, then, are two major attributes of the poor or even bad responsibility among the speakers of handicapped English. Such defective responsibility, in turn, means that speakers of basilect Modern American English are inept in their handling of the *styles or keys of discourse* (see Joos, 1961, 1962, 1967; Gleason, 1965, Ch. 15). This ineptitude is further evidence of the fact that they fail to achieve an appropriate image of the linguistic roles which they should assume.

Styles or Keys of Discourse

As Martin Joos first (1961) demonstrated and then H.A. Gleason, Jr. (1965) corroborated, speakers of the full range of the national language do not all talk the same way all the time. Indeed if they did, they would probably soon be locked up for not being in touch with reality. Speakers of acrolect Modern American English have, in fact, several different ways of organizing and transmitting their messages, depending upon the influence of such factors as these: the context situation they are in, the audience they are addressing, the psychological distance they wish to maintain, the attitude they take toward their subject, the emotional mood they are in, and the formality of tone they wish to establish. The different ways in which the speakers of acrolect cast their messages are known to linguists as the *styles or keys of discourse* and may be illustrated (see Marckwardt, 1966, Ch. 3) in the following five dramatic scenes:

1

MR. GRIFFIN: Well, Bill, what do you think of Simpson?

BILL: Mr. Griffin, in my opinion he is not the man whom we want.

MR. GRIFFIN: After having studied the man's credentials and read his anemic recommendations, I fear that I must concur with your estimate of Mr. Simpson's potential. Thank you, and good day.

2

MR. GRIFFIN: Well, Tom, what do you think of Simpson?

TOM: Mr. Griffin, I believe he is not the man we are looking for.

MR. GRIFFIN: It seems to me that your creed is not unwarranted in this case. Thank you, and good day.

3

MR. GRIFFIN: Well, Floyd, what do you think of Simpson?

FLOYD: Mr. Griffin, I don't believe he's the man we're looking for.

MR. GRIFFIN: You know, Floyd, you're right. That's why I'm not making him an offer.

FLOYD: You're not?

MR. GRIFFIN: No, I'm not. Whatta ya say to that?

FLOYD: That's a good idea.

MR. GRIFFIN: Thank you, Floyd. So long for now.

4

MR. GRIFFIN: Well, George, what does the nineteenth hole tell you about Simpson?

GEORGE: Some golf game yesterday, wasn't it? But about Simpson—look, J.B., I don't think he's our man.

MR. GRIFFIN: Don't *think?* Come on, George. You *know* he isn't.

GEORGE: Well, J.B., if you put it that bluntly—yes, he isn't.

MR. GRIFFIN: Glad to hear you say it. With four recommendations against Simpson, I think I can get Cliff to go along with me in the Board Meeting this afternoon.

GEORGE: Oh, Cliff 'll come around all right. See you later.

MR. GRIFFIN: Like at noon for lunch?

GEORGE: Swell.

5

MR. GRIFFIN: Well, if it ain't "the nemesis on me premises," as me old sainted Irish grandmother used to say.

CLIFF: Hiya, clown! You know, J.B., I'd like to get you really bombed on a fifth of good scotch some night.

MR. GRIFFIN: I know better 'n to ask, why?

CLIFF: 'Cause then I'd have a real live hushpuppy.

MR. GRIFFIN: *Hushpuppy?* What's a hushpuppy?

CLIFF: A fried cornball.

MR. GRIFFIN: (*Enjoying the wit*) Well, I see you're in a two–martinis–before–lunch mood, so I'll ask you to join George and me for a steak in the Executive Club at noon.

CLIFF: Why the bribe? Oh, I get it—you want my support on hiring that Simpson twerp. Sorry, pal. 'Fraid you've picked a lemon.

MR. GRIFFIN: (*Breathing a sigh of relief*) Picked, hell. I don't want the silly jerk. I was afraid *you* might, but now——

CLIFF: Now we can dump him at the Board Meeting, and you won't have to buy me that steak after all.

MR. GRIFFIN: Now wait a minute, Cliff. That offer still goes. In fact, I'll drink *three* martinis, and you'll have your "real live hushpuppy!"

Running throughout these five dramatic scenes is, of course, *a hierarchy of formality* (see Nist, 1969b, pp. 5–7), which means that the younger, junior officers tend to be more formal with "Mr. Griffin"—more formal, that is, than George and Cliff, who will be having lunch with "J.B." Bill, of course, is the most formal; Tom, the next most formal; Floyd, somewhat informal; George, the next most informal; and Cliff, the most informal. The sensitive business executive responds, in turn, to each man's speaking style with a similar style of his own. As "Mr. Griffin" he is most formal with Bill, next most formal with Tom, and somewhat informal with Floyd; as "J.B." he is next most informal with George and most informal of all with Cliff. Within this two–way hierarchy of formality, then, exist examples of the five styles or keys of discourse, first characterized and described by Martin Joos (1961, 1962, 1967) and later refined in nomenclature and description by H.A. Gleason, Jr. (1965, Ch. 15): (1) oratorical or rhetorical, (2) deliberative, (3) consultative, (4) familiar or casual, and (5) intimate. The following extractions (see Marckwardt, 1966, p. 40) from the foregoing dramatic scenes, serve as illustrations:

Examples of the Five Styles or Keys of Discourse

1. *Oratorical* or *rhetorical.* Said by Bill:
   "In my opinion he is not the man whom we want."
2. *Deliberative.* Said by Tom:
   "I believe he is not the man we are looking for."
3. *Consultative.* Said by Floyd:
   "I don't believe he's the man we're looking for."
4. *Familiar* or *casual.* Said by George:
   "I don't think he's our man."
5. *Intimate.* Said by Cliff:
   " 'Fraid you've picked a lemon."

Now the point of all this discussion is simply this: socially disadvantaged speakers of basilect Modern American English are generally incapable of encoding the first two messages (those of Bill and Tom) and tend to mix the last three messages (those of Floyd, George, and Cliff) into one confusing blend of a statement, dominated by a high emotive function (see Nist, Nov. 1969, p. 8). Why? Because such speakers of the basilect are not only linguistically handicapped, but are also usually emotionally handicapped. Many of the culturally deprived in the United States today grow up in an "emotional pressure cooker" (Nist, June 1969, p. 17) in which such negative commands as "Shut up!" and "Get the hell outa here!" are not the exception but the rule. This "emotional pressure cooker," especially in the ghettos of the big cities of America, is the environment where children are spawned into a highly emotive one–keyed incubator of nihilism and despair. Fed upon negative reactions to almost everything and terribly undernourished on the semantic deficiency of their handicapped English, these children quite naturally tend to respond with raw gut energy and very little mind. As Charles E. Osgood (1960, pp. 298–300) has suggested, such response is marked by the following linguistic features: shorter words, smaller vocabulary, repetition of phrases, higher noun–verb usage, greater stereotyping in diction, higher predictability of structuring, categorical inclusiveness, higher incidence of common–meaning value terms, many egocentric assertions, faulty time orientation, and many ethos–begging mands. Often under an immense drive motivation, speakers of handicapped English are, in short, *deprived of stylistic choice*.

This stylistic deprivation among speakers of the basilect in the United States today means that they do not handle their own socially disadvantaged code well *in relating to other people* through the message. Such failure to relate effectively to other people is mirrored, of course, in the fact that speakers of handicapped English do not usually achieve any of the clear–cut styles represented in the following discussion of the foregoing five dramatic scenes about the possible hiring of Simpson. Taking these examples in reverse order, we would say that the first style or key of discourse which speakers of the basilect fail to master well is the intimate, or the method by which J.B. and Cliff constantly express their deep mutual affection for one another. As Nist (1969a, p. 13) has previously indicated, the intimate style or key "denotes the closest of ingroup relationships, with no need for background insertions of information or for revisions of expression because there is a complete rapport between the *two* speakers (or some small–group equivalent) of their private language." Conveying *feeling* in preference to information, the intimate style or key is often extremely elliptical and code–like. It tends to keep words at a minimum, as in this passage:

CLIFF: Why the bribe? Oh, I get it—you want my support on hiring that Simpson twerp. Sorry, pal. 'Fraid you've picked a lemon

MR. GRIFFIN: (*Breathing a sigh of relief*) Picked, hell. I don't want the silly jerk. . . .

The high emotive function and the emotional rapport between J.B. and his pal Cliff immediately label their conservation as being in the *intimate* style or key. They are such very close friends that they can afford to *playfully* insult one another with dysphemism (see Bolinger, 1968, p. 112), or the hyperbolic use of derogatory terms as marks of intimacy and affection. Thus J.B. calls Cliff "the nemesis on me premises," and Cliff responds in kind by calling J.B. a "clown" and, by implication, a "cornball." In short, they like each other so much that they can afford to dispense with the *outward show* of courtesy and respect—they know where they stand with each other. That is why their dysphemism can spread, in mutual agreement, into an attack on "that Simpson twerp," who is "the silly jerk." Such an extension of dysphemism ultimately involves J.B. and Cliff in such highly emotive terms as the metaphorical *lemon* and the mildly profane *hell*.

J.B. and George, however, are not nearly on such intimate terms with one another. That is why they discuss the Simpson affair in the *familiar* or *casual* style or key of discourse. As Nist (1969a, pp. 13–14) has previously indicated, this style or key shows the close "ingroup" relationship and rapport that make background information and carefully chosen wording almost completely unnecessary between friends. Highly elliptical and slangy, though not nearly so emotional in tone as the intimate key, casual style nevertheless conveys a good deal of feeling along with factual information, as in this passage:

GEORGE: Some golf game yesterday, wasn't it? But about Simpson—look, J.B., I don't think he's our man.

MR. GRIFFIN: Don't *think?* Come on, George. You *know* he isn't.

GEORGE: Well, J.B., if you put it that bluntly—yes, he isn't.

MR. GRIFFIN: Glad to hear you say it. . . .

The immediate lack of a high emotive function and the brief search for emotional rapport label this conversation between J.B. and George as being in the familiar or casual style or key. George is not and never will be of the same emotional intensity as J.B. Hence he cannot move into the intimate key with J.B., not the way Cliff does. The emotional qualifier "if you put it that bluntly" marks George's speech as casual rather than intimate. Such casualness, of course, is extremely informal and characterized by these adult slangy idioms: "Some golf game yesterday," "But about Simpson," "Look, J.B.," "Well, J.B.," and "Yes, he isn't." Such casualness makes use of word–form contractions and syntactical clippings, as in J.B.'s rather emotional responses: "Don't *think?* Come on, George. You *know* he isn't." And again, "Glad to hear you say it. . . ." These responses obviously show that J.B. would like to get into intimate key with George, but is kept at too great a psychological distance by his friend. For friends they are, though not pals.

Because he is neither on intimate nor on familiar terms with Mr. Griffin, Floyd forces the business executive to speak in the *consultative* style or key of discourse. As Nist (1969a, p. 14) has previously indicated, the consultative style or key

. . . denotes an attempt to achieve a kind of ingroup relationship among the several speakers of their semipublic language, through an exploration of the area of their rapport by means of background insertions of information and revisions of expression. This is the key that we speak in most often away from home, at work in the office among our colleagues or at play among a party of casual acquaintances. Avoiding emotional tone whenever possible and constantly on guard against offensive connotations, the consultative

key is nevertheless colloquially idiomatic. Its most distinguishing
trait, perhaps, is its concern for a neutral subject matter, summed
up in the U.S. naval officers' code: "Never discuss sex, politics,
or religion at the dinner table." It is precisely because we can do
nothing about the weather that we can find it such a safe topic
for conversation in the consultative key.

The stylistic tipoff to the consultative key in the talk between
Floyd and Mr. Griffin is in the idiomatic informality of their
speech patterns. Both men, that is, resort to syntactical clippings, contractions, and idiomatic verbs with directive particles, as in *think of* and *looking for*. Even though Floyd keeps
his superior in this key, Mr. Griffin relaxes to the point of
slurring his articulation: "Whatta ya say to that?" As business
acquaintances, Floyd and Mr. Griffin like and respect each
other, but the consultative key they speak in reveals that
they are not close friends.

It is precisely because he is a junior officer in the company
and not even on consultative terms with Mr. Griffin that Tom
speaks in the *deliberative* style or key of discourse in order
to maintain a respectful psychological distance from his boss.
Indeed as Nist (1969a, p. 14) has previously indicated, it is
this deliberative style or key which

> . . . denotes the psychological distance of a speech, at least par-
> tially planned in advance, for a rather large group of people who
> are permitted little opportunity for response. Requiring complete-
> ness in expression, the deliberative key aims for detachment from
> the audience and for cohesion of ideas; usually it imposes a rhetorical
> mastery at the level of the paragraph.

The sentence patterns of the deliberative key, furthermore,
are generally of a semiformal and rather standard variety:

MR. GRIFFIN: Well, Tom, what do you think of Simpson?
TOM: Mr. Griffin, I believe he is not the man we are looking
    for.
MR. GRIFFIN: It seems to me that your creed is not unwar-
    ranted in this case. . . .

Tom's formality is almost total, but not quite. He leaves out
the relative pronoun *whom* as the marker of formal syntactical
linkage, and he also ends his sentence on the idiomatic adverb
for (often misthought by the mythic schoolmarm Miss Fid-

ditch to be a preposition). His semiformal manner, however, is a cold and distant response to Mr Griffin's attempt to be consultative, and so the sensitive executive responds in an even more formal construction, beginning with the time–honored formula, *It seems to me that*. The term *unwarranted*, of course, is another sign of the deliberative style or key.

Because he is very unsure of himself, Bill casts his message in the *rhetorical* or *oratorical* style or key of discourse. As Nist (1969a, p. 14) has previously indicated, the rhetorical key "denotes an even greater psychological distance between speaker and audience in the elaborateness of a declamation that is professional in nature and rules out the possibility of any sort of language response," that is, under *normal* conditions for that key:

> With complete formality, as in a State of the Union Address, the rhetorical or oratorical key organizes the entire discourse in advance, through several versions and revisions, until the style is as polished as that of formal written work. Utterances in this key are usually designed for publication. It is thus in the rhetorical or oratorical key that speech fully intersects with writing.

Bill retreats to this key, of course, because it is a way of giving his opinion to Mr. Griffin without incurring anything but the same sort of antiseptic formality in response:

MR. GRIFFIN: Well, Bill, what do you think of Simpson?

BILL: Mr. Griffin, in my opinion he is not the man whom we want.

MR. GRIFFIN: After having studied the man's credentials and read his anemic recommendations, I fear that I must concur with your estimate of Mr. Simpson's potential. . . .

Unlike Tom, Bill uses the relative pronoun *whom* to establish syntactical linkage; he also substitutes the formal *in my opinion* for the semiformal *I believe*. These two signs of the rhetorical key, plus Bill's avoidance of any contractions, syntactical clippings, and idiomatic verb phrases, lead Mr. Griffin into a frozen response, in which he sounds like a professor of oratory reading from his own textbook. So long as Bill and Mr. Griffin address each other in this formal key, they will never establish much emotional rapport or become even casual friends.

Thus, through the use of both the rhetorical and the deliberative styles or keys of discourse, a degree of formality is maintained in interrelationships, which is less noticeable in consultative discourse and practically nonexistent in the casual and intimate styles.

THE SELF AND LINGUISTIC ROLES: A SUMMING UP

Now the application of all the preceding discussion to the problem of handicapped English in the United States today is simply this: because they are woefully deficient in verbal planning, cannot readily detach themselves from their audience, and do not seek coherence of ideas, speakers of basilect Modern American English are usually utterly incapable of handling both the *rhetorical* and the *deliberative* styles or keys of discourse. Because of their generally high emotive function and their rather constant suspicion of "outsiders," speakers of handicapped English often also fail to master the requirements of the *consultative* style or key; they frequently fail to avoid offensive connotations and will "blunder into" topics of discussion that are normally forbidden for this key. And even in the *familiar* (casual) and *intimate* styles or keys, where they are assuredly more at home, the socially disadvantaged speakers of the basilect still have a tendency to "goof up" in their organization and transmission of the intended message.

With regard to these last mentioned informal styles or keys, in both instances expressive symbolism tends to devour the *verbal* content of the basilect message, with the result that inexplicitness often leads to a breakdown in communication even among members of the ingroup. In the familiar style or key, for example, slang frequently degenerates into criminal argot; whereas, in the intimate style or key, what we have called "dysphemism" (or hyperbolic use of derogatory terms as marks of affection or intimacy) customarily decays into mere name–calling—a process in which offensive vulgarity, profanity, and obscenity abound. In other words, *I*

don't know do he work out worth shit, or some other equivalent manifestation of the basilect, is not an appropriate
response to Mr. Griffin's question about the possible hiring
of Simpson. And yet it is just this sort of a "bastard blend"
of the three lower styles or keys of discourse which is liable
to inform the messages of socially disadvantaged speakers
of basilect Modern American English.

Such a "bastard blend," in turn, means that most speakers
of handicapped English suffer from a terrible esthetic
deficiency. They do not realize, for example, that style itself
is like a kaleidoscope, constantly shifting its patterns and
colors from the influences which are brought to bear upon
it. Deprived of a mastery of the full range of the national
language and therefore unaware of the *formal elevation* of
the consultative, deliberative, and rhetorical keys of spoken
discourse into the informal, semiformal, and formal styles
of written discourse (Nist, 1969a, pp. 15–16), these same
speakers of the basilect are generally ignorant of the following
facts (Nist, 1969b, p. 7):

> A man does not write a letter in the same style in which he
> composes a telegram; the code for each contact is different. That
> same man does not tell an anecdote to his wife in the same style
> he uses for his six–year–old son; the aesthetic expectancy and
> critical intelligence of his addressees are different. Neither does
> he, once engaged in running for political office, speak in the same
> manner to a small audience of labor leaders as he does to a national
> audience of television viewers; each occasion demands a style that
> will fit the cultural context and the medium. In like manner, he
> shifts his style to suit the genre of his discourse when he turns
> professional writer—that is, he does not write an essay in the same
> way in which he writes a short story or a lyric poem. His purpose
> and his rhetorical mode make him adjust the code of his message
> to meet their demands. Just as description differs from narration
> and drama differs from lyricism, so the same person's style differs
> from occasion to occasion, from purpose to purpose, from audience
> to audience, from subject to subject, from contact to contact, from
> rhetorical mode to rhetorical mode, from emotional state to emo-
> tional state, and from age to age.

In their disregard for these esthetic facts, speakers of handicapped English usually fail to exercise the *limited freedom*
which underlies stylistic choice. From that failure, further-

more, these same speakers of handicapped English fall short of asserting their right to a full humanity (see Nist, 1969b, p. 7). And, in failing to assert that right, speakers of basilect Modern American English inevitably also rarely achieve what the great philosopher Alfred North Whitehead (1861–1947) thought a clear–cut mastery of style to be: THE ULTIMATE MORALITY OF THE HUMAN MIND.

In summary, then, failure to achieve this ultimate morality of the human mind among speakers of handicapped English is a direct result of an earlier failure to achieve an appropriate image of themselves and of the various linguistic roles which they should assume.

Chapter 6

CAUSES OF HANDICAPPED ENGLISH

BOTH EXPLICIT AND IMPLICIT in the argument of this book so far is the fact that handicapped English is the result of the direct interference of a *native* language with the learning of the *national* language within the period of resonance (from 2 to 12 years of age) of the child so handicapped. Such interference, of course, constitutes an *environmental deprivation,* as distinct from a deficiency in biological inheritance. It is thus within the phenomenon of environmental deprivation that the linguist must look for the several individual causes of handicapped English. Neither are these causes very hard to find. Indeed, as Bernstein (1968; 1969; 1970), Labov (1970b), Lawton (1968), Lenneberg (1967), and many other authorities in the study of psycholinguistics and sociolinguistics (see, e.g., Bright, 1966; Fishman, 1968; Halsey, Floud, and Anderson, 1961, 1965; Lieberson, 1969; Reed, 1971; Saporta, 1961; and Shuy, 1964) have already indicated, the major causes of handicapped English within the phenomenon of environmental deprivation are these (see Nist, Nov. 1969, pp. 8–9): (1) the lack of an adequate language model in each of the child's important phases of linguisitc development within the period of resonance; (2) the lack of emotional security that comes from the deprivation of normal parental love and care; (3) the lack of richness and variety in the play

179

materials available to the child at home; (4) the damaging influence of a restricted code, together with its inordinate emphasis on expressive symbolism, which is inherent in the closed systems of communication and imperative modes of behavior control in positional– or status–oriented families; (5) the cultural warfare or conflict of value systems in the public schools of the United States, together with the self-fulfilling prophecies of failure in the educability of the socially disadvantaged; and (6) the peer–group reinforcement of various forms of basilect Modern American English and therefore of their local kinds of environmental deprivation. These major causes of handicapped English are the subject of the present chapter.

LACK OF ADEQUATE LANGUAGE MODEL

As Lenneberg (1967, p. 135) has said, "It is obvious that a child cannot acquire language unless he is exposed to it." In other words, genotypical capacity to acquire a language is not enough; phenotypical modeling of a specific language is an absolute requirement. So important is genotypical capacity, however, that it *regulates the age of onset of speech* within the child, quite independently of the quality of his modeling environment. Hence Lenneberg (1967, pp. 135–136) believes that it is reasonable to assume the following:

> . . . that in most instances an initially poor language environment does not cripple the child's basic potentialities forever. If the social environment is enriched early enough, he will at once improve his language habits. The important point here is that intuitively the notion can be accepted that language potentialities do develop regularly and in spite of certain environmental deprivations. A closer look at the empirical investigations support [sic] precisely this view.

The key phrase in Lenneberg's assertion, of course, is *early enough*. Why? Because within the phenomenon of constancy and stability in the emergence of language *capacity*, there is also the phenomenon of independent incremental growth in the *exercise and expression* of that capacity. The latter phenomenon, which relates directly to the quality of the phenotypical modeling, means that damage in the exercise

and expression of language capacity tends to be *irreversible.*
Indeed, as Carroll (1971, p. 99) has said,

> Human characteristics have an apparent stability: the child who
> is gifted in language development at the age of 5 tends to be, on
> the average, gifted also at later ages. Likewise, the child who is
> retarded at age 5 will probably be retarded at later ages.

Despite the overwhelming influence of genotypical capacity
upon the emergence of the onset of the period of resonance,
what the child attains within that period of resonance depends
in large measure upon the quality of the phenotypical modeling he encounters. This seems, at least, to be the claim of
Carroll.

And Lenneberg (1967, p. 136) agrees:

> Morley [1957] found that the language habits which emerged at
> the common time soon showed signs of impoverishment in the
> underprivileged, and unintelligibility occurred more commonly in
> second and subsequent children than in first. Thus the influence
> of the environment upon speech habit is undeniable, even though
> the onset of speech habits is relatively unaffected.

The impoverishment of language habits discovered by Morley
(1957) is attributable, according to Nisbet (1961, 1965, p. 274),
to a deprivation in these three factors: "the size of the family
itself, the amount of contact between adult and child
and the consequent stimulation of the child's verbal
development." In other words, the larger the family, the
smaller the amount of contact with an adult model, and the
less the stimulation of verbal development—the *more
impoverished* the child will be in the exercise and expression
of his language capacity. Nisbet (1961, 1965, p. 274) makes
it very clear, moreover, that "family size has a direct effect
on the environmental aspect of mental development" in the
child himself, as he adds:

> This hypothesis derives from the view that language and words
> afford a system of symbols which greatly increases the efficiency
> of abstract thought. Limitation of opportunities for verbal develop-
> ment is therefore likely to exercise a depressive influence on ability
> to score in a test of general mental ability. It has been established
> that the only child enjoys a much greater verbal development than
> the child from an orphanage, because of greater opportunities of
> contact with adults and of acquiring adult vocabulary. The large

family is considered here as an environment midway between that
of the only child and the orphanage.

Insofar as family size contributes to a deprivation in phenotypical modeling, Carroll (1971, p. 146) corroborates the conviction of Nisbet:

> Almost every study of environmental influences leads one to con-
> clude that the primary factor in language development, aside from
> native abilities, is the *quality* of the language exposure that the
> child receives. The richer this quality of language exposure, other
> things being equal, the faster and better the individual's language
> development.

What Nisbet and Carroll are both saying, then, is this: within
the early stages of the period of resonance, THE CHILD
WILL LEARN THE BASICS OF HIS LANGUAGE, OR
FAIL TO DO SO, *IN DIRECT PROPORTION TO THE
INTENSITY OF HIS ONE–TO–ONE RELATIONSHIP WITH
THE PHENOTYPICAL MODELING OF A LINGUISTIC
ADULT.*

As all the world of literary criticism knows, the great French
short–story writer Guy de Maupassant (1850–1893) learned
the craft of his art from an intense one–to–one relationship
of literary apprenticeship to the acknowledged nineteenth
century master of French prose, the great novelist Gustave
Flaubert (1821–1880). The older and far more experienced
Flaubert, that is, made the younger and far less experienced
De Maupassant rewrite and rewrite and *re*–write one story
after another until that day when the disciple had learned
all that the master could teach him. Then, when De Maupassant had reached the point of critical maturity and creative
independence, Flaubert told him that he was "on his own"
and free to publish as he would. As it was with De Maupassant and Flaubert in the phenotypical modeling of
nineteenth–century literary French, so it is with every American child and his parent(s) or some surrogate equivalent(s)
in the phenotypical modeling of twentieth–century spoken
English: the intensity of that one–to–one relationship is
everything.

Such intensity, or the lack thereof, means that handicapped

English is not necessarily the monopoly of the poor. Indeed, Carroll (1971, p. 147) makes this point very clear:

> Early language deprivation is not necessarily correlated with low socio–economic status; it can occur even in children of the very wealthy who have minimal contact with their parents. Children who are for any reason placed in orphanages during their early years also are likely to exhibit retarded language development, and according to Goldfarb (1943), this handicap may persist even up to adolescence.

The key phrase in the foregoing quotation from Carroll, of course, is *minimal contact with their parents.* By extending the term *parents* to include any and all adults who act as phenotypical models, linguistic science can say that the most important language deprivation within the family environment is that of a profound reduction of contact between the learner child and the teacher adult. Such a profound reduction lies at the heart of the fact that twins, on the whole, show a marked retardation in verbal development when contrasted with the performance of single–birth children (see Nisbet, 1961, 1965, p. 275). In similar fashion, a baby in a large family that permits the conflict of contrasting language models, will tend to be verbally retarded: shall he talk and segment reality like Grandma, like Mom, or like Aunt Mabel, or Big Sis? If all four share the role of phenotypical modeling, then the child is most assuredly deprived of that intense one–to–one relationship upon which optimum progress depends. If all four neglect the role of phenotypical modeling, on the other hand, and leave it to Little Sis, then the child may experience an intense one–to–one relationship—but not with a linguistic adult. In short, with an inadequate model.

So important is this factor of an intense one–to–one relationship with a linguistic adult for the language development of the child within the early stages of the period of resonance, that it becomes the *sine qua non* for the attainment of superiority in both competence and performance. Indeed—again as Nisbet has said (p. 275)—it is precisely because of this factor (an intense one–to–one relationship with a linguistic adult) that "only children show a striking superiority in language development, and children from institutions a marked retardation."

Because of the extent to which they encourage language development in their children, moreover, parents from various ethnic groups—in New York City, for example—will tend to be good phenotypical models, whereas others will not be. According to Carroll (1971, p. 147),

> Jewish children were found to be significantly better in English verbal ability than all other groups studied, followed by Negroes, Chinese, and Puerto Ricans, in that order. In each group, middle–class children were superior to lower–class children, but the class difference was most marked among Negroes. . . .

At the heart of Carroll's observation is the well–known fact that Jewish families, not only in New York City but also throughout the United States as a whole, tend to be close–knit and child–development oriented; such families, therefore, tend to foster the intense one–to–one relationship in phenotypical modeling we have been speaking of. On the other hand, close-knit and child-development oriented or not, many Chinese and Puerto Rican families in New York City permit the gross interference of an ancestral and/or native *foreign* language with the child's learning of national Modern American English and so defeat the purpose in single-language mastery. Because Negro families generally do not permit such foreign–language interference, their children tend to develop a better English verbal ability than do their Chinese and Puerto Rican peers. Yet the class difference among the Negro population of New York City is the most marked, simply because within families that speak the basilect more than half of the children grow up without at least one of their parents. Hence among these socially disadvantaged Negro children an inadequate phenotypical modeling joins with an inferior lect to deprive them of a mastery of the national language.

Inadequate phenotypical modeling, in turn, is not necessarily conditional upon the absence of the parent(s). In fact, both parents may be *present* with the young child much of the time, but say little or nothing to each other *or* to the child, with the result that the child will be permanently retarded in the acquisition of Modern American English. There are, for example, such extreme cases as that of a seven–year–old Negro girl in rural south Alabama who COULD NOT SPEAK A SENTENCE OF HER NATIONAL LANGUAGE (personal observation, 1969) at the time she was admitted into a summer program of Head Start. Restricted to the expressive symbolism of kinesics and paralanguage, this terribly disadvantaged child grew up in a family situation which offered *no* real verbal stimulation whatsoever: her inarticulate parents merely gestured and made holophrastic animal–like noises to one another and to her.

Less rare than this extreme case of inadequate phenotypical modeling, of course, are those instances in which doting parents prolong infantile "baby–talk" beyond the period of the onset of resonance (18 to 24 months), thereby hindering the child's growth and development in the phonology, morphology, syntax, and semantics of Modern American English. At the opposite extreme, but surely just as damaging, are those "ultra modern" parents who persist in sophisticatedly "talking over the child's head" and who thereby refuse to simplify the child's acquisition of the national language by means of a *judicious and appropriate* use of overarticulation, exaggerated intonation, slower pacing, basic rather than derived sentence structures, explicit lexical words rather than inexplicit substitute words, and repetition of key words and phrases. Among the socially advantaged, moreover, there is the added probem of *bilingualism*, or the probability that a native foreign language in one or both of the parents may interfere with the child's acquisition of an unaccented acrolect version of Modern American English. Complicated as this problem of bilingualism can be, here again Carroll (1971, p. 147) is eminently sane, as in the following assertion:

> Available data are not inconsistent with the hypothesis that the degree to which bilingualism affects native language development is a function of the amount and kind of exposure such a condition allows the child to get to his native language, quite independently of how much exposure he receives to the other language involved.

In other words, Carroll is saying that if Parent A is master of the acrolect version of Modern American English and Par-

ent B is master of the acrolect version of Foreign Language
X, then each parent must act as the phenotypical model of
that language and *only that language* which is acrolectly
native to him: Parent A for Modern American English and
Parent B for Foreign Language X. It is precisely when Parent
B or some surrogate equivalent nurse with a foreign accent
tries to do the phenotypical modeling of Parent A that deprivation in the acquisition of the national language occurs.
Because of the phenomenon of basilect interference, it is
a notorious fact that among many well–to–do Southern white
families such deprivation has occurred historically, and may
continue to occur today, through the undue influence of the
phenotypical modeling of a Negro "Mammy" maid or nurse.

From all available evidence in both theory (see Chomsky,
1965; 1968, 1972) and research (see Lenneberg, 1967), it is
apparent that insofar as the child's acquisition of his
native—and hopefully, national—language is concerned
PERFORMANCE PRECEDES AND INDEED DETER-
MINES COMPETENCE. This existentialist, even phenom-
enologist, view of language acquisition means that whatever damage is done to the child's mastery of Modern
American English is DONE EARLY AND PERMANENTLY
AND CUMULATIVELY. Indeed one of the saddest observations on the phenomenon of independent incremental growth
in the development of competence through performance is
that of Carroll (1971, p. 99), who claims the following:

> It would appear, for example, that by the age of about 4, the
> typical child has acquired half of all the mental growth he will
> ever acquire; the amount of mental growth he gains in any given
> year is almost completely independent of what he has acquired
> up to the start of that year. The increments of growth are, so to
> speak, accidents of the particular maturational and environmental
> influences that happen to obtain during a particular period of
> growth.

A very sad observation indeed, because, as Lenneberg (1967,
Ch. 4) has shown, the prime time for the acquisition of any
language is the period of resonance, which runs from about
age 2 years to age 12 years. Within this ten–year period,
then, the child suffers *the full range* of linguistic
deprivation: dialectal and lectal "foreign" accent, if any; pau-

city of vocabulary; narrow range of syntactic structures and therefore heavy reliance on expressive symbolism; dyslexia, dysscriptsia, and illiteracy; rhetorical and semantic deficiency; inadequate segmentation of reality; and inappropriate image of the self and of the linguistic roles which the self *should* assume.

Within this ten–year period of the full range of linguistic deprivation, moreover, the tragedy of "cumulative deficit" emerges. Indeed the scores of research articles summarized by Williams and Naremore (1970, pp. 416–456) in their annotated bibliography all tend to support these important conclusions drawn by Davenport Plumer (1970, pp. 297–298):

> 1. The five preschool years are the most important in a child's language development.
> 2. Hence, poor children who spend these five years in homes which lack the conditions necessary for full language development enter schools poorly prepared for the challenges of the traditional school curriculum. There is, in short, a consistently high correlation between poverty (and often race) and poor language performance.
> 3. This correlation persists throughout a child's schooling. In other words, schools have, at best, a very modest impact in terms of their ability to educate poor children. That is, a poor child who begins school with submedian tests scores will, in all likelihood, end his school career even further below the median score for his age and grade. The Coleman report (1966) indicates that this is true for middle–class as well as lower–class children. Irrespective of the child's social status, schools do not account for much of the variance in achievement scores.
> 4. Finally, there are exceptions to the poverty cycle (and to the prosperity cycle). The poor children who "make it" may be genetically superior, or they may have had an unusually supportive environment. Thus far, however, research has not been able to distinguish between these causes or to specify in detail the characteristics of a supportive environment.

Implicit throughout Plumer's conclusions is the fact that the lack of adequate phenotypical modeling within the child's period of resonance lies at the very heart of the phenomenon of "cumulative deficit" in handicapped English. First of all, the child suffers from an inadequate model at home; then he enters public school, defective in his command of the national language, and gets "turned off" by his teachers. Despite Plumer's claim that current research cannot "specify in detail the characteristics of a supportive environment," it is fairly obvious that children who are exceptions to the deprivation pattern outlined above are those fortunate enough to experience somewhere in an "extended family" situation an intense one–to–one relationship with a linguistic adult —perhaps in the *adopting personality* of a minister or priest, youth counselor or athletic coach, playground supervisor or off–duty policeman, homeroom teacher or "neighborhood mother." No matter who that person may be, the adopting personality will be there as the key factor in the efficacy of the supportive environment. Why? Because a prerequisite for the adequacy of the phenotypical model of the national language is a loving and protective temperament, the temperament of one who cares.

LACK OF EMOTIONAL SECURITY

As a corollary to the inadequacy of the phenotypical modeling on the part of the parent(s) or some surrogate equivalent(s), then, is the lack of emotional security on the part of the child who is deprived of love and affectionate care. Since emotional security is of extreme importance during the intonational stage (ca. 6 to 12 months) of the child's "phatic priming" for the eventual resonant acquisition of the modeled language, any real deprivation of love and affectionate care within the family environment *automatically* results in a diminution in the child's sense of fate–control and therefore in a loss in his own self–image (see Plumer, 1970, p. 296). Such a diminution and such a loss, furthermore, lead to a weakening of the motivation to learn—that is, to achieve competence in the modeled language by means of an exercise in performance.

So crucial is this problem of motivation, moreover, that the research of O.C. Irwin (1948a; 1948b; 1952) indicates, in the summary language of Williams and Naremore (1970, p. 438) that infants (1 to 30 months) "from laboring–class families develop speech sounds at a slower rate than infants from families representing business, clerical, or professional class." Not only do these socially disadvantaged infants develop speech sounds at a slower rate, but they also, according to Irwin (see Williams and Naremore, 1970, p. 438), "have a lower frequency of speech–sound utterances than do infants from families representing a business, clerical, or professional class." Of utmost importance, however, is the fact that Irwin's research shows that *the age of eighteen months is the crucial turning point* within the pre–resonant linguistic life of the child. Up to that age, as Irwin indicates (see Williams and Naremore, 1970, p. 438), there exists "no difference according to occupational status of parents" in the language acquisition of the children studied, but after eighteen months "then those infants reared in a home where the occupational status is unskilled tend to lag in development behind higher status counterparts," whereas differences in performance reveal "delayed development in orphanage children, as compared with infants living in their own homes."

From a judicious interpretation of the research of Irwin (1948a; 1948b; 1952), Lenneberg (1967), Plumer (1970), and the summary findings of Williams and Naremore (1970) in scores of research articles on handicapped English, it is possible for linguistic science to say that the language damage done to a child WITHIN HIS PERIOD OF RESONANCE follows the general outlines of the following scheme:

Age Period	Language Function	Amount of Damage
birth–18 months	"phatic priming"	negligible linguistic but considerable emotional
18–24 months	onset of resonance	considerable phonological and emotional
2–4 years	learning of language	50 percent of verbal and cognitive deficit
4–8 years	overlearning of language, start of reading and writing, onset of "code switching"	30 percent of verbal and cognitive deficit
8–12 years	formal mastery of grammar, rhetoric, logic; cognitive maturation	20 percent of verbal and cognitive deficit

From the foregoing scheme, then, it is apparent that most of the damage, both linguistically and emotionally, which is done to the child within his period of resonance is done to him BEFORE HE EVER ENTERS THE FIRST GRADE. Most of the emotional damage, furthermore, may very well take place even *BEFORE THE ONSET OF RESONANCE* and the ensuing crucial two years (from two to four) during which the child learns his preferred resonant language (geographical dialect and social–class lect). Such emotional damage, moreover, relates directly to the weakening of the child's motivation "to learn" anything at all.

In other words—as an increasing body of evidence from the experience of Head Start (better named "Late" Start) programs and nursery school encounters (personal observation) shows—if the "timing mechanism" within the child's central nervous system is not "turned on" to the acquisition of language and knowledge by the time he is 18 months old, then the child will be, to some degree or other, permanently retarded in his own linguistic development. Retarded, that is, in relation to his own *potential but unactualized* capacity for competence and performance.

The emotional security that comes from love and affectionate care within the family environment during the first eighteen months of "phatic priming," then, is of extreme importance to the later linguistic development of the child. If the mother, who normally does most of the phenotypical modeling, does not want the child and therefore does not love him, she may very well not give him more than minimum care. In addition to letting him lie around in unchanged diapers and cry for a withheld feeding, the mother may not give the child any real vocal stimulation or smiling attention. If so, then most assuredly she will not reward and hence reinforce his early vocalizations. The usual result of this sort of "denial of phatic presence," of course, is a permanent retardation in the language growth of the child.

At the conclusion of his great mystical poem "Song of the Open Road," Walt Whitman (1819–1892) says:

"I give you my love more precious than money,
I give you myself before preaching or law. . . ."

These eloquent lines should be the motto of every parent

toward his child, the universally actualized ideal of human behavior. It is precisely because Whitman's vision of the importance of love in the actual physical presence of the loving person is denied in so many present–day American families that handicapped English in the United States is so widespread a phenomenon. Poorly educated and out–of–work fathers abandon their families, with the result that the innocent children become linguistic victims of absentee mothers, of mothers who must work or keep hounding the Welfare Office. A similar result occurs, though for different reasons, among many middle–class families in which the mother either works long hours away from home—perhaps to put a husband through graduate or professional school or to help pay off the debts incurred by trying "to live too high on the hog"—or travels prolongedly. Emotional insecurity on the part of the child and its accompanying language deprivation may be the unintended by–product of a long hospitalization of one or both parents, or the outgrowth of the sudden death of both the mother and the father—a death which commits the child to the relative emotional anonymity of an orphanage.

Worst of all for the child, of course, is the emotional warping which results from a distorted or unhealthy relationship with the parent who does most of the phenotypical modeling. Perhaps the parent is overly protective and "baby–talks" the child into an exaggerated emotive reliance on the expressive symbolism of intonation and paralanguage, with the twin effects of damaging both articulatory transmission and auditory reception. Maybe the parent is overly anxious for the child to "get ahead" and hence pushes the child into linguistic stages for which the child is not ready, thereby swamping the child's capacity to perform, undermining the child's sense of fate–control, diminishing the child's own self–image, and ultimately deadening the child's motivation to "learn." Conceivably the parent shows only concern when the child is sick; if so, then the child will probably suffer from a case of induced hypochondria, together with its distorted segmentation of reality and emotionally twisted image of the self and of its linguistic roles. Rarely, though possibly, the parent may affectionally abuse the child by making him into a psychological and/or physical mate–substitute, with verbal and cognitive consequences too hideous to contemplate. But regardless of the exact cause of the emotional insecurity and the affectional warping, this much is certain: as M.M. Lewis has demonstrated in his classic *Infant Speech: A Study of the Beginnings of Language* (1951), ONLY THOSE CHILDREN WHO HAVE EXPERIENCED THE MOST INTENSE CARE IN THE ONE–TO–ONE RELATION-SHIP OF PHENOTYPICAL MODELING SHOW THE MAXIMUM AMOUNT OF GROWTH AND DEVELOPMENT IN THE ACQUISITION OF THE PREFERRED RESONANT LANGUAGE. In other words, the conditions which are most favorable to a child's acquisi-tion of an acrolect version of Modern American English include the emotional security which stems from that parental love and affectionate care which strike an even balance between not helping enough and helping too much, between lack of concern and overanxiety.

LACK OF PLAY MATERIALS

Such emotional security, in turn, will be accompanied by a richness and variety in the play materials available to the child in his home. Indeed, it is this very lack of richness and variety in the play materials available to him at home which is one of the major causes of handicapped English in the socially disadvantaged child. As Ponder (1967, p. 28) has said, "the economic 'have nots' are often the verbal 'have nots' as well." Why? Because for one reason, according to Ponder (1967, p. 26), the economically "have–not" child is often a victim of his own "extended family":

> The extended family is not uncommon in the family structure of the disadvantaged child. Uncles, aunts, grandparents, cousins, and sometimes very close friends are a part of the family structure. It would appear that the disadvantaged child has only advantages regarding language development with so many people around. The extended family structure, however, may cause serious discontinuity in the language development of the child. He learns language from the many people around him, likely speaking in varied pitches and accents. Lost in the shuffle of so many people, often in a crowded space, the child has limited opportunities for help in learning to

label the objects in his environment. His opportunities for enrichment within and outside the encapsulated, socially impoverished environment are also limited.

Impoverished, then, in space and in time and in attention and therefore in opportunity, the socially disadvantaged child of the "extended family" is not only deficient in his labeling of the objects about him, but also—even more importantly—at a loss to cope with the higher level of abstraction involved in what Ponder (1967, p. 28) calls "the labeling of similarities and differences in objects and functions of objects." This basic failure at classification is truly rampant among speakers of basilect Modern American English. Such failure among their children in the public schools of the United States has been well analyzed in the research of Mukerji and Robison (1967, pp. 19–20):

> They generally were quite limited in their knowledge and use of classifying terms. For example, they did not know that they, as individuals, made up their kindergarten class or that apples, bananas, and oranges are classified as fruit. Most children, unlike their middle-class counterparts, had so little familiarity with written symbols that they could neither recognize nor write their own names, failed to use picture clues in many instances, and could not identify a map by name or by its use. In addition to language symbols, the children needed to become aware of other nonverbal forms of symbolic representation. They also needed to gain awareness that maps and globes, signs, pictures, numerals, tallies, and arbitrary symbols are important ways of representing real things and ideas so that their ability to acquire and utilize important data could be broadened.

At the heart of their failure to label and to classify, of course, is the fact that most socially disadvantaged children of the basilect do not enjoy a richness and variety in their play materials at home. Since all quality is posited upon a crucial quantity (see Chardin, 1959, *passim*), this lack of sheer physical number and variety in the toys available to poor children of the "extended family" generally results in their being handicapped both in the experience of and discrimination among colors, sizes, shapes, amounts, weights, textures, motions, speeds, distances, and characteristic actions and mechanical relationships. In short, in their being handicapped in Aristotle's categories of observation (see pp. 142–144). Such hand-

icapping, furthermore, immediately shows up in the results
of I. Q. tests conducted upon young speakers of the basilect,
simply because, as Metz (1967, p. 14) has indicated, "group
tests of intelligence measure the young child's language
deprivation." Indeed, as Metz (1967, p. 14) irrefutably contends, such deprivation is rooted often in the child's failure
to acquire *geometric* terms and concepts from his grossly
inadequate play materials:

> Analysis was made of the oral vocabulary required to complete
> successfully five different group tests of intelligence. In one, the
> child must understand fourteen geometric terms to comprehend
> the teacher's oral directions. Language–deprived children often lack
> the concepts of such terms; for example, *pointed, oval–shaped, open-
> ing* (noun), or *partly curved*. This same test includes more than
> twenty directional words and phrases, among which are *toward
> the left, opposite from, the next after*, and *exactly under*. How,
> when we know such tests are valid as predictors of academic success,
> can we fail to teach the language–deprived child this vocabulary?

The question upon which Metz concludes the foregoing passage is, of course, the all–important one which *the parents
rather than the teachers* of socially disadvantaged children
should be made first to ask themselves and then to answer
with affirmative action. Why? Because, as this chapter has
already indicated, most of the linguistic damage done to the
child within his period of resonance is done to him before
he ever enters a public school in the United States.

This linguistic damage, furthermore, stems to a large degree
from the fact that the socially disadvantaged child is unmerci-
fully penalized in his achievement of a sense of relationship
through the *connective system* (see Whitehall, 1956, Ch. 5)
of Modern American English, simply because he is deprived
of the *sensuous basis* for forming such verbal abstractions.
In other words, it is precisely because the socially disadvantaged child does not have a rich and varied experience with
such toys and playthings as swings and slides, building blocks
and erector sets, modeling clay and finger paints, coloring
books and crayons, sand boxes and dump trucks, rocking
horses and electric trains, teddy bears and dollhouses *before
he enters public school* that he is so demonstrably inferior
to the socially advantaged child in both labeling and classi-

fying. Without a firsthand and sensuous apprehension of the crucial quantity of things (including such pets as dogs and cats, goldfish and guinea pigs, calves and riding ponies), the young speaker of the basilect is almost automatically doomed to suffer a marked deficiency in his control over an understanding of the new kind that is the quality of their abstract relationship to one another and, above all else, to the language which seeks to segment their reality. Hence as an outgrowth of this lack of richness and variety in the play materials available to him at home, the socially disadvantaged child will almost inevitably be retarded in his mastery of the concepts conveyed by the *prepositions* and the *conjunctions* of Modern American English.

The above named concepts, moreover, are fundamental not only to the child's nonverbal segmentation of reality, but also to his verbal expression of that segmentation and to his academic performance in school. Indeed, as Whitehall (1956, Ch. 5) has so brilliantly indicated, the following basic concepts within the connective system of Modern American English are of utmost importance for the child's ultimate mastery of the national language (cf. Diagram 9 below). Failing to master these simple connectives, together with their attendant expression of the *generally explicit* relations involved, the socially disadvantaged child inevitably fails to graduate into a deeper understanding of how compound and complex connectives express *even more specifically explicit* relations, whereas group and paired connectives express *the most specifically explicit* relations. Accompanying such failure, of course, is the young speaker of basilect's inability to make the necessary transferral from concrete to abstract, from spatial to temporal to logical.

Surely this inability to make the necessary transferral from concrete to abstract, from spatial to temporal to logical on the part of the socially disadvantaged speaker of basilect Modern American English is a major reason why he fails so consistently in those intelligence tests which require him to perform so–called *nonverbal* tasks that are necessarily based upon a successful *verbal* mediation of the very tasks themselves. Such consistent failure on the part of the socially

Connective	Category	Relation	Symbol
at	preposition	location	
by	preposition	location	
in	preposition	location	
on	preposition	location	
between	preposition	location	
among	preposition	location	
to	preposition	direction	
from	preposition	direction	
up	preposition	direction	
down	preposition	direction	
off	preposition	direction	
through	preposition	direction	
out	preposition	direction	
of	preposition	association	
for	preposition	association	
with	preposition	association	
and	conjunction	addition	
but, yet	conjunction	subtraction	
as, than	conjunction	comparison	
or, nor	conjunction	alternation	
for, so	conjunction	illation	
if, since	conjunction	qualification	
that	conjunction	incorporation	
who, when	conjunction	incorporation	

DIAGRAM 9.

IMPORTANT RELATIONAL CONCEPTS IN MODERN ENGLISH CONNECTIVES

disadvantaged child is discussed with penetrating insight in the following quotation from the published research of Metz (1967, pp. 14–15):

> Most group tests of intelligence include tasks called *nonverbal* which involve ability in abstraction or classification. The task may involve the selection of an object or design from a series because it is *different* or *not like the others*. It may require the selection of two items from a series because they are related as are no other items in the series. Such tasks involve the ability to relate or isolate items on the basis of multiple determinants. Choice must sometimes be made on the basis of *use;* for example, isolating an *eraser* from a series of *tools for writing*. In other tasks the choice might be determined by *direction*, up or down or left and right. *Spatial* factors such as symmetric–asymmetric may be involved. Examples of still other determinants are: spatial–numerical; reality testing; series–patterning. Are these tasks really *nonverbal?* Let us compare the responses of children from adequate language environments with those of language–deprived children. On a relatively simple task such as selecting a *tiger* as different from a *pig*, a *horse,* and a *sheep*, both children will probably succeed. When the first child is told, "Tell why," he can easily explain, "Well, the pig and the sheep and the horse are all farm animals, but the tiger is a jungle animal." Many language–deprived children, on the other hand, will be unable to give a verbal explanation of their thought processes. One child responded by pointing to each farm animal saying, "Him here," then pointing to the tiger and saying, "Him not here!" Can we doubt that some quality of inner–language is being employed by a child when he performs such so–called *nonverbal* tasks? On more complicated items of a test, the language–deprived child will probably fail the task even without verbalization.

Such intelligence tests as those described by Metz are really *cultural deprivation* tests. Basically unfair to the native *capacity* of the socially disadvantaged child to form abstract concepts that depend upon his verbal mediation of concrete experience, these tests do nevertheless reveal that unless that capacity is nourished by a richness and variety of concrete experience and exercised by the linguistic support of an attentive phenotypical modeling, then the resultant damage in both competence and performance will make the child both verbally and cognitively retarded.

Such retardation among the young speakers of basilect Modern American English, as Dale (1967, p. 31) has indicated, stems from the fact that "the actual physical range of the underprivileged child is restricted." Who, for example, takes this underprivileged child to see the animals in a zoo? As Dale (1967, p. 31) has said,

> . . . If he lives in a broken home, there may be no father to do this. Or even if he is in an intact home, there may be no method of easy transportation, such as the middle–class child has.

Quite obviously, then, the socially disadvantaged child is impoverished in the very range of his *active contact with things*. He generally has very little opportunity before his entrance into a public school, in the words of Dale (1967, p. 33), "to work with wood of various kinds, to paint, to cut out things with scissors, to eat varied foods or prepare foods . . ., make visits, go on study trips—and to discuss all these activities." Deprived of this active–contact–with–things method of learning, a most important method for the inquisitive and acquisitive little "animal sensorium" that he is, the socially disadvantaged child undergoes a tragic blunting of his power to perceive structure, to sustain interest, to segment reality—in short, in his power to motivate himself "to learn." Such blunting, furthermore, shows up linguistically in what Martin P. Deutsch (1963) has discovered as the socially disadvantaged child's *syntactical disorganization* and *discontinuity of subject* (see Ponder, 1967, p. 28).

DAMAGE OF RESTRICTED CODE

Such syntactical disorganization and discontinuity of subject within the messages of basilect Modern American English are the direct result of the damage which that socially disadvantaged code inflicts upon the grammar, rhetoric, and logic of its users. In the terminology of the great modern British sociologist Basil Bernstein, as a socially disadvantaged code the basilect is "restricted" rather than "elaborated." Such a code, furthermore, is the outgrowth of an intricate set of relations among the members of the lower class and their peculiarly closed family role system. Indeed, Bernstein (1970, pp. 28–29) himself reveals the sources of this phenomenon of restriction in the code in the following X–ray of social disadvantage:

> If a social group, by virtue of its class relation—that is, as a result of its common occupational function and social status—has developed strong communal bonds; if the work relations of this group offer little variety, little exercise in decision making; if to be successful, assertion must be collective rather than an individual act; if the work task requires physical manipulation and control rather than symbolic organization and control; if the diminished authority of the man at work is transformed into an authority of power at home; if the home is overcrowded and limits the variety of situations it can offer; if the children socialize each other in an environment offering little intellectual stimuli—if all these attributes are found in one setting, then it is plausible to assume that such a social setting will generate a particular form of communication which will shape the intellectual, social, and affective orientation of the children.

So eminently sound are Bernstein's observations that it would be *implausible* to assume any other conclusion than the one he does.

That conclusion, in turn, rests upon the incontrovertible fact that the father in a basilect family, more likely than not, will be engaged in manual labor, will have little or no experience in selective education, and will enjoy little or no occupational training in a specific skill (see Lawton, 1968, p. 83). The mother in such a basilect family, furthermore, will in all probability have little or no experience in selective education, little or no specific training for a skilled occupation, and little or no experience in work that is non–manual (see Lawton, 1968, p. 83). Sensitive to *content* rather than to *structure,* both parents in a basilect family generally will be unaware of the importance between means and long–term ends and of the need for self–discipline to achieve individual differentiation. Such parents, therefore, will usually let their children grow up outside a formally articulated structure, will normally not orient their children's behavior toward an explicit set of goals and values and thus will not impose a *stable* set of rewards and punishments. Such parents, moreover, will usually not think of the future in direct relation to the educational development of their children, who tend to grow up in an emotive rather than in a rational atmosphere, expressing their hostility and aggression through kinesics and paralanguage and *seldom verbalizing* their deepest feelings.

As a result of their verbal impoverishment through being reared in the restricted code of a basilect family, socially disadvantaged children in the United States today suffer cognitively from A MARKED DEFICIENCY IN THE ABILITY TO ABSTRACT AND GENERALIZE, TO PERCEIVE THE WORLD AS AN ORDERLY AND RATIONAL ENTITY, TO BELIEVE IN THE REWARD OF INTELLIGENT AND VIRTUOUS ACTION, TO PLAN AHEAD, AND TO EXERCISE SELF–CONTROL (see Lawton, 1968, pp. 14–15). Dominated by the senses, these same socially disadvantaged children are very likely to ignore obscure objects and hidden functions, and both the temporally and the logically more remote consequences of their present actions (see Lawton, 1968, p. 15). Thus they tend to satisfy immediately their current wishes, needs, and moods rather than control them or defer them for the sake of ultimately satisfying potentially more valuable and important future (i.e., absent and abstract) wishes, needs, and moods (Lawton, p. 15). Such satisfaction, furthermore, is mirrored linguistically in the kind of *phatic communion* in which speakers of the basilect, both young and old, indulge—i.e., the "phatic communion" of a "public language" that is notorious for the inexplicitness of its meaning.

Accompanying such inexplicitness in the restricted code of the basilect, of course, is the fact that *things and events tend to predominate over ideas and over reflections on events.* This predominance is dramatically apparent in the immature "it–itis" of the following essay from the pen of a fifteen–year–old British lad (see Lawton, 1968, pp. 112–113) who is a victim of handicapped English:

My Life in Ten Years' Time

I hope to be a carpenter just about married and like to live in a modern house and do a ton on the Sidcup by–pass with a motor–bike and also drinking in the Local pub.

My hobby will be breeding dogs and spare time running a pet shop. And I will be wearing the latest styles of clothes.

I hope my in ten years time will be a happy life without a worry and I have a good blance behide me. I am going to have a gay and happy life. I am going to work hard to get somewhere in the world.

One thing I will not do in my life is to bring disgrace and unhappiness to my family.

In addition to the obvious errors in spelling, the egregious failures in mood and aspect, the mental lapses that produce incomplete constructions, and the "bird-brained parroting" of clichés, the foregoing discourse is a classic example of the basilect's preoccupation with the concrete details of inconsequence, of its inability to abstract a pattern of generalized thought, of its pathetic verbal imprisonment in a very narrow range of structures and an underlying constriction of choice and rigidity of alternatives, and of its ultimate reliance on the inarticulate "good will" of a group solidarity with which it so strongly identifies—hence the closing appeal for ethos in the unconcious bit of bragging self–righteousness: "One thing I will not do in my life is to bring disgrace and unhappiness to my family."

Sad. So very sad. Especially when contrasted with the following excerpt from the pen of another fifteen–year–old British lad (see Lawton, 1968, p. 113), one whose English is a curious mixture of adult acrolect and adolescent mesilect:

My Life in Ten Years' Time

As I look around me and see the wonders of modern science and all the fantastic new developments I feel a slight feeling of despondency. That is because I am beginning to wonder who will be in control of the world in ten years time, the machine or man. Already men are being shot round earth in rockets and already machines are being built that will travel faster and faster than the one before. I wonder if the world will be a gigantic nut–house by the time I'm ten years older. We are told we will be driving supersonic cars at fantastic speeds, with televisions, beds, and even automatic driving controls. Do we want this, do we want to be ruled by machinery. Gone will be the time when the family go out for a picnic on a Sunday Afternoon, we will be whisked along wide flat autoroads, we will press a button in a wall and out will come a plate of sandwiches ready prepared. you may think that this is a bit far–fetched but if things keep on improving men will not have to think for themselves and we will become a race of boseyed mawrons. There is, if this is going to happen, no way to stop it. Men say we will have just one or two more luxuries and it never stops. I enjoy the luxuries of to–day, but in my opinion there is a limit. But who decides what that limit will be. No one knows its just a lot of men all relaying on someone to stop this happening, but no–one is going to. We're doomed. No prayers can save us now, we'll become slaves to great walking monstrosities. Powerless in the hands of something we helped to create. I'm worried about 'my life in ten years time'.

Despite the minor blemishes in punctuation and capitalization, despite the occasional lapses into inappropriate slang and the malapropism of misspelling, despite the illogicality of overgeneralization and the high emotive function that makes a "tennis match" of categorical claim and rhetorical question, despite the almost paranoid vagueness of pronoun references and the nearly schizophrenic clash between hyperbole and litotes, despite the thematic incongruity of positive details and negative conclusions—this discourse is vastly superior to its predecessor: its young author is capable of genuine speculation. Unlike his rather inarticulate basilect contemporary, this British teenager can generalize what happens and prophesy what may happen. In short, he can "think."

This capacity to think, in turn, separates the acrolect–mesilect lad from his basilect peer—separates him through a difference in competence and performance that is both quantitatively and qualitatively as dramatic as the Grand Canyon. This difference, moreover, is the direct result of the influence of the following eight characteristics of what Bernstein has called the "elaborated code" of social advantage (see Lawton, 1968, p. 85):

Eight Characteristics of the Formal Language of "Elaborated Code"

1. Accurate grammatical order and syntax regulate what is said.

2. Logical modifications and stress are mediated through a grammatically complex sentence construction, especially through the use of a range of conjunctions and relative clauses.

3. A discriminate use of prepositions frequently indicates logical relationships as well as temporal and spatial contiguity.

4. Such *impersonal* pronouns as *it* and *one* are in frequent use.

5. There is a discriminate selection from a rather wide range of adjectives and adverbs.

6. Individual qualification is verbally mediated through the struc-

ture and relationships within and between sentences. The meaning of such qualification, therefore, is *explicit*.

    7. The expressive symbolism that is conditioned by the linguistic form of an "elaborated code" distributes *affectual support* rather than logical meaning to what is said.

    8. The use of language in such a code constantly points to the possibilities inherent in a complex *conceptual hierarchy* for the purpose of *organizing experience*.

Deprived of an intense one–to–one phenotypical modeling in these eight characteristics of the formal language of an "elaborated code," the socially disadvantaged speakers of the basilect—both in Great Britain and in the United States—suffer from an enormous retardation in linguistic maturity: verbally and cognitively. Relatively infantile in contrast with the speakers of acrolect, these same speakers of the basilect, no matter what their actual physical age, *seldom grow beyond the mental and emotional age of twelve.* In other words, they are trapped within the narrow prison of their own language–impoverished period of resonance.

    A strong and depressing claim? Of course. But one that is fully supported throughout the entire range of Bernstein's theory and research. Indeed, a summary of that theory and research makes clear—almost at a cursory glance—the enormous deprivation that is inherent in the "restricted code" of the basilect, especially when contrasted with the tremendous enrichment that accompanies a mastery of the "elaborated code" of the acrolect:

Summary of Bernstein's Theory and Research on the Codes

Elaborated/Formal/Acrolect	*Restricted/Public/Basilect*
Associated with middle class and above.	Associated with lower class.
Accessible through intense one–to–one phenotypical modeling.	Accessible to everyone.
Reguires long period of informal, formal, and even technical training.	Requires relatively short period of informal training only. Becomes well–habituated readily.
Speaker has an extensive range of alternatives in language	Speaker has a limited range of alternatives in language orga-

Elaborated/Formal/Acrolect | *Restricted/Public/Basilect*

organization. Difficult to predict his choice of structural elements.

nization. Fairly easy to predict his choice of structural elements.

Functions to facilitate the construction and exchange of individuated symbols. Explicit and highly personal.

Functions to reinforce the forms of social ingroup relationship. Implicit or inexplicit and highly communal, even ritualistic.

Does not necessarily presuppose shared and self–consciously held identifications. Cannot take for granted the intent of the addressee.

Relies heavily on shared and self–consciously held identifications of the ingroup. Can and does take for granted the intent of the addressee.

Requires verbal planning on the part of the speaker, who plays an active role and assumes personal responsibility for what he says.

Does not require verbal planning on the part of the speaker, who plays a passive role in the group conformity which protects him from assuming personal responsibility for what he says.

Speech reflects the hesitations of verbal planning as the speaker seeks to organize the increase of information.

Speech does not reflect the hesitations of verbal planning; the speaker cannot tolerate the delay normally associated with the increase of information.

Teaches the speaker to make generalizations, to move from concrete to abstract levels of speaking and thinking.

Does not teach the speaker to make generalizations but inhibits this ability at the higher levels by increasing the relevance of the concrete and the descriptive at the expense of the abstract and the analytical.

EFFECT is to increase linguistic ability, to exercise capacity.

EFFECT is to diminish linguistic ability, to let capacity atrophy.

From this summary of Bernstein's theory and research on the contrasting attributes of the two different codes, it is apparent that real social disadvantage is fundamentally linguistic disadvantage. In other words, that to be reared in the language atmosphere of the basilect is to be handicapped severely in the acquisition of any truly national version of Modern English.

Such handicapping, in turn, is a direct result of the impoverishment of *audience relationship* which is inherent in the
informal immersion in the basilect. As John B. Carroll (1961,
p. 339) has indicated, in their evolution as communicative
beings most speakers of the acrolect pass through at least
five stages of audience relationship:

> In the early childhood (2 to 5 years) communication is with one
> person at a time; in later childhood (6 to 12 years), the child learns
> to communicate with groups; the adolescent (12 to 18 years) resumes
> communication with agemates of the opposite sex; in young adult-
> hood communication is mostly with age–superiors; in middle and
> later adulthood there is a gradual change–over from intake to output
> of information.

In commenting on Carroll's foregoing analysis of language
development, Nist (1969a, p. 27) has revealed that "These five
stages of audience relationship can be said to occur along
two major axes: that of *solidarity,* in which people communicate with their peers in an ingroup situation, and that
of *power* or *authority,* in which they communicate with either
their superiors or their inferiors in a divergence–of–groups
situation." These two axes, furthermore, may be depicted
as follows (see Nist, 1969a, p. 27):

Axes of Audience Relationships

```
                    elders      P      strongers
                   teachers     O      masters
                high rankers    W      employers
equals                          E                      friends
similars        S O L I D A R I T Y  A X I S           relatives
sames                           A                      lovers
                   juniors      X  weakers
                  learners      I  servants
                low rankers     S  employees
```

Now it is precisely because speakers of basilect Modern
American English tend to be trapped in the "restricted code"
of the solidarity axis that they suffer so terribly when they
try to switch to the "elaborated code" that is demanded by
the power axis imposed by the public schools of the United

States. Impoverishment of audience relationship, then, lies at the very heart of the fifth major cause of handicapped English in this country: the cultural warfare or conflict of value systems in the public classrooms of America, together with the self–fulfilling prophecies of failure in the educability of the socially disadvantaged.

CULTURAL WARFARE IN SCHOOL

Upon his first entering a public school in the United States today, the socially disadvantaged child who usually speaks some form or other of basilect Modern American English immediately runs into three enemies of, or blocks to, his ever learning anything of lasting value in the classroom: (1) the cultural insecurity of his mesilect–reared but acrolect–ambitious teacher, (2) the ethnocentrism of WASP supremacy, and (3) the social ostracism inherent in his own stereotyped patterns of nonstandard, if indeed not *sub*standard, language competence and performance (see Williams, 1970, pp. 380–399). As Labov (1964) himself has indicated, these enemies produce that conflict of value systems which ultimately prevents the socially disadvantaged child from ever acquiring an acrolect version of so–called Standard English. This conflict, moreover, is characterized by Labov (1964, p. 95) as "the difference between the teachers' speech and the students'." Believing that the basilect she hears in the classroom is "incorrect" and "sloppy" and "bad," the average teacher, in the words of Labov (1964, pp. 95–96),

> . . . struggles to impose a fixed standard, which she mistakenly believes she follows herself, upon youngsters who mistakenly believe that they also make no concession to the other side in daily life. In the data from the New York City survey, we see some evidence for the view that teachers may be transferring to the students their own inner conflicts; they recoil from a kind of behavior that is still very much a part of their own personalities. On the other hand, the student may rightfully feel that the teacher threatens him in trying to abolish completely the speech pattern that identifies him as a member of his own group: this is the group that he respects, that awards him prestige, that establishes his masculinity.

The fact that the majority of the classroom teachers in the United States are women, moreover, merely intensifies the conflict and therefore complicates even further the problem of language–learning for the male–student speakers of the basilect.

In general support of Labov's view about the centrality of this conflict of value systems in preventing real education in the classroom, Allison Davis (1967) contends that it is the basilect culture itself which comes under attack in the public schools of the United States today. Whether black or white, in the words of Davis (1967, p. 58), the chief obstacle to the school achievement of the socially disadvantaged child

> . . . is his *first–learned culture*, that language and way of life which he already has learned in his family. In school, the child is expected to change the behavior which his own father, mother, and peer group have taught him. He has to learn to speak and understand a new language, "standard" English, and to learn increasingly complex middle–class behavior, with respect to study habits, control of aggression, and sexual values.

The basilect culture of the socially disadvantaged child in the classroom, therefore, is the source of the following vicious circle involving speech types and stereotypes (see Williams, 1970, p. 383): (1) The basilect speech of the child serves as a social identifier; he is poor and from the lower class. (2) This social identifier that is his language elicits stereotypes held by his teacher concerning speakers of the basilect; he is therefore judged as being inferior in intelligence, interest, and motivation. (3) Such stereotypes make the teacher behave in accordance with her own negative attitude toward the socially disadvantaged child; thus he is scarcely worth her professional attention and instructional patience. (4) This negative attitude, in turn, is translated into a social reality; hence the child becomes *uneducable.*

The consequences of such a vicious circle of social reality, of course, are those *self–fulfilling prophecies* (see Rosenthal and Jacobson, 1968) which produce the phenomenon of "cumulative deficit," or the further linguistic handicapping, of the socially disadvantaged child in the classrooms of present–day America. Because he cannot identify with the school (i.e., with its activities, methods, and teachers), the culturally isolated and alienated young speaker of the basilect usually suffers from the following four weaknesses in educational capacity and performance (see Davis, 1967, p. 59): (1) a relative lack of attention to the details of solving a problem; (2) no real apparent interest in learning the school procedures for carrying out routine tasks; (3) failure to demonstrate a truly competitive drive to excel, with an attendant lack of confidence in his ability to achieve; and (4) relatively poor work habits. These four weaknesses, in turn, show that in education, as in everything else in life, *the goals must appear attainable before motivation and drive come fully into play.* One of the first tasks, if indeed not *the* first task of the classroom teacher, therefore, is to convince the socially disadvantaged speaker of the basilect that HE *CAN* "LEARN."

If the public schools of the United States are ever to so convince their basilect–culture students, then they will have to first realize how horrible are the consequences of their not fully understanding and sympathizing with the following four major principles of education itself (Davis, 1967, p. 59):

1. All learning is stimulated or hindered by the teacher's feelings toward the student. They must trust and have faith in each other.

2. All school learning is influenced by the cultural attitudes which the teacher has toward the student, and which the student experiences toward the teacher. Often in rejecting the student's cultural background, the teacher appears to reject the student himself, as a human being. In return, and as early as the first grade, the student may reject the culture of the school, and of the teacher. Both teacher and pupil must learn to *respect* the ability and position of the other.

3. All school learning is influenced by the degree of interest and drive with respect to schoolwork which the student has learned in his family and peer group.

4. All school learning is influenced by the presence, or absence, of intrinsic motivation in the curriculum itself. Neither the teacher nor the student can create interest in dull, unrealistic texts in reading, social studies, or arithmetic.

In direct contravention of these four sound principles of education, however, is the fact that many American public school teachers bear the hostile feelings of their own emotional hangups against their students, do not respect the various basilect cultures of the minority ethnic groups represented in their classes, and "couldn't care less" whether there is any intrinsic motivation in the curriculum itself. From such contravention flows the high negative emotive function of their students as addressers and the low negative conative function of these same students as addressees. The following passage of Black English, from the recording hand of Roger W. Shuy (1970, p. 347), bears eloquent witness to the preceding value judgment:

> Sometimes we thinks she's absolutely crazy. She *come* in the classroom *she be* nice and happy, she never *have* a smile though cause *she be* nice and happy . . . the next minute *she be hollering* at us for no reason, she'd be giving us a lecture on something that happened twenty years ago. . . .

This sort of confused and potentially hostile reaction on the part of the socially disadvantaged student toward his insecure and unpredictable teacher is rampant throughout the classrooms of the United States today.

Such, at least, is the claim of James Sledd (Dec. 1969), who has argued with a good deal of emotional conviction that much of the problem of "cumulative deficit" among speakers of the basilect in the American public schools is traceable to what he calls "the linguistics of white supremacy." Insecure in her own lower middle–class and mesilect background, the mythic Miss Fidditch, in the view of Sledd (Jan. 1972) and other linguists (e.g., see Wayne O'Neil, Jan. 1972), demands an almost hypercorrect form of acrolect in the classroom, even when not functionally effective or socially appropriate. Ignorant of the kinds of *systematic* departures from the so-called "standard" norms of Modern American English, departures which are part of the grammar of the basilect she faces, Miss Fidditch drills her deviant students in the *wrong* sets of rules (see Labov, 1970b, pp. 28–30), tries to suppress their natural and native way of speaking, and creates cultural warfare in the classroom instead of a healthy climate for learning.

A linguistic snob because of her own cultural insecurity, this same Miss Fidditch tries to teach an unanalyzed class, and therefore a linguistically unknown class, *her speech and hearing patterns,* when she should be trying to teach that same class *how to read and write according to its own speech and hearing patterns.* As in personal loyalty, so in language performance—no man or child can serve two masters. Thus so long as Miss Fidditch continues to give pronunciation lessons in her usually adopted acrolect version of English, she will go on failing in her central task of teaching basilect students how to read and write. Multiply Miss Fidditch thousands of times over, aid and abet her views with the emotional prejudice of a mesilect majority of linguistically insecure WASP Americans, and intensify these views with the stereotypes of an ugly racism that pervades the cultural climate of the United States today, and any intelligent layman can see why a conflict of value systems in the public schools continues to further handicap the already socially disadvantaged student: HIS CLASSROOM IS A MICROCOSMIC MIRROR OF HIS MACROCOSMIC ISOLATION AND ALIENATION.

Such isolation and alienation, furthermore, are directly related to the fact that the basilect child has been reared in a *particularistic* system of meaning. The school he enters, however, operates by means of a *universalistic* system of meaning. The conflict between the acrolect school and the basilect child, therefore, is inevitable; their different ways of valuing things carry within themselves the sources of cultural warfare. Indeed, the theory and research of Bernstein (1970, pp. 55–56) makes this point very clear in the following terms:

> The school is necessarily concerned with the transmission and development of universalistic orders of meaning. It is concerned with making explicit and elaborating, through language, principles and operations as these apply to objects (the science subjects) and to persons (the arts subjects). One child through his socialization is already sensitive to the symbolic orders of the school, whereas another child is much less sensitive to the universalistic orders of the school. The second child is oriented toward particularistic orders of meaning which are context–bound, in which principles and operations are implicit, and toward a form of language use through which such meanings are realized. The school is necessarily trying to develop in this child orders of relevance and relation as these apply to persons and objects which are not initially the ones he spontaneously moves toward. The problem of educability at one level, whether it is in Europe, the United States, or newly

developing societies, can be understood in terms of a confrontation between the universalistic orders of meaning and the social relationships which generate them, of the school, and the particularistic orders of meaning and the social relationships which generate them which the child brings with him to the school. Orientations toward metalanguages of control and innovation are not made available to these children as part of their initial socialization.

Deprived of experience with universalistic systems of meaning, therefore, the young speaker of basilect Modern American English becomes—ironically, tragically—the unwitting and often the unwilling victim of his own deprivation once he enters the public school. It is as though Miss Fidditch were specially appointed by the official prejudice which she represents to be the avenging archangel who makes sure, insofar as a mastery of the national language is concerned, that from those who have little even that little will be taken away.

In short, the handicapped speaker of the basilect is not "at home" in his educational world. Indeed, as Bernstein (1970, p. 57) himself has said,

> . . . if the contexts of learning, the samples, the reading books, are not contexts which are triggers for the child's imaginings—are not triggers on his curiosity and explorations in his family and community, then the child is not at home in the educational world. If the teacher says continuously, "Say it again darling, I didn't understand you," then in the end the child may say nothing. If the culture of the teacher is to become part of the consciousness of the child, then the culture of the child must first be in the consciousness of the teacher. This may mean that the teacher must be able to understand the child's dialect, rather than deliberately attempt to change it. Much of the context of our schools is, unwittingly, drawn from aspects of the symbolic world of the middle class; when such a child steps into school he is stepping into a symbolic system which does not provide for him a linkage with his life outside.

Failure to provide such a linkage for the socially disadvantaged child in the public schools of the United States today means that, insofar as his middle–class–values oriented education is concerned, such a child is a stranger and afraid, in a world he never made. Out of his estrangement and fear, the speaker of basilect learns, even as early as kindergarten or the first grade, the importance of masking the constant

threat of failure, based upon his teacher's stereotype of him
and his own inferiority at abstraction, behind the highly concrete style of speech which is generated by the *context–bound.*
As Frederick Williams (1970, pp. 393–394) has said, the
socially disadvantaged child speaker of handicapped English
soon learns that one *safe* role for him to assume is this:

> ... to stay close to context, to make a minimal commitment verbally
> in the situation, for the more that the child's speech transcends
> context the more he is committing himself to behavior based upon
> not only psycholinguistic but also sociolinguistic knowledge, and
> the greater is the potential for failure. A context–bound type of
> speech offers the guarantee of shared referents for speech, less
> reliance upon stereotypes, and the context even assumes part of
> the communicative load. This line of speculation is one way of
> unravelling the puzzle about an oft–cited observation of the speech
> of poverty children—that they employ a highly concrete style of
> speech.

This highly concrete style, in turn, is the inevitable result
of the child's exclusive rearing in the "public language" and
"restricted code" of the basilect. When the context–
boundedness of his style fails him, furthermore, the socially
disadvantaged child will then retreat or withdraw into the
group solidarity of his peer group. Such a withdrawal, of
course, is but another cause of his "cumulative deficit," of
his further deprivation in both verbal and cognitive growth
and development.

PEER-GROUP REINFORCEMENT

As linguistic science knows full well, during the age–span
of from six to twelve years, the peer group reshapes the
phenotypical modeling of the parents so that by the time
the child emerges from the period of resonance his language
is no longer that of his family, but rather that of his generation.
As Labov (1971, p. 214) has said, "children's speech resembles
that of their peers in their own dialect area." If that speech
has no access to an acrolect version of the national language,
however, then the resultant context–bound code of group solidarity will suffer from conformity and triviality, self–induced
isolation and alienation, perhaps even covert contempt or
overt hostility. To be sure, along a rather restricted scale of

oral performance, the peer group offers linguistic growth and development for its members. As Labov (1971, p. 214) has observed,

Within the peer group, we find that there is a rich development of special vocabulary: taboo language, slang and argot, rhymes and rituals of varied sorts. Narrative skills are developed—skills in joke telling, various types of rhymes, chants and songs; all of these skills are differentially rewarded by the members of the group.

But these same members of the peer group are not concerned with developing an awareness of the differences and the correlations between Modern American English spelling and phonology, of inculcating a respect for the fact that an exterior standard of "correctness" does exist, of providing an enrichment in the terms and meanings of an immense Latinic and Romance vocabulary, of training both the emotive and the conative function to adjust to the fact of social stratification in language usage, of perfecting the skills of reading and writing. In short, they are not concerned with the universalistic symbols of the school.

This almost total lack of concern for the universalistic system of values inherent in the public school education in the United States today means that the peer group merely serves to reinforce the handicapped English of the speakers of the basilect. These speakers are handicapped precisely because they have been deprived of a rich linguistic experience in that intense one–to–one phenotypical modeling by an adult which underlies almost all learning of an acrolect version of Modern American English. Once they reject Miss Fidditch and her colleagues in the public schools, they then turn to an intense *many*–to–one phenotypical modeling IN THEIR OWN SOCIALLY DISADVANTAGED SPEECH, and *not* with a linguistic adult. As Labov (1964, p. 98) has recorded, the result is liable to be the kind of infantile arrestment in both competence and performance that is evident in the following oral narrative of an eighteen–year–old Irish–Italian boy from the Lower East Side:

I went ice skatin' in Jersey—Hoboken. Came back two o'clock in the mornin'. Whole bunch of guys went—I come back, everybody says, "I'm hongry, I'm hongry." I say, "I'll be right back." I go next door for a pizza. I come out, and there's five big niggers

standin' there. They say, "Gimme that!" I say, "Give you *wot.*"
Yerr whop! I went down. They kicked me, everything. Boom!

I got up, 'n' ran in the house, 'n' grabbed a steak knife and chased
them. A guy jumped into his car and chased them. Spanish guy named
Rickey, he took out a bread knife, ran down the subway, and scared
an old lady silly. Thought he was gonna kill her.

Bright cop comes over—cullud cop. "Wha' happened?" I say,
"Five of your bright people jumped me." He says, "What were
dey?" I say, "Yeah, they were colored." He says, "Den they—they
ain't my people." I said, "You cullud." He says, "They ain't my
people." I say, "O.K., g'bye, f'get everyt'ing. Went t'the hospital."

As the narrative itself shows, Jimmy Riley, the *white* basilect
narrator, drifts unconsciously into the very style of his *black*
basilect adversaries. The product of peer–group reinforcement of handicapped English, such a style, in the words of
Labov (1964, p. 99), leads almost inevitably to "low educational achievement, lack of occupational skills, and unemployment."

Because the drop–ins of group solidarity are too frequently
the drop–outs of power and authority, a major problem faces
the public schools in the United States today: how to remove
the *social forces* that impede language learning and therefore
hinder the acquisition of an acrolect version of Modern American English. Any solution for this problem, moreover, is beset
with its own difficulties, for as Labov (1964, p. 99) himself
has said:

> It is not likely that any change in the methods of teaching English
> will be powerful enough to cope with problems such as
> these. . . . No amount of research into the mechanism of language
> learning will remove these larger social forces from the scene. The
> polarization of linguistic behavior serves as an excellent indicator
> of the social processes that are occurring, but these indicators do
> not give us any immediate program for corrective action, or even
> for amelioration.

Beset with such difficulties, educators and scholars today will
find the solution to the problem of handicapped American
English long and hard to unmask. But if linguists are something more than mere language analysts and if educators are
not just retail information dispensers, then together they *can*
find a workable solution.

In the spirit of that belief, then, the following chapter will
venture into some pretensions at pedagogy.

Chapter 7

PRETENSIONS AT PEDAGOGY

URING THE LAST THIRD of the twentieth century
in the United States a tremendous debate has
arisen among both linguists and educators about the
desirability of making every child in the public schools
—regardless of race, ethnic origins, native and/or
ancestral language—both a listening and reading *in-
terpreter* and a speaking and writing *performer* of some
form of acrolect Modern American English. As Roger
W. Shuy (Spring/Summer 1969, pp. 81–83, 160–161) has
indicated, proposals for dealing with the problem of nonstandard (i.e., substandard or "handicapped") English
present their own problem—namely, the problem of what
might be called "lect engineering" (see Sledd, Dec.
1969). These proposals, in turn, fall into the following
three categories, which are summarily characterized by
their italicized head word: (1) *eradication* of all forms
of the basilect in Modern American English; (2) *cultivation* of a multilectal mastery of the national language
of the United States by members of socially disadvantaged communities (e.g., urban ghetto Negroes; rural
Southern blacks and whites; Spanish–speaking Americans of Puerto Rican, Cuban, and Mexican ancestry;
Indians on Government reservations); and (3) *inculcation* of functional knowledge about, performing mastery
of, and emotional respect for all forms of nonstandard
Modern American English by speakers of standard. Now
since Proposals 1 and 2 are impossible of achievement

unless the classroom teachers in the United States first adopt Proposal 3 as their central guide to formal phenotypical modeling in the various psycholinguistic and socialinguistic dimensions of the acrolect, this chapter shall discuss Proposal 3 first.

INCULCATION

He who degrades another degrades himself. Thus those linguists and educators in the United States today who believe in the inculcation of functional knowledge about, performing mastery of, and emotional respect for all forms of nonstandard Modern American English within the acrolect community itself, must extend their goal to encompass the countless millions of speakers of the mesilect within the American public at large. Furthermore this goal must operate to fulfillment by the means of love rather than by the method of fear. Love for the speakers of handicapped English as sacred persons must be expressed not with condescension as to broken linguistic dolls which somehow need the professional care of "fixing up and mending." Such condescension, fostered by an ethnocentric sense of WASP supremacy, is like pinning one's opponent's shoulders to the wrestling mat. And yet, to continue the metaphor, in such a contest even the victor comes out a loser, because in his very conquest he is forced to remain on his hands and knees all his life. Once again, he who degrades another, degrades himself.

A keen sensitivity to this kind of self–inflicted degradation is the *sine qua non* of bringing the inculcation proposal to national fruition in the public schools. Linguistically speaking, Miss Fidditch and her colleagues must realize— profoundly—that the Word was indeed made flesh. And that It dwells among us even now. How? In the form of the socially disadvantaged and the culturally deprived. In other words, Miss Fidditch and her colleagues must never forget, indeed must never be allowed to forget, that Jesus of Nazareth was born in a stable and that He "talked funny" and WITHOUT MUCH PRESTIGE AMONG THE SCRIBES AND PHARISEES OF HIS OWN TIME. And why? Because He spoke the despised Northern or Galilean dialect of Aramaic.

As a boy, then, the Christ Himself grew up speaking a native rather than a national language!

Functional Knowledge

An understanding of the difference between *native* and *national* lies at the heart of Miss Fidditch's acquisition of a functional knowledge of the basilect Modern American English which she faces in her classroom. In fact, this functional knowledge must be acquired if she is to succeed in her task of teaching the socially disadvantaged child the universalistic system of values he will need to enable him to learn the national language of the United States and thereby to make himself eligible to enter the mainstream of its acrolect culture. To expedite such an acquisition, furthermore, Miss Fidditch must come to realize the importance of certain propositions which, in the words of Jane W. Torrey (1971, p. 252), apply to "children in preschools or elementary schools where the language used is different from the language of their homes, where before the children can learn any subject matter, they must first learn the language forms in which it will be taught." These propositions (Torrey, 1971, pp. 253–261) run as follows:

PROPOSITION I: *Some aspects of learning capacity change with age.* This proposition involves two practical questions: (a) timing and (b) methods. When and how should the socially disadvantaged child speaker of the basilect be submitted to a formal immersion in acrolect? As Torrey (p. 253) says, "the practice of starting first grade instruction entirely in a new language is a sound one,"and yet "overemphasis on English at the expense of Spanish may so threaten and alienate a Spanish–speaking child that he cannot learn anything from his school. In a case like this, the advantages of early instruction must be weighed against other considerations." Closely related to timing, of course, is methods, which "should be designed to fit the age of the learner." Younger children, for example, "will need shorter sentences to imitate, shorter dialogues to memorize, and material that is conceptually simpler."

PROPOSITION II: *The learning of one thing may influence the later learning of something else.* Again in Torrey's words (p. 254), "Interference effects are greater for partially learned than for well–learned material." Because of the "balance effect" in bilingual children, "the learning of a second language is always somewhat at the expense of the first." Thus Miss Fidditch must realize that "the native language may suffer as well as the second language

[the national language], and neither has the chance of full development in vocabulary and syntax that occurs in children schooled
in their native language." Furthermore, "with children especially,
a command of the target language is not sufficient qualification
to teach it as a second language." Since special linguistic training
is necessary for effective language teaching, Miss Fidditch "should
have a *technical* knowledge of the school language as well as of
the contrast between it and the children's language in order to
organize lessons and evaluate results." Even more importantly,
because of the similarity between acrolect and basilect in many
respects, socially disadvantaged "children are even less clearly
aware that a difference in language exists and certainly not of the
detailed nature of the difference." In the light of this fact, therefore,
"teachers of children who speak a substandard dialect also need
special training."

PROPOSITION III: *All behavior, including learning behavior, is
guided by the purposes of the learner and evaluated by him in
relation to his own goals.* Since, in the words of Torrey (p. 255),
motivation "is energy with direction," in order to be successful
in the classroom Miss Fidditch "must be able to persuade the children that the school activities are worthy of their effort." Because
intrinsic reward "is the commonest and most effective type of
reward," the socially disadvantaged child must not only know the
goals of instruction "but also accept them as his own in order to
get any feeling of success or personal satisfaction out of learning."
In summary, this proposition "states one of several reasons why a
teacher must be in accurate and friendly communication with the
child. Neither detailed exchange of information nor positive mutual
feeling is enough by itself, since a child must both understand and
accept the goals of each task in order to be able to profit from
it. A language barrier, a culture barrier, a class barrier, or all three
are very difficult and very necessary to overcome."

PROPOSITION IV: *Language behavior is highly systematic, not a
set of loosely related responses, associations, or concepts.* Corollary:
*The single system that is a language may have many overt manifes-
tations in performance, including producing speech, understanding
spoken and written material, writing, translating, and other skills.*
This proposition is extremely important in relation to the basilect
child and his problem of learning how to read an acrolect version
of Modern American English in the first grade. As Torrey (p. 255)
has indicated, "Since reading is the key to all other learning, a
child who does not grasp the principle early is crippled for life.
To be introduced to it under difficult circumstances imposes an
unnecessary burden where it is least tolerable." J. B. King (1967,
p. 56) is emphatically more specific—and condemnatory: "To try
to teach a child to read a . . . language which he neither understands

nor speaks is wasteful of the best efforts of, and inevitably harmful to, both the learner and the teacher." According to Torrey (1971, p. 256), many linguists agree "that school instruction should always be begun in the mother tongue with the second language introduced only gradually and with instruction by means of it waiting upon mastery of the specific words and structures needed" and that "the particular material to be read at any time be within the linguistic competence of the child. . . ."

PROPOSITION V: *The rules employed by the user of a language are not necessarily conscious.* Although not elaborated upon by Torrey, this proposition means that the child speaker of basilect is usually completely unaware of those *habits of performance* which make him deviate from the modeled norms of the acrolect school register. If Miss Fidditch will bear this phenomenon in mind, she will refrain from trying to make the child feel guilty over every unconscious lapse in his so–called "duty" to learn her brand of Modern American English.

PROPOSITION VI: *Learning a language is learning to understand and to be understood by other speakers of that language.* Quite simply, this proposition means that the child is completely *message–oriented* rather than *code–directed*. In other words, as Torrey (p. 257) has indicated, "Explicit grammatical rules are necessarily highly abstract, and few teachers need a warning not to try to use them with young children. . . . For a child, apparently, language has only the function of communication; it has no perceivable structure or existence of its own." Hence Miss Fidditch must beware of using pattern drills that focus attention on an abstract competence rather than upon a concrete performance. For the child speaker of basilect, language is merely a means to an end.

PROPOSITION VII: *Learning a language is accepting a culture and therefore, in some degree, a personal identity.* This proposition relates directly to the problem of acculturation and self–image among student speakers of the basilect in the public schools of the United States today. Because mastery of an acrolect version of Modern American English is so important for the child's future success in life, in the words of Torrey (p. 258), "The school must do more than just teach him the dominant language and inform him about its culture; it must also teach him to identify himself as a worthy member of that culture." Miss Fidditch, therefore, must avoid exerting excessive early pressure upon the basilect child in order to make him learn the acrolect of the school. Why? Because, as Torrey (see p. 258) has indicated, "A child cannot feel accepted by a teacher who does not speak his own language or by a school that forbids him to use it. His whole present identity is tied up in his language and culture. Rejection of it is rejection of him. Under such conditions, he cannot perceive himself as 'belonging' in school. A first grader

is still a very dependent creature. The teacher's personal acceptance
is for him his passport to citizenship, and his motivation in school
depends heavily on his desire to please her. All this is lost if the
teacher makes him an alien." In summary, then, this proposition
means that Miss Fidditch and her colleagues must keep from inciting
the educational riot of social–class–lect alienation and its attendant
cultural warfare in the classroom. Unless they prevent such
alienation, the socially disadvantaged child will surely retreat into
his basilect as the only refuge he has from the feeling of insecurity.

PROPOSITION VIII: *Language is a tool of thought.* Because the
child, socially disadvantaged or not, is moving from intuition to
conception in the early grades, this proposition means that, in the
words of Torrey (see p. 260), if this child is "not allowed to build
upon the language skill he already has but is forced instead to start
again from scratch, he is at a serious disadvantage in the intellectual
development appropriate to his age." Such a serious disadvantage,
in turn, means, according to Torrey (1971, p. 260), that "If a child's
conceptual development is severely retarded, the price for early
acquisition of the new language may be too great. It follows that
the introduction to science and mathematics as well as other abstract
subjects should not be exclusively through the medium of a language
not thoroughly known to the child." In summary, then, this proposition means, in the words of Torrey (1971, p. 260), "that a firm linguistic foundation should be laid for each step of conceptual learning."
Such a firm foundation cannot be laid, however, unless Miss Fidditch is as bilectal as she wants her socially disadvantaged students
to become. In other words, she must "speak their language."

As a conclusion to the argument that is implicitly paramount
in the foregoing propositions, it is apparent that Miss Fidditch
and her colleagues cannot be truly effective classroom
teachers of student speakers of basilect Modern American
English unless they themselves are also capable of speaking
this language of social disadvantage. Such a capability,
moreover, will remain out of reach unless Miss Fidditch and
her colleagues first acquire a functional knowledge of the
native lect that is interfering with their own modeling of an
acrolect version of the national language.

This acquisition of a functional knowledge of the interfering
native lect means that the classroom teacher of Chicanos or
Tex–Mexicans, for example, will have to know the key points
of contrast to Modern American English which are inherent
in the phonology, morphology, syntax, and semantics of New
World Spanish. By the same token, the classroom teacher

of speakers of Black English will have to know the key points of contrast between this form of the basilect and her own modeled acrolect. Why? Because as Labov (1970b, p. 61) has said, "the most efficient use of teaching materials will always presuppose the teacher's knowledge of the language of students in his class." Such a presupposition likewise emphasizes this implicit rule of education: AN UN-ANALYZED CLASS IS AN UNTAUGHT CLASS; AN UNANALYZABLE CLASS IS AN UNTEACHABLE CLASS.

Knowing the Student's Language

When Miss Fidditch and her colleagues come to realize the full significance of the foregoing rule, then they will more readily see that insofar as their acquisition of a functional knowledge of the language of social disadvantage is concerned, they must first systematically learn *just which forms of the basilect are facing them in the classroom.* As Labov (1970b, p. 61) has already indicated, such a process of systematic learning will engage these teachers in answering the following three main questions of linguistic research:

1. What is the set of contrasting vowels and consonants used by children to distinguish different words, in both perception and production?
2. What nonstandard rules of grammar are used by children in this school, and how firmly are these rules established?
3. What are the main differences between the speech used outside of school among peers and that used in the classroom?

Hopefully, from their answers to these three questions, the classroom teachers of socially disadvantaged children will achieve a far more effective instructional program than currently exists in the United States. So important are these potential answers, moreover, that they must be studied, along with their underlying questions, individually and in some measure of detail.

The possible answers to question 1, of course, make important intersections with the problem of teaching the basilect child to read an acrolect version of Modern American English. Inherent in the discussion of the phenomenon of *resonance* (see Lenneberg, 1967, Ch. 4) is the fact that every child in the United States today should first learn to read and write

in the code of his own *preferred* resonant language (i.e., geographical dialect and social–class lect) before he learns to read
and write in the code of some *nonpreferred* resonant language or, even worse, of some nonresonant language. Since
the socially disadvantaged child needs to learn that he *can*
learn, perhaps more than he needs to learn anything else at
the outset of his formal schooling, it is—or should be—clear
that this child's *initial* language of instruction, the language
he achieves *literacy* in first, should be his own native
tongue—that is, his own preferred resonant language, whether
it be Spanish, French, German, Polish, Czech, Yiddish,
Ukrainian, some Indian language, or still some other
non–English method of communication. As of 1960, according
to A. Bruce Gaarder, Chief of the Modern Foreign Language
Section of the U.S. Office of Education, there were about
six million *bilingual* children of school age and under in the
United States. Millions of these youngsters, as Gaarder
(Spring/Summer 1969, p. 33) asserts, "have been cheated or
damaged or both by well–intentioned but ill–informed educational policies which have made of their bilingualism an ugly
disadvantage in their lives." Such disadvantage is primarily
the result of the fact that, contrary to the law of resonance,
almost all instruction in first–grade literacy in the United
States today is conducted in an acrolect version of Modern
American English. Such unrealistic instruction, obviously,
is one major reason why the National Advisory Committee
on Mexican–American Education, in its report to the U.S.
Commissioner of Education (see Rodriguez, Spring/Summer
1969, p. 36), has recommended the training of at least one
hundred thousand bilingual–bicultural teachers and educational administrators for the American public schools.

This basic principle for motivating the socially disadvantaged bilingual child to learn, and therefore to reinforce his
ego and enhance the image that he has of himself, *by letting
him first learn to read in his own preferred resonant
non–English language,* applies equally well to the socially
disadvantaged child who speaks some preferred resonant nonstandard Modern American English geographical dialect or
social–class lect. Miss Fidditch and her colleagues, so demon-

strably incompetent in answering question 1 as it pertains to the *native* language of the bilingual child, must therefore not try to teach the speaker of basilect to read (and write) acrolect until they have first made him a competent speaker, or at least a full understander, of acrolect. Ideally, of course, they should teach him to *read his own lect first,* and then move him up the scale of social acceptability and prestige. If they have no books in the appropriate form of basilect to begin with (a very common complaint), then Miss Fidditch and her colleagues should let the children make their own (see Nist, June 1969, p. 22). That is, members of the class should be allowed to tell and to have their fellow students tell stories in their own social–class lect and tape–record them for ultimate transcription into writing for their own class-room–made books. This kind of a joint effort will motivate the children to learn and hence establish the necessary climate of mutual respect and affection that must exist before Miss Fidditch and her colleagues dare venture any further into the potentially dangerous process of "lect engineering."

Classroom–made books like these will, of course, enjoy such educational advantages as the following: (1) The materials will reduce foreign code interference to a minimum. (2) They will draw upon the child's own vocabulary and thus get him to read *at the level of his oral comprehension.* (3) They will motivate the child to learn to write, to want to see his "talk made visible" on paper. (4) They will teach the child that he *can* learn and thus avoid in the early stages of his education the terrible psychological depression and lowered self–image which accompany the inevitable failure at *immediate* acculturation in the value systems of the school–register acrolect. In summary, then, these four educational advantages, and any others which may attend upon them, mean that if the basilect child is first taught to read and write in his own native language, then he may avoid entirely what Johnnie M. Sharpe (Oct. 1972, p. 273) has so accurately characterized as his first stage of acculturation—namely, *bewilderment.*

If Miss Fidditch and her colleagues should choose, how-ever, to teach the basilect child to read acrolect Modern American English first, then they *must,* in the best of well–informed professional conscience, LET HIM PRONOUNCE THE WORDS AND SENTENCES THAT HE CAN DECODE IN THE PHONOLOGY OF HIS OWN LECT FIRST. Miss Fidditch and her colleagues cannot really teach the basilect child to read well at all if they are constantly correcting and fussing him with niceties of pronunciation that are *foreign to him.* If an acrolect sentence in a reader says, for example, that *John always comes back from the woods,* and if the child reads aloud that *John alway come back from duh wood,* then his teacher must rest content with her achievement with him at this stage. HE CAN READ! It is merely the deviant phonological realization of his basilect grammar that is showing—not his so–called (and misnamed) "illiteracy."

Performing Mastery

Functional knowledge that such deviant phonological realization does not constitute illiteracy, must go hand in hand with a performing mastery of the basilect grammar underlying this deviance, if, that is, Miss Fidditch and her colleagues are ever to become ideal classroom teachers of the socially disadvantaged in the United States. Such a performing mastery, in turn, presupposes the fact that these ideal teachers will be able to answer question 2 above (see Labov 1970b, p. 61): "What nonstandard rules of grammar are used by children in this school, and how firmly are these rules established?" Being able to answer this question, Miss Fidditch and her colleagues can thus both receive and transmit such basilect sentences as the following, knowing all the time that they are perfectly logical in their different acrolect wording:

BASILECT	ACROLECT
He know sumpn.	He knows something.
He don' know nuttin.	He doesn't know anything.
He *don'* know *nuttin.*	He doesn't know nothing.
Das Nick boy.	That's Nick's boy.
It don't all be her fault.	It isn't always her fault.
It hit him upside duh head.	It hit him in the head.
I'm a hug you.	I'm going to hug you.
He pass me yesterday.	He passed me yesterday.
I ax Tom do he know how to play footall.	I asked Tom if he knew how to play football.
I wanna be a POlice.	I want to be a policeman.

This knowledge of the logicality of the basilect will go a long way in helping the ideal classroom teacher to isolate the crucial area of language learning for the socially disadvantaged.

This crucial area of language learning obtains also in the fact that Miss Fidditch and her colleagues must know, in the words of Labov (1970b, pp. 28–30), of different types of linguistic rules underlying the generation of any basilect or acrolect grammar. Indeed, as Labov (1970b, p. 29) has said, "Most linguistic rules . . . are automatic, deep–seated patterns of behavior." Hence the ideal classroom teacher of socially disadvantaged children must know *which rules* are properly within her province of instruction. From an analysis which categorizes all language rules into three different types, in the following scheme Labov (1970b, p. 30) makes it implicitly clear that it is the Type II rules which constitute the crucial area of language learning—and teaching:

Rule Type	How Often Rule Operates	Violations	Response to Violations	Example
I.	100 per cent	None in natural speech	Wha'?	Rules for when one can contract *is:* "He is" *vs* "He's."
II.	95 to 99 per cent	Rare and reportable	He did?	"Why you ain't never giving me no A's?"
III.	5 to 95 per cent	None by definition and unreportable	So what?	"He sure got an A" *vs* "He surely got an A."

Since Miss Fidditch and her colleagues are obviously wasting their time in trying to teach basilect children acrolect rules of Types I and III, they must concentrate on those of Type II. Why? Because these are the very rules in both acrolect and basilect which in their permission of violations allow *the conflict of structural norms* in the systematic transmission of the message.

There is, of course, another kind of conflict which occurs

between basilect Modern American English and its acrolect equivalent—namely, that of *functional norms.* In the words of Labov (1967, p. 142), this conflict constitutes an "interference with the desire to learn standard English stemming from a mismatch in the functions which standard and nonstandard English perform in a given culture." Basically a value–system alienation, this conflict of functional norms lies at the heart of the fact that Miss Fidditch and her colleagues constantly try to teach not only the socially disadvantaged child but also the socially advantaged speaker of acrolect itself, those petty niceties of usage which occur almost exclusively among the Type III rules of Modern American English grammar. Their laborious drilling of the children in these petty niceties usually succeeds in "turning off" all the students, no matter what their native lect, from taking any deep and abiding interest in eventually mastering the full range of the national language. Why? Because in the classroom the *natively natural* is forced to give way too often, and with little apparent justification, to the *formally stuffy,* as may be seen in the following paradigm of contrasts:

STUDENT	MISS FIDDITCH
He pitched real good.	He pitched really well.
Who'd ja give it to?	To whom did you give it?
I won't go to the game if it rains.	In the event of rain, I shall not attend the game.
It's me.	It is I.
I don't like him doing that.	His doing that is distasteful.
I'll be back.	I shall return.
John's different than me.	John is different from me.
I didn't even have a dollar.	Not even a dollar did I have.
Everybody took their seat.	Everybody took his seat.
She wanted to falsely accuse me.	She wanted falsely to accuse me.
Any car whose engine won't run ain't worth a damn.	Any car the engine of which will not function is worthless.

In short, as the foregoing paradigm of contrasts reveals, Miss Fidditch and her colleagues cannot, or at least do not, distinguish grammar from style, level of usage from functional variety.

From the preceding discussion it is apparent that the fundamental situation facing the average classroom teacher of acrolect Modern American English and her basilect–speaking students is one of *reciprocal ignorance.* That is, the public school in the United States today, in the words of Labov (1967, p. 140), is all too frequently a place "where teacher and student are ignorant of each other's system, and therefore of the rules needed to translate from one system to another." Out of their insecure share in this reciprocal ignorance, of course, Miss Fidditch and her colleagues *impose rules,* as Labov (1967, p. 141) has said, "upon chaotic and shapeless speech, filling a vacuum by supplying rules where no rules existed before." The result of this imposition of rules is a national disaster. A national disaster in which even the educators themselves seem to have lost sight of *the priorities which must be honored* before any real solution to the problem of handicapped English can be achieved. These priorities, in turn, may be listed, with brief commentary, as follows (see Labov, 1967, pp. 141–142):

Educational Priorities of the Basilect Classroom

1. The children must be able to understand the spoken code of their teacher. Since the very process of instruction itself depends upon this priority, Miss Fidditch must be both willing and able to "switch" into the basilect of the children whenever they fail to understand her school–register acrolect.

2. The children must be able to read and comprehend the written code of the classroom. Since this priority is of extreme importance for the ultimate literacy of the students, Miss Fidditch must be willing and able to let the children under her instruction read in their own lect whenever their progress in decoding the printed word is endangered.

3. The children must be able to communicate with their teacher by means of a daily spoken performance—first of all (and always) in their own preferred resonant lect and gradually in the modeled school register, which will become their nonpreferred, but *resonant* lect. Here, of course, Miss Fidditch will have to be willing and able to make compassionate allowances for any and all failures in the children's mastery

of the target lect. She will also have to be willing and able to tell her struggling students whenever their linguistic security is threatened to "Say it in your own way, dear."

4. The children must be able to communicate with their teacher first, then with one another, and eventually with the world at large through the medium of writing. Quite obviously, their early attempts at any form of written composition will tend to be overwhelmed by the grammar, style, and usage of their native basilect. Miss Fidditch must encourage *fluency* and *amplitude* of expression rather than a so–called acrolect "correctness." Trying to force the children to perform in writing beyond their native capacity will inevitably result in their "clamming up" or in their retreating to the mediocre haven of trivial conformity.

5. The children must eventually learn to write according to the so–called standard norms of the grammar of acrolect Modern American English. Quite obviously, this is a long-range goal, and therefore one which must not be allowed to intrude unjustly upon the fundamental short–range goals of fluency and amplitude in composition.

6. The children must be able to spell correctly. This too is a long–range goal that must not be allowed to make the children "uptight" and hence to "turn off" their fluency and amplitude. If Miss Fidditch will just remember that F. Scott Fitzgerald (1896–1940) was a devil of a speller who wrote like an angel, she will keep a healthy perspective on this problem.

7. The children must eventually be able to use a so–called "standard" acrolect grammar when they speak their own idiolect versions of Modern American English. This is another long–range goal, which must be approached AS EARLY IN THE PERIOD OF RESONANCE AS POSSIBLE so that the children will not speak in a stilted and uncomfortable manner, feeling "alien" to the grammar they have learned.

8. The children must eventually be able to speak with a prestige pattern of pronunciation and hence avoid those

basilect forms of phonological realization which are stigmatized. Once again, this is a long–range goal, one which
must be approached AS EARLY IN THE PERIOD OF
RESONANCE AS POSSIBLE so that the children will not
speak their prestigious school–register acrolect with "a
foreign accent"—namely, that of the nonprestigious basilect.

9. Miss Fidditch and her colleagues must be ready to
change the foregoing order of priorities at any time when
the classroom situation shows that a lower priority is really
a higher one. As the history of man shows, a wise person
changes his mind many times in the light of new facts; a
fool never does.

Good and effective as these educational priorities in the
basilect classroom may be, they can become worthless in
themselves if the teacher does not nurture an *emotional
respect* for the nonprestigious language of her socially disadvantaged students.

Emotional Respect

Such an emotional respect means that Miss Fidditch and
her colleagues will want to be able to answer this third question of linguistic research posed by Labov (1970b, p. 61):
"What are the main differences between the speech used
outside of school among peers and that used in the
classroom?" It is these main differences, of course, which
set up the interference in the learning of the target lect modeled by Miss Fidditch and her colleagues. Such interference,
furthermore, is a result of the fact that, as Labov (1970b, p.
34) has said, "it is the local group of their children's peers
which determines this generation's speech pattern." That
speech pattern, in turn, may not only interfere with the modeling of the school–register acrolect in the early grades,
but may also offer resistance to its acquisition in the later
grades. Indeed, Labov (1970b, p. 34) makes this point very
clear in the following observation:

> The full force of peer group influence may not indeed appear
> in the speech of the six–year–old in the first grade. It is in the
> fourth and fifth grade, when the ten–year–old begins to come under
> the full influence of the preadolescent peer group, that we obtain

the most consistent records of his dialect. It should also be pointed out that it is at this age that many school records show sharp downward trends, and this is not unconnected with the fact that peer groups present a more solid resistance to the schoolroom culture than any individual child can.

From the foregoing observation, then, it is apparent that classroom knowledge of the language of the peer group is essential for the purposes of effective teaching.

Such knowledge, of course, must join with emotional respect. In other words, Miss Fidditch and her colleagues must never make fun of the basilect of the socially disadvantaged children under their instruction (see Nist, June 1969, pp. 22–23). To make fun of the basilect is to turn their speakers off forever, and Miss Fidditch and her colleagues in this circumstance will fail miserably in their every attempt to motivate their students to speak a more socially acceptable version of their speech variety, regionalism, or geographical dialect. Therefore, when a speaker of basilect says in the classroom, "I ain't got no pencil," Miss Fidditch and her colleagues must *not* jump to "correct" his English. They should give the child a pencil in order to show that they too are more message–oriented than code–directed. With such emotional respect as an ally of their intelligent pragmatism, they are then in a favorable educational position to lead the child *gently* into other ways of saying the same thing. Both emotional respect and intelligent pragmatism demand, in such instances, that Miss Fidditch and her colleagues should encourage the child to *accept his own lect* as a useful tool for communication within the total context situation of his cultural environment. In short, his teachers must help make him proud of his way of "talking funny" for what it truly is: a *limitedly effective* method of expressing himself and of segmenting the world of reality about him.

CULTIVATION

But once Miss Fidditch and her colleagues have succeeded in making the child proud of his way of "talking funny," they must go on to convince him that *we all* "talk funny," but not with the same amount of social acceptability, not with the same amount of prestige, and therefore *not with the same effectiveness in the immediate context situation.* Such convincing, however, is emotionally loaded with educational dangers. Since the truth about the social inferiority of one's own preferred resonant lect constitutes a potential attack on one's parents, family, way of life, and personal identity, it must be approached in the compassionate manner of great art: implictly, indirectly, self–discoveringly, and therefore self–instructionally. Otherwise, the result of any attempt to cultivate a multilectal mastery of the national language of the United States among socially disadvantaged speakers of the basilect will be a severe loss of self–image and a terrible psychological depression among the culturally deprived students of Miss Fidditch and her colleagues. Indeed such loss and depression are the inevitable outcome of instructional ignorance and prejudice in the classroom, for Sharpe (Oct. 1972, p. 272) is eminently correct in claiming the following:

> As teachers, one of our weaknesses is lack of awareness of the socioculture of disadvantaged students who, because of isolation, experience educational suicide in our middle–class oriented schools where they are made to feel out of place or trapped. Differences in the socioculture of the disadvantaged and the schools lead to negative attitudes, defensiveness, anxieties, and even hostility. If teachers remain apathetic, indifferent to the chasm between the socioculture of the school in contrast to that of disadvantaged students, they will inflict deeper wounds by creating cultural conflict through their teaching methods.

To help avoid the creation of such cultural conflict, the following discussion of the goal of cultivation will concentrate on these three important areas: (1) linguistic roles, (2) general rules for language teaching, and (3) specific suggestions for target–lect modeling.

Linguistic Roles

In preparing the child to accept emotionally the sociolinguistic fact that his basilect is inferior and disadvantaged, Miss Fidditch and her colleagues should work on the natural "ham" in him. With peer–group speakers of the target lect as models *(for children teach each other more than their teachers* can teach them in the way of remodeling a systematic set of language habits), Miss Fidditch and her colleagues should get the child to assume linguistic roles other than those he is used to playing. These linguistic roles, in turn, will center in the mastery of a *spoken* code rather than a written one, for it goes without saying that the child, under ideal instruction, will be learning to read in his own preferred resonant lect or will be permitted to pronounce his reading of acrolect in the phonology of his native basilect. Using the child's own peer–group speakers of the target lect as models whenever possible, Miss Fidditch and her colleagues should make the basilect child pay special attention to forms of MITIGATION and POLITENESS (see Labov, 1970b, pp. 51–59), particularly since these forms relate to the child's awareness of *need, obligation* (duty), *ability,* and *right.* Such attention will do much to lower the basilect child's high and negative emotive function as a speaker and to raise his low and negative conative function as a listener.

As Labov (1970b p. 51) has also indicated, the socially isolated and alienated speaker of basilect Modern American English "is undoubtedly handicapped in many ways by his lack of control over mitigating forms which are more highly developed in middle class and school language." Indeed the strong points of brevity and clarity, two attributes so admired by Labov in the basilect, frequently force the socially disadvantaged child into a DIRECT REFUSAL, simply because his restricted code *permits him no other pattern of behavior.* Since such a direct refusal is lacking in the politeness necessary for maintaining good relations between teacher and student, Miss Fidditch and her colleagues must protect the child, themselves, and the learning situation by becoming experts in the kind of *discourse analysis* that will reveal the structural relationship between the implicative (signs to signs) and the designative (signs to referents) ranges of meaning on the one hand, and the pragmatic or expressively behavioral (signs and referents to their users) range of meaning on the other. To be effective teachers of the culturally deprived, then, in the words of Labov (1970b, pp. 54–55), Miss Fidditch and her colleagues must be willing and able to draw upon the most recent discoveries in the following areas of ongoing sociolinguistic and psycholinguistic research:

. . . the rules for commands, and for refusing commands, which prevail for standard English and the middle class society in which that language is embedded. Commands and refusals are actions; declarations, interrogatives, imperatives are linguistic categories—things that are said, rather than things that are done. The rules we need will show how things are done with words and how one interprets these utterances as actions: in other words, relating what is done to what is said and what is said to what is done. This area of linguistics can be called "discourse analysis"; but it is not well known or developed. Linguistic theory is not yet rich enough to write such rules, for one must take into account such sociological, nonlinguistic categories as roles, rights, and obligations. What small progress has been made in this area is the work of sociologists and philosophers who are investigating informally the Type I rules [see p. 225] which lie behind everyday "common sense" behavior.

No matter how small the progress in the ongoing research in the language rules which support everyday "common sense" behavior in the classroom, Miss Fidditch and her colleagues must not only keep up with this progress but also, ideally, contribute to it.

The research itself, moreover, must concentrate attention upon these four areas of the conative function which relate so closely to the emotive function itself: need, obligation or duty, ability, and right. Why? Because it is these four areas of the conative function which help so immeasurably to determine whether any command has validity for the addressee—in this case, the basilect child who is working to achieve the educational goals of his classroom teacher. These four areas, in turn, may be illustrated as follows (see Labov, 1970b, p. 55):

Four Areas in the Conative Function of the Addressee

1. NEED. *Something should or must be done.*
   a. **Nonmitigated forms:**
      Teacher: This work simply must be done over.
      Student: I don't think it's sloppy enough to do over.
   b. **Polite forms:**
      Teacher: Shouldn't this work be done over?
      Student: It's not that sloppy, is it?
2. OBLIGATION *Someone has the obligation or duty to do something.*
   a. **Nonmitigated forms:**
      Teacher: You'll simply have to do this work over.
      Student: I'm not supposed to be doing that kind of work today.

    b. Polite forms:

      Teacher: Don't you think you should try to do neater work than this?

      Student: If it's correct it doesn't have to be too pretty, does it?

3. ABILITY. *Someone has the ability to do something.*

    a. Nonmitigated forms:

      Teacher: You can do better than this.

      Student: I hurt my hand and I can't write.

    b. Polite forms:

      Teacher: Don't you think you can do neater work than this?

      Student: That's the best I've done so far, isn't it?

4. RIGHT. *Someone has the right to request that somebody else do something.*

    a. Nonmitigated forms.

      Teacher: It's my job to get you to do better than this.

      Student: You have no right to tell me to do that.

    b. Polite forms.

      Teacher: Can't I ask you to do this work over?

      Student: Aren't you telling me to do everything twice?

From the foregoing illustrations, it is apparent that the conative function of the addressee is inseparable from the emotive function of the addresser. In other words, a high and negative emotive function will almost invariably draw a low and negative conative function in response. When such a stimulus draws such a response, then the classroom teacher and her basilect student are no longer allies in the process of education; instead, they have become enemies.

To avoid any further alienation of their socially disadvantaged students, Miss Fidditch and her colleagues must realize that if the speakers of basilect *cannot* talk in acrolect at first, then they have no *obligation* to do so. Indeed, under these circumstances such students have the *right* to be taught the target lect first, whereas their teachers *need* to know how to go about that teaching in the best possible manner. If Miss Fidditch and her colleagues do realize the various kinds of relations among these four areas in the conative function, especially as they pertain to the various linguistic roles of instructor and pupil, then they will become much more effective in achieving their goals in the classroom. And one of the most important goals, as Labov (1970b, pp. 56–59) has indicated, should be an appropriate command of the question–and–answer technique. Such a command, in turn, presupposes that Miss Fidditch and her colleagues understand that a question itself, in the words of Labov (1970b, p. 57), "may be used to execute many different kinds of speech acts, including commands, insults, jokes, and challenges." After such a realization, these teachers will refrain from using questions as information–seeking surface masks of noninformation conveyers of deeper and baser motives, which are usually emotionally related to their own hidden feelings of cultural insecurity and therefore to the unstated need for personal aggrandizement at the expense of their own students.

These students, moreover, culturally deprived and socially disadvantaged though they may be, are not fools. Behaving under the principle of the *dramatic audience,* which means that the collective intelligence of the class is higher than that of even the brightest member in that class, the student speakers of basilect Modern American English *instinctively* know, even though they may not be able to verbally articulate their knowledge, that Miss Fidditch and her colleagues have a habit of asking any one of the following three kinds of questions discussed by Labov (1970b, p. 58):

Three Kinds of Questions Asked in the Basilect Classroom

1. *A known–answer question.* The teacher believes that she knows the answer and that the basilect–speaking student she is questioning may not know it. This form of question is fundamentally A REQUEST FOR PROOF.

2. *A no–answer question.* The teacher believes that there is no really correct answer to the question. This form of question is fundamentally A REQUEST FOR DISPLAY, designed to "draw the student out."

3. *A rhetorical question.* The teacher believes that she knows the answer and that her basilect–speaking student knows it too. Plurisignificant in its import, perhaps even a means of entrapping the student, this form of question is fundamentally A REQUEST TO BE ALLOWED TO CONTINUE DEVELOPING AN ARGUMENT.

From the foregoing discussion of the three kinds of questions in the basilect classroom, it is apparent that Miss Fidditch and her colleagues must learn which kind of question is *appropriate* in any given immediate context situation and then ask it in such a polite and encouraging manner as to charm the conative function of the student into permitting a charming emotive–function response. They will need to intensively study also the relationship of these questions to the verbal skills and the linguistic habits of their students, because as Labov (1970b, p. 59) has said:

> If we are to understand verbal behavior in the schoolroom situation, we must begin to solve the general question posed here. How do students know, in a given situation, what kind of question is being posed, and what is requested of them? When we have the answers to this, we may simultaneously begin to understand some of the reasons for failure, confusion, and rejection in the classroom.
>
> We will also be in a better position to carry out research on the verbal skills and linguistic habits of school children.

These verbal skills and linguistics habits, of course, relate directly to the classroom goal of cultivation in the more prestigious forms of the national language that is Modern American English.

General Rules

Once Miss Fidditch and her colleagues have trained the socially disadvantaged child to *accept* the various linguistic roles expected of him in the classroom, then they are ready to make him a speaker of both mesilect and acrolect. In short, to make him multilectal, both in reception and in transmission. In an emotionally hyperbolic statement, induced by a well–meaning but misguided linguistic liberalism that would keep the speaker of basilect Modern American English in the figurative ghetto of his social isolation and alienation, James Sledd (Jan. 1972, p. 441) claims that the completely multilectal speaker, "with undiminished control of his vernacular and a good mastery of the standard language, is apparently as mythical as the unicorn: no authenticated specimens have been reported." Apparently both Sledd and Labov whom he cites (1972, p. 441, n. 3) have looked for this mythical linguistic unicorn *only among the admitted failures of the current public school system* of the United States—that is, among speakers of the basilect who were neither properly motivated nor adequately trained in more prestigious versions of the language within the early and hence most effective stages of the period of resonance. Scores of professional actors and athletes, however, contradict by their example Sledd's outlandish and potentially pernicious claim. As do scores of doctors, lawyers, merchants, and chiefs—including those like Sledd himself, who are entrusted with the education of American youth.

Indeed, in the summer of 1967 the author of this book was privileged to have a whole classroom full of multilectal teachers of English, in an NDEA Institute in Hilo, Hawaii. Speakers of creolized forms of pidgin English in childhood, these same teachers showed themselves to be masters of the acrolect, who could revert to their childhood basilect *with perfect control* upon a moment's notice. One of them is Mr. Tojiro Motoki of Captain Cook, Hawaii. An "authenticated specimen," but not a unicorn. Rather a warm and sympathetic teacher, with intelligence and humor. A fine human being.

And a symbol of the fact that once the basilect–speaking child is *willing to pretend* that he is also a speaker of both mesilect and acrolect, then Miss Fidditch and her colleagues can draw upon his native instinct for drama and motivate him to become multilectal. Ideally, *in an integrated class*, they should DO THE SAME THING FOR THE STUDENTS WHO NATIVELY SPEAK MESILECT AND ACROLECT. From such a two–way learning process between lect and lect among the peer group, can come much mutual understanding and respect, as well as the best kind of linguistic enrichment. The peer group itself, moreover, must have MORE THAN ONE KIND OF LECT in it; therefore, it must be integrated.

The biggest question facing American education today, perhaps, is not that of busing, but rather that of *what comes after* the busing. Or as Father Theodore M. Hesburgh, President of the University of Notre Dame and former Chairman of the President's Commission on Civil Rights, has repeatedly said in one national forum after another, the biggest question facing American education today is the *quality of instruction* at the end of the ride! What is potentially so pernicious about the Sledd claim, of course, is simply this: if accepted as true, it will merely serve to fuel the fires of prejudice and racism.

Ironically so. For if the WASP majority comes to believe that
nothing can be done to remodel the language of the socially
disadvantaged speaker of basilect Modern American English,
then that group will gladly embrace the liberal linguist's doc-
trine of "Let the so–called 'culturally deprived' child's language alone!" Why? Because to let his language alone is to
let the child alone. And to let the child alone is precisely
what prejudice and racism want—namely, to keep the child
a member of some minority group or other, rather than to
help make him an American with free access to the mainstream of the national culture.

In their attempts to give the socially disadvantaged child
such an access, Miss Fidditch and her colleagues must
become experts in the general rules which govern effective
language teaching. At the very outset of their self–education
they will learn that they must *not* make any child, no matter
what his native language, *talk about* Modern American En-
lish *before* they have him speaking the target lect they want
him to master. Indeed, so important is this general rule that
Lenneberg (1967, p. 324) himself would place a ban on all
"grammatical meta–language until a basic proficiency in language is fully established." Such a ban, of course, means
that the American *grammar* school is, by its very name and
definition, a national disaster. Within its confines, in Chomskyan terminology, Miss Fidditch and her colleagues have
been attempting—with the sorriest of results—to teach all
children, no matter what their preferred resonant lect, AN
ABSTRACT COMPETENCE RATHER THAN A
CONCRETE PERFORMANCE.

This Quixotic mission in the absurd violates the fundamental linguistic principle that *a maximum of informal practice*
in receiving and transmitting the target lect is essential to
success. In other words, Miss Fidditch and her colleagues
need to learn immediately that they must keep all formal
and technical talk about the niceties of acrolect grammar and
style to an absolute minimum. The younger the child, the
more this absolute minimum should approach the
methodology goal of zero. Because the socially disadvantaged
child is like a cunning language computer that NEEDS TO

BE PROGRAMMED TO PERFORM, Miss Fidditch and her colleagues should bend all their efforts into inducing him *to actively synthesize* sentences and discourses in the target lect rather than to merely *passively analyze* them.

In the process of programming the socially disadvantaged child to perform in the target lect(s) of the classroom, to actively synthesize sentences and discourses rather than merely to passively analyze them, Miss Fidditch and her colleagues must put into effect, insofar as is humanly possible, certain general rules for the promotion of optimum language teaching. The most important of these rules, in turn, may be summarized and commented upon as follows:

General Rules for the Promotion of Optimum Language Teaching

1. Keep your classes to a manageable size—ideally, to a maximum of 12 students in each class. Since an intense one–to–one relationship in phenotypical modeling is the goal, if your classes are too large (e.g., 30 to 40 students or more per class), divide them up into smaller discussion groups and transmission units and USE STUDENT-TEACHER SPEAKERS OF THE TARGET LECT(S) TO HELP YOU CONDUCT ALL INFORMAL PATTERN PRACTICES, MIMIC-MEMORIZE DRILLS, AND MINIMAL-PAIR CONTRASTS IN PRONUNCIATION.

2. Engage each student in the production of as many target–lect discourses as possible everyday. Feel free to make use of the choral–reading technique whenever you need to reduce murmuring and inattention in the classroom.

3. Give your students as much *native*-lect modeling as possible, ESPECIALLY THAT WHICH IS MOST NATURAL FOR YOU OR YOUR STUDENT-TEACHER HELPERS. Since this modeling is designed to sharpen the child's ability at reception as well as in transmission, do not "baby talk" or speak with a slow and exaggerated articulation. Such poor practice distorts the entire intonational system of

the target lect and makes a mockery of its normal features of delivery.

4.   Get as much natural *paralanguage* as you can into your intonational modeling; it steps up emotive function and increases student interest. Since you should also teach the culture which supports acrolect Modern American English, try to accompany your paralanguage with as much *appropriate* "body language" as possible. Remember that socially disadvantaged speakers of the basilect rely heavily upon the expressive symbolism of nonverbal communication; they are hip to paralanguage and kinesics.

5.   Do *not* model long pronunciation lists that emphasize single and often unknown words OUT OF THEIR NATURAL CONTEXT. Such poor practice allows the lexemic domain of maximum stress to invade the syntactic domain, with the usual result that normal intonational contours are distorted and the students suffer some damage to their "sentence sense" in its all–important relationship with reading.

6.   Teach *colloquial idioms* whenever possible so that the basilect–speaking children can see that acrolect Modern American English can be just as "natural" and expressive as their own preferred resonant language. Avoid at all costs the impression that the acrolect is to be equated with a formal school register known as "classroom English."

7.   Do *not* be afraid to correct your textbooks if they are guilty of using stuffy or stilted or unnatural sounding acrolect. The greatest of authors "fall asleep" at times; for the sake of your students, wake such authors up.

8.   Do *not* adopt any textbook(s) for classroom use in the target lect if such flaws as these prevail: (a) lack of high "reader interest" in the dialogues; (b) constant plethora of grammatical explanation; (c) a banal and repetitious quality in the exercises; (d) a critical scarcity of reinforcing pictures and illustrations; (e) failure to teach something of the culture

that produces acrolect Modern American English; (f) lack of proper gradation according to increasing difficulty in the modeling exercises; (g) no systematic allowance for review, so that material becomes old and forgotten through disuse; (h) lack of variety in the language drills; (i) reinforcement of "bad English" by means of WRONG ANSWERS in multiple–choice testing.

9. Remember always that "negative testing" is bad. Seek, therefore, to elicit correct responses from your students by means of their *positive transmission* in the target lect. Any reasonable answer to a well–considered question should be accepted.

10. Give as much correct *visual reinforcement* to the target lect as possible. Whenever possible, draw objects on the blackboard to visually strengthen your pattern practice in acrolect Modern American English.

11. Be alert to the attention span of your students; when their interest flags on repeating an exercise, begin a new discourse.

12. Build, whenever you can, "natural discourses" from the objects you bring to class (e.g., toys, sensory boxes, foods), thereby giving your students an *informal and unself–conscious* growth in vocabulary and in pattern practice.

13. Whenever you show several different "correct" acrolect forms or expressions of the same content message, make clear to the students whatever usage constraints may obtain through the imposition of style and the degree of formality involved.

14. Keep your students close to you and to one another in the classroom in order to reduce the contact noise of the outside world to an absolute minimum.

15. Remember always to be *courteous but firm* in main-

taining order and discipline in the classroom. Loss of temper forfeits *ethos,* your most priceless asset as a teacher.

If Miss Fidditch and her colleagues will put the foregoing fifteen general rules into effect, then their entire language–teaching program could become one that is geared to the cultivation of English as a *worldwide phenomenon,* one that is incomparably rich in national dialects and social–class lects, in literary achievements and scientific contributions: British, American, Commonwealth. Such a program should become THE ULTIMATE GOAL of the public schools in the United States, for such a program would teach all students, no matter what their preferred resonant lect, that there are several major versions of the English language which are effective, graceful, prestige–bearing, and therefore *completely acceptable.* In the long run, this kind of language–teaching program in the public schools would do much to help break the American psyche itself out of its own culturally deprived isolation and alienation—two attributes of its own current social disadvantage, induced by a false sense of WASP supremacy.

Specific Suggestions

In addition to their putting into effect general rules for the promotion of optimum language teaching in the classroom of basilect–speaking children, Miss Fidditch and her colleagues will have to become masters of specific techniques in the art of target–lect modeling. To become such masters, furthermore, they will need to know the differences between the two major methods of teaching: (a) the *indirect* and (b) the *direct.* These two methods, in turn, may be summarily characterized as follows:

Characteristics of the Two Major Methods of Language Teaching

Indirect	*Direct*
Emphasizes *grammar* and *translation:* analysis.	Emphasizes *audio–lingual* approach: synthesis.
Fosters translation from native	Fosters pattern practice in the

lect to target lect, from target lect to native lect.	target lect, with no translation allowed.
Operates by the memorization of abstract rules.	Operates by the promotion of habits of concrete perfor- mance.
Believes that the language is fundamentally *vocabulary* and that words can be trans- lated from one language to another, from one lect to another.	Believes that the language is fundamentally *system* and *structure* and that even though words can be trans- lated, they should be learned directly in relation to both system and structure.
Places emphasis on the *written* code.	Places emphasis on the *spoken* code.

Once Miss Fidditch and her colleagues understand the differ-ence between these two major methods of language teaching, they will then be in a better professional position to accept the inherent superiority of the direct method.

Once Miss Fidditch and her colleagues come to accept the inherent superiority in this method of teaching the target lect, they will then be ready to proceed to make the following five educational practices effective in the classroom: (1) con-trastive linguistic analysis: native lect *vs* target lect; (2) teach-ing the problem areas of difference between the two lects; (3) playing down the role of meaning in the acquisition of the target lect; (4) minimizing the memorization of rules, with about 85 per cent of the time spent in practice and about 15 per cent of the time spent in grammatical explanation; and (5) the habit of pattern–practicing all language structures LARGER THAN SINGLE UNITS. If they are teaching basilect speakers of Hawaiian creole, for example, Miss Fid-ditch and her colleagues will learn from a contrastive linguis-tic analysis between this native language and the national acrolect that the creole supports the following ten areas of difficulty, based upon an underlying ancestral pidgin: the confusion of *say/tell, no/not, like/want;* the substitution of *get* for *have;* the use of *go* as an auxiliary verb and of *no more* as a general negative; the substitution of *stay* for *be* and *went go* for *went to;* the use of double comparatives and superlatives; the replacement of *a/an* with *one.* Concentrating on these problem areas of difference, Miss Fidditch and her colleagues will want to model the acrolect equivalents of the basilect expressions, get their students to listen to these modeled equivalents and learn to recognize them so that they can produce them on their own, first *in isolation* and then, AS SOON AS POSSIBLE, *in context*. This sort of procedure will quite naturally involve an avoidance of meaning–based translation from the target lect to the native lect, a minimization of rule–memorizing, and a maximum of practice in transmission at sentence and discourse level, rather than at word or idiom level.

This sort of procedure will also involve Miss Fidditch and her colleagues in the problem of *lesson–planning*, especially as it relates to the *sequencing of learning* for their students. As a specific suggestion for effective classroom performance, the following overall lesson plan is offered as a *possible* sequence, not as an infallible guide to instant success:

Sequencing of Learning: A Possible Overall Lesson Plan

1. REVIEW of the preceding lesson, in order to guarantee continuity, transition, and cumulative mastery in the target lect. The general review of all preceding lessons should be built into the overall sequencing and should be practiced at regular intervals.

2. PRONUNCIATION LESSON. Minimal–pair drills in the phonology of the target lect should be designed to elicit both an auditory and an articulatory discrimination among the students. Using such sound contrasts as *leak/lick, cheek/chick, feast/fist, green/grin*—this kind of lesson should proceed in the following sequence: (a) listening on the part of the students, (b) testing of their auditory discrimination on the part of the teacher, (c) production of the target sounds in isolation, and (d) production of the target sounds in verbal context by the students. The teacher should get the students to produce the target sounds in verbal context as soon as possible and spend most of her time in this area of the pronunciation lesson.

3. PRESENTATION OF NEW VOCABULARY. Growing mastery in the phonology of the target lect should be supported by an increasing experience in the lexicon, especially in its

morphological invasion of the grammar, of the target lect, in order that the socially disadvantaged students may enjoy a further development of their segmentation of reality. An appropriate sequencing of this vocabulary lesson runs as follows: (a) the unlocking of new words in the experience of the students by means of their *identification* of objects, actions, and places visualized in class, either actually or representationally; (b) the *presentation* of the words which signify these objects, actions, and places in the target lect of the teacher; and (c) the asking of *comprehension* questions to make sure that the students understand the new terms. As a general rule, IT IS POOR PRACTICE TO DRILL STUDENTS ON MISUNDERSTOOD OR NONUNDERSTOOD MATERIAL.

4. REPETITION DRILLS. The teacher should now engage the students in pronouncing the new items in their growing target–lect vocabulary. Although "practice makes perfect," the repetition drills in the morphophonemic shapes of these acrolect words should constantly by accompanied and reinforced by the *visual referent equivalents* of their designative meaning. Such accompaniment and reinforcement is essential for the promotion of the best method of target–lect learning—namely, that of an informal "linguistic osmosis."

5. INDIRECT GRAMMATICAL PREPARATION. Since all target–lect words, like all native–lect words, inhabit a grammatical system of class structures that depends upon their occurrence in syntactic context, the teacher should prepare her students for an ultimate conscious mastery of acrolect grammar by an immediate *sub*conscious submersion in it through contrastive use of the various vocabulary items just learned. The following syntactic occurrences of *got*, for example, can prepare the students for an eventual understanding of the different functions of transitive, intransitive, middle, copular, and reflexive verbs in Modern American English: *I got a dollar. I got. I got myself in trouble. I got sick. I got me a horse.* In the early stages of formal schooling, no matter what the native lect of the child, the keeping of formal and/or technical grammatical analysis to a minimum is absolutely essential. Hence, ironically enough, in the direct method of language

teaching, grammatical indirection truly finds grammatical directions out!

6. PATTERN PRACTICE. After the indirect grammatical preparation, the teacher should now engage her students in the generation of target–lect sentences that make good use of the newly acquired phonology and vocabulary. Particular attention should be paid to an *orderly* exercise in the processes of *substitution* and *transformation* so that the students can become the informal and unself–conscious masters of the basic structures of acrolect Modern American English and their derived transforms, both singulary and generalized.

7. CUMULATIVE PRACTICE. As an extension of the pattern practice, the teacher should now engage her students in the generation of target–lect sentences *based upon review material.* Such cumulative practice will ensure the constant presence of "the linguistic forest among the individual language trees."

8. "FREE EXPRESSION." After the cumulative practice, the teacher should let her students converse, ask questions, supply answers, tell anecdotes and stories in the target–lect. While the students are having their informal fun, the teacher can quietly check on how well they have generalized acrolect grammar rules from the limited corpus modeled for them and see which habits of performance need further reinforcement or remodeling. The "free expression" period thus becomes a means of constantly testing the efficacy of the preceding seven stages of the overall lesson plan and is a preparation for the following two closing stages.

9. READING IN THE TARGET LECT. In directing the reading in acrolect Modern American English, the teacher should always remember that her basilect–speaking students understand the speech of the target lect and that the orthography of the national language crosses all native dialect barriers. She must therefore let her students be rewarded from time to time with basilect pronunciation of what has just been read out loud in acrolect pronunciation, to show that EVEN THOUGH THE CODES ARE DIFFERENT, THE MESSAGE IS THE SAME.

10. WRITING IN THE TARGET LECT. In directing the writing

(i.e., penmanship and composition) in acrolect Modern American English, the teacher should seek to induce her students to achieve the following goals: (a) self–reliance and independence in drawing upon their own private worlds of the content of their writing; (b) use of a vitally expressive vocabulary that is constantly expanding and specializing; (c) continual growth in the mastery of a grammar which will generate the basic and derived sentences that are appropriate to the rhetorical demands of the message; and (d) conceptual development to ultimately achieve an adequate segmentation of reality and a proper image of the self and the linguistic roles it must or should assume in the social institution of the written code.

In the execution of this possible overall lesson plan, Miss Fidditch and her colleagues will need to employ *visual aids* for at least the following five reasons: (1) to provide their students with a fuller immediate context situation; (2) to induce a keener memory recall through the mnemonic reinforcement of sight; (3) to stimulate the generation of discourses about the visual aids themselves; (4) to give the classroom routine an esthetic brightening and an added air of informality; and (5) to provide the socially disadvantaged children with keener insights into the culture of the socially advantaged speakers of acrolect Modern American English.

Such visual aids, in turn, may include such items as a house-with–rooms poster and movable figures to reinforce the pattern practice in the target lect. Presumably, of course, Mother in the kitchen will talk of different things than will Father in the den. Many teachers find that flash cards with arrows for the indication of tense are helpful in the modeling of acrolect verbs. Equally useful are a series of flash cards which represent a story for the children to tell in the target lect; a roulette wheel of objects that can naturally induce the generation of sentences; and a cardboard clock with movable hands that can reinforce pattern practice in directive particles and prepositions, all–important items in the connective system of the acrolect version of the national language. Many teachers allow their students to bring appropriate objects to class so that they can talk about them during the period of "free expression." But perhaps potentially the most valuable ally of effective instruction is the "scapegoat" puppet that makes all the mistakes in transmitting an as–yet–unmastered target lect. Miss Fidditch and her colleagues, therefore, should allow their students to make hand puppets for use in classroom dialogues. With the sensory reinforcement of the puppets as a teaching–and–learning aid, the students can then assume roles and play parts and *not be hurt* when mistakes occur, because THE PUPPETS ARE SPEAKING! This sort of fun will also help to increase classroom interest and attention. The dramatic mode, furthermore, will tend to greatly reduce inhibition and shyness.

All of the foregoing commonsense pretensions at pedagogy take for granted, of course, that Miss Fidditch and her colleagues will be sufficiently well trained in linguistics and emotionally unbiased enough to put them into effect in the best possible blend of the scientific and the humanistic manner. The scientific side of that blend means that they will KNOW THE RIGHT QUESTIONS to ask concerning the pre–school language development of the children under their instruction. For each child in the classroom, these questions will run as follows: Can the child form complete sentences, or does he merely gesture and speak in monosyllables? Are the child's sentences kernel and simple or transformed and complex? Can the child understand prepositions, directive particles, and other connectives? Can he qualify his statements with the use of adjectives and adverbs? Does he articulate clearly, or does he mumble or lisp or resort to "baby–talk"? Is his speech fluent and smooth or halting and stammering? Is the child relaxed in his conversations with adults and with other children, or is he tense enough so that his speech becomes blocked and repetitious? Is he spontaneous in the expression of his thoughts and feelings? Does he ask questions in order to gain information or merely to command adult attention? Does the child ignore his classmates and/or his teacher? And finally, does he shut himself off from others in talking–to–himself fantasies?

From the answers they receive to the foregoing set of questions, Miss Fidditch and her colleagues can operate within well-informed guidelines for teaching their socially disadvantaged students how to read in the target lect of the classroom. These guidelines will then help to bring a measure of professional serenity to the teachers themselves, who will know such important matters as these: (a) That boys are likely to be slightly more immature in their language development than are girls—particularly in syntax and articulation, even though the male vocabulary is likely to be a bit more advanced. (b) That children from upper socio–economic groups are usually more linguistically developed and ready for reading than are children from lower socio–economic groups. (c) That an only child is frequently quite advanced in his language development, whereas twins and children who were prematurely born are more liable to be retarded. (d) That orphans from institutions or from foster–homes are usually less ready to begin reading than children who have always lived in family settings. (e) That children who have recently moved to a new home or who have had to recently accept a new baby in the family are liable to be less ready to start reading. And finally, (f) that left–handed children or those who are ambidexterous are liable to experience some difficulty in starting to read.

The humanistic side of such classroom expertise will tell Miss Fidditch and her colleagues that entrance into school usually turns off the child's voluminous transmission and practice in the *oral* code of his preferred resonant lect. In transferring the child's attention to the *written* code of the non-preferred resonant lect of the classroom, therefore, they should guard against these customary defects in the pre–primer and primer literature of the school: simple–mindedness, lack of narrative interest, repetitious vocabulary far below the child's level of oral comprehension, and lack of relevance to the child's total context situation. Thus Miss Fidditch and her colleagues face a constant challenge to maintain motivation and interest in the written code of the classroom.

This challenge, moreover, means that their humanistic expertise must be matched with a scientific one. Drawing upon the deepest insights of linguistics (see LeFevre, 1964; Smith, 1968), Miss Fidditch and her colleagues must *act as models, not as policemen* in their teaching of reading. Further-more, they should work with their socially disadvantaged stu-dents in the following *chronological* or *order–of–importance* stages:

Chronological Stages in the Teaching of Reading

1. INTONATION. In the cultivation of "sentence sense," teach the basilect–speaking child the "melodies" of the printed page, especially as they relate to their oral counter-parts among the suprasegmental phonemes (i.e., the entire intonational system of stress, pitch, juncture) of acrolect Modern American English.

2. SENTENCE PATTERNS. In the deepening of the child's mastery of "sentence sense," teach him the analytic system of functional word order in Modern American English, espe-cially as this word order relates to cadence and rhythm and the organizing principle of maximum stress within the various word groups of the language (see Nist, 1972, pp. 191–195).

3. STRUCTURE OR FUNCTION WORDS. In deepening the child's mastery of the function of various structures within the analytic word order of acrolect Modern American English, teach him the all–important 300 or so word–level markers of noun phrases, verb phrases, connective phrases, subor-dinate clauses, questions and the like. *Never teach* the struc-ture or function words of the language *in isolation,* but always in their typical orders and patterns.

4. WORD–FORM CHANGES. In deepening the child's mas-tery of the various parts of speech within the lexicon of the national language, teach him the inflectional and derivational markers of the four open classes of Modern American English words: nouns, verbs and verbals, adjectives, adverbs.

5. SPELLING, WORD–ANALYSIS, PHONICS. And finally, in polishing up the child's mastery of the written code of the target lect, drill him in the niceties of spelling, word–analysis, and phonics. But always remember that THESE SKILLS DO *NOT* CONSTITUTE READING.

In executing these five stages in the teaching of reading, of course, Miss Fidditch and her colleagues will have to draw upon the scientific certitude of linguistics that GRAPHS ARE *NOT* SOUNDS, but only poor abstract approximations of the phonemes and morphophones (see Smith, 1968) of the national language.

From both their scientific and their humanistic expertise, Miss Fidditch and her colleagues will know better than to give up the ghost of hope if progress in making their student speakers of basilect Modern American English become multilectal is slow and filled with many setbacks. They will know better simply because they will understand that by the time a child enters kindergarten he has already had about 20,000 hours of practice in speaking his own preferred resonant lect. And that is much reinforcement to be overcome in the task of remodeling his systematic set of language habits.

ERADICATION

Before closing out this present chapter and the study as a whole, the author must make the following cautionary observations. If after a nation–wide adoption of the inculcation and the cultivation proposals, speakers of basilect Modern American English as the preferred resonant language still show marked handicapping (at least 20 points in I.Q.) in their segmentation of reality and in the image which they develop of themselves and of the linguistic roles which they must or should assume, then the United States as a whole must consider the adoption of our first proposal—namely, *the eradication of all forms of the basilect* in the country.

Should the day ever come for a massive adoption of this proposal, the entire American educational system will have to undergo an enormous revision. Why? Because if "lect engineering" along the lines of inculcation and cultivation proves to be a failure—AND IT MAY VERY WELL SO PROVE—then it will be unmistakably clear, even as it should be now, that the most important years for a child's linguistic growth and development are those from the onset of resonance to the age of entrance into the public schools, or from about two years old to five. If such a failure in "lect engineering" occurs, then the United States will have to seriously consider the desirability of supporting NATIONWIDE PRE–SCHOOL NURSERIES along the lines of those now operating in Israel, Scandinavia, Mainland China, and the Soviet Union—nurseries which inculcate a love for the national language, cultivate a mastery in some acrolect version of it, and reduce the level of peer–group rivalry and personal aggression among the youngsters attending them.

Radical as the concept of such nationwide pre–school nurseries may appear, it may very well offer the only hope of ever solving the problem of handicapped English in the United States. In fact, in the considered opinion of the author, adopting such a program of eradicating the basilect from Modern American English would result in success within one or two generations, with such beneficial social side effects as these: (1) the true achievement of "one language, one people, one nation," instead of the currently fragmented society in which minority groups become "little sub–nations" at constant war with one another; (2) the general raising of the average national intelligence, with the result that a more capable and better informed electorate could better ensure the fulfillment of the democratic ideals of the nation's Constitution and its republican form of government; (3) the drastically needed reorganization of values and priorities within the nation itself, with increasing emphasis on encouraging mind over muscle, sacrifice over success, hard inquiry over easy discovery, lasting achievement over ephemeral accomplishment, ethics of motive over pragmatism of action, love–freedom over fear–boundedness; (4) the emotional maturation of millions of otherwise puritanical and puristic adults, with an attendant renaissance in both the creative (as distinct from the performing) arts and the speculative (as distinct from the applied) sciences; (5) the overall improvement of the egalitarian system of public education in the country, from the first grade through the graduate and professional schools; and (6) the ever–increasing focusing of the national resources upon the needs of diplomacy and peace, rather than upon the demands of militarism and war.

In conclusion, it can be said that the foregoing six advantages envisioned in a nationwide adoption of pre–school nurseries as the best method to rid the United States of handicapped English and all the socio–economic ills which issue from it, relate directly to an observation made by Dorothea McCarthy in a paper presented at the English Curriculum Study Center of the University of Georgia on January 16, 1964:

> . . . Children who are very secure and who have learned to trust loving parents are quite superior in their use of time words. Those who have been shunted around from one foster home to another, those raised in institutions, and those who are juvenile delinquents have been found to be inferior in their knowledge of and use of time words. Somehow this ability to wait, to trust, to predict events, and to foresee the consequences of one's actions, and to postpone gratifications appears to be basic to the moral development of the child and to the development of his conscience (1967, p. 123).

Like the socially disadvantaged child, who is inferior in his command of time words, the United States today needs to develop its own moral conscience. Sick with single–minded selfishness and compulsive greed, the nation must stop the psychological murder of its children in the classroom equivalents of foster homes, orphanages, and juvenile detention camps. In other words, insofar as handicapped English is concerned, the blackboard jungles of the country produce the fire–bombings in its city streets.

REFERENCES

1. Collections of Essays

Aarons, Alfred C., Barbara Y. Gordon, and William A. Stewart, eds. *Linguistic-Cultural Differences and American Education.* Special Anthology Issue. *The Florida FL Reporter*, Vol. 7, No. 1 (Spring/Summer 1969).

Alatis, James E., ed. *Report on the Twentieth Annual Round Table Meeting on Linguistics and Language Studies.* Monograph Series on Languages and Linguistics, Number 22, 1969. Washington: Georgetown University Press, 1970.

Baratz, Joan C., and Roger W. Shuy, eds. *Teaching Black Children to Read.* Washington: Center for Applied Linguistics, 1969.

Bright, William, ed. *Sociolinguistics.* Proceedings of the UCLA Sociolinguistics Conference, 1964. Second Printing. The Hague and Paris: Mouton & Co., 1971.

Evertts, Eldonna L., ed. *Dimensions of Dialect*. Champaign, Ill.: National Council of Teachers of English, 1967.

Fishman, Joshua A., ed. *Readings in the Sociology of Language*. The Hague and Paris: Mouton & Co., 1968.

Frazier, Alexander, ed. *New Directions in Elementary English*, Champaign, Ill.: National Council of Teachers of English, 1967.

Gregory, Emily, and Mary J. Tingle, eds. *Foundations for a Curriculum in Written Composition, K–6*. Athens, Ga.: English Curriculum Study Center, University of Georgia, 1967.

Halsey, A.H., Jean Floud, and C. Arnold Anderson, eds. *Education, Economy, and Society*. A Reader in the Sociology of Education. New York: The Free Press, 1961.

Hechinger, Fred M., ed. *Pre–School Education Today*. New York: Doubleday & Co., 1966.

Hill, Archibald A., ed. *Linguistics Today*. New York and London: Basic Books, 1969.

Hymes, Dell, ed. *Language in Culture and Society*. A Reader in Linguistics and Anthropology. New York, Evanston, and London: Harper & Row, 1964.

Lieberson, Stanley, ed. *Explorations in Sociolinguistics*. Second Edition. Bloomington: Indiana University Press, 1969. The Hague: Mouton & Co., 1969.

Nist, John, ed. *Style in English*. Indianapolis and New York: Bobbs-Merrill Co., 1969b.

Postman, Neil, Charles Weingartner, and Terence P. Moran, eds. *Language in America*. New York: Pegasus, 1969.

Reed, Carroll E., ed. *The Learning of Language*. A Publication of the National Council of Teachers of English. New York: Appleton–Century–Crofts, 1971.

Saporta, Sol, ed. *Psycholinguistics: A Book of Readings*. New York: Holt, Rinehart and Winston, 1961.

Sebeok, Thomas A., ed. *Style in Language*. Cambridge, Mass.: M.I.T. Press, 1960.

Shuy, Roger W., ed. *Social Dialects and Language Learning*. Proceedings of the Bloomington, Indiana, Conference 1964. Champaign, Ill.: National Council of Teachers of English, 1964.

Williams, Frederick, ed. *Language and Poverty: Perspectives on a Theme*. Chicago: Markham Publishing Co., 1970.

Wilson, Graham, ed. *A Linguistics Reader*. Introduction by Paul Roberts. New York: Harper & Row, 1967.

2. Individual Publications

Atwood, Elmer Bagby. "The Methods of American Dialectology." In Harold Hungerford, Jay Robinson, and James Sledd, eds. *English Linguistics:*

An Introductory Reader. Glenview, Ill.: Scott, Foresman and Co., 1970. Pp. 176–214.

Baratz, Joan C. "Teaching Reading in an Urban Negro School System." In Baratz and Shuy, eds. *Teaching Black Children to Read.* 1969. Pp. 92–116.

Bereiter, Carl, and Siegfried Engelmann. *Teaching Disadvantaged Children in Preschool.* Englewood Cliffs, N.J.: Prentice-Hall, 1966.

Berko, Jean. "The Child's Learning of English Morphology." *Word,* Vol. 14(1958), 150–177. Reprinted in Saporta, ed. *Psycholinguistics.* 1961. Pp. 359–375.

Bernstein, Basil. "Elaborated and Restricted Codes: An Outline." In Lieberson, ed. *Explorations in Sociolinguistics.* 1969. Pp. 126–133.
———. "A Sociolinguistic Approach to Socialization: with Some Reference to Educability." Chapter 3 in Williams, ed. *Language and Poverty.* 1970. Pp. 25–61.
———. "Some Sociological Determinants of Perception. An Inquiry into Sub-cultural Differences." In Fishman, ed. *Readings in the Sociology of Language.* 1968. Pp. 223–239.

Birdwhistell, Ray L. *Introduction to Kinesics.* An Annotation System for Analysis of Body Motion and Gesture. Washington: Department of State, Foreign Service Institute, 1952.
——— "Kinesics and Communication." *Explorations: Studies in Culture and Communication,* III (1954), 31–41. Reprinted in Edmund Carpenter and Marshall McLuhan, eds. *Explorations in Communications: An Anthology.* Boston: Beacon Press, 1960. Pp. 54–64.

Bloomfield, Leonard. *Language.* New York: Holt, Rinehart and Winston 1933, 1962.

Bolinger, Dwight. *Aspects of Language.* New York: Harcourt, Brace & World, 1968.

Braine, Martin D.S. "The Acquisition of Language in Infant and Child." Chapter 2 in Reed, ed. *The Learning of Language.* 1971. Pp. 7–95.
———. "The Ontogeny of English Phrase Structure: The First Phase." *Language,* Vol. 39 (1963), 1–13.

Bruner, Jerome S. *The Process of Education.* Cambridge, Mass.: Harvard University Press, 1963.

Carroll, John B. "Development of Native Language Skills beyond the Early Years." Chapter 3 in Reed, ed. *The Learning of Language.* 1971. Pp. 97–156.
———. "Language Development in Children." *Encyclopedia of Educational Research.* Third Edition. New York: Macmillan Company, 1960. Pp. 744–750. Reprinted in Saporta, ed. *Psycholinguistics.* 1961. Pp. 331–345.

Chardin, Pierre Teilhard de. *The Phenomenon of Man.* Tr. Bernard Wall. With an Introduction by Sir Julian Huxley. New York: Harper & Row, 1959, 1961.

Chomsky, Carol. *The Acquisition of Syntax in Children from 5 to 10.* M.I.T. Research Monograph No. 57. Cambridge, Mass.: M.I.T. Press, 1969.

Chomsky, Noam. *Aspects of the Theory of Syntax.* Cambridge, Mass.: M.I.T. Press, 1965.

————. "The Formal Nature of Language." In Harold Hungerford, Jay Robinson, and James Sledd, eds. *English Linguistics: An Introductory Reader.* Glenview, Ill.: Scott, Foresman and Company, 1970. Pp. 107-150. Reprinted, with editorial commentary, from Eric H. Lenneberg. *Biological Foundations of Language.* New York: John Wiley & Sons, 1967. Pp. 397–442.

————. *Language and Mind.* New York: Harcourt, Brace & World, 1968. Second Edition, 1972.

————. *Syntactic Structures.* The Hague: Mouton & Co., 1957, 1962.

Chomsky, Noam, and Morris Halle. *The Sound Pattern of English.* New York: Harper & Row, 1968.

Church, Joseph. *Language and the Discovery of Reality.* New York: Random House, 1961.

Corbett, Edward P.J. *Classical Rhetoric for the Modern Student.* New York: Oxford University Press, 1965.

Crosby, Muriel. "English: New Dimensions and New Demands." In Evertts, ed. *Dimensions of Dialect.* 1967. Pp. 1–6.

Dale, Edgar. "Vocabulary Development of the Underprivileged Child." In Evertts, ed. *Dimensions of Dialect.* 1967. Pp. 30–38.

Davis, Alison. "Teaching Language and Reading to Disadvantaged Negro Children." In Evertts, ed. *Dimensions of Dialect.* 1967. Pp. 57–63.

Davis, Flora. "How to Read Body Language." *Reader's Digest,* Vol. 95, No. 572 (December 1969), 127–130. Condensed from *Glamour,* September 1969.

Deutsch, Martin P. "The Disadvantaged Child and the Learning Process." In A. Harry Passow, ed. *Education in Depressed Areas.* New York: Bureau of Publications, Teachers College, Columbia University, 1963. Pp. 163–179.

Dillard, J.L. *Black English: Its History and Usage in the United States.* New York: Random House, 1972.

Entwisle, Doris R. "Semantic Systems of Children: Some Assessments of Social Class and Ethnic Differences." Chapter 7 in Williams, ed. *Language and Poverty.* 1970. Pp. 123–139.

Ervin, Susan M., and Wick R. Miller. "Language Development." In Fishman, ed. *Readings in the Sociology of Language.* 1968. Pp. 68–98.

Erwin, Selma, and John E. Lee. "Language of the Pre–school Child (2–4)" Unpublished report of a study made as a part of the work of the English Curriculum Study Center, University of Georgia, 1964.

Francis, W. Nelson. *The English Language: An Introduction.* Background for Writing. New York: W.W. Norton & Co., 1963, 1965.

Gaarder, A. Bruce. "Statement Before the Special Subcommittee on Bilingual Education of the Committee on Labor and Public Welfare of the United States Senate, Thursday, May 18, 1967, 11:00 A.M. DST." In Aarons, Gordon, and Stewart, eds. *Linguistic–Cultural Differences and American Education.* Spring/Summer 1969. Pp. 33–34, 171.

Gesell, Arnold, M.D., and Frances T. Ilz. *Child Development.* New York: Harper & Row, 1959.

Gleason, H. A., Jr. *Linguistics and English Grammar.* New York: Holt, Rinehart and Winston, 1965.

Gottschalk, Louis A., M.D., and Goldine C. Gleser, M.D. *The Measurement of Psychological States Through the Content Analysis of Verbal Behavior.* Berkeley and Los Angeles: University of California Press, 1969.

Hall, Robert A., Jr. *Hands off Pidgin English!* New York: Albert Daub, 1956.

————. *Melanesian Pidgin English: Grammar, Texts, Vocabulary.* Baltimore: Linguistic Society of America, 1943.

————. "Pidgin Languages." *Scientific American,* Vol. 200 (February 1959), 124–134.

Hawkins, P.R. "Social Class, the Nominal Group and Reference." *Language and Speech,* Vol. 12 (1969), 125–135.

Hayakawa, S.I. *Language in Thought and Action.* Third Edition. New York: Harcourt–Brace–Jovanovich, 1972.

Heise, David R. "Social Status, Attitudes, and Word Connotations." In Lieberson, ed. *Explorations in Sociolinguistics.* 1969. Pp. 99–111.

Hertzler, Joyce O. *A Sociology of Language.* New York: Random House, 1965.

Hockett, Charles F. *A Course in Modern Linguistics.* New York: Macmillan Company, 1958.

Hook, J.N. "The Steps Toward Composition." *English Journal,* Vol. 55, No. 4 (April 1966), 417–424.

Hunt, Joseph McV. *Intelligence and Experience.* New York: Ronald Press Company, 1961.

Irwin, O.C. "Infant Speech: The Effect of Family Occupational Status and of Age on Sound Frequency." *Journal of Speech and Hearing Disorders,* Vol. 13 (1948a), 320–323.

————. "Infant Speech: The Effect of Family Occupational Status and of Age on Use of Sound Types." *Journal of Speech and Hearing Disorders,* Vol. 13 (1948b), 224–226.

————. "Speech Development in the Young Child: 2. Some Factors Related to the Speech Development of the Infant and Young Child." *Journal of Speech and Hearing Disorders,* Vol. 17 (1952), 269–278.

Jacobs, Roderick A., and Peter S. Rosenbaum. *English Transformational Grammar.* Waltham, Mass.: Blaisdell Publishing Co., 1968.

Jakobson, Roman. "Closing Statement: Linguistics and Poetics." In Sebeok, ed. *Style in Language.* 1960. Pp. 350–377.

———. *Phonological Studies*. Volume I of *Selected Writings*. The Hague and Paris: Mouton & Co., 1962.

Jakobson, Roman, C. Gunnar M. Fant, and Morris Halle. *Preliminaries to Speech Analysis*. Cambridge, Mass.: M.I.T. Press, 1963.

Jespersen, Otto. *Language: Its Nature, Development and Origin*. The Norton Library, New York: W.W. Norton & Co., 1964.

John, Vera P., and Vivian M. Horner. "Bilingualism and the Spanish–Speaking Child." Chapter 8 in Williams, ed. *Language and Poverty*. 1970. Pp. 140–152.

Joos, Martin. *The Five Clocks*. Introduction by Albert H. Marckwardt. Harbinger Edition. New York: Harcourt, Brace & World, 1961, 1962, 1967.

———. "Homeostasis in English Usage." *College Composition and Communication*, XIII, No. 3 (October 1962), 18–22. Reptinted in Nist, ed. *Style in English*. 1969b. Pp. 14–17.

Katz, Jerrold J. *The Philosophy of Language*. New York and London: Harper & Row, 1966.

Kenyon, John S. "Cultural Levels and Functional Varieties of English." *College English*, Vol. 10, No. 1 (October 1948), 31–36. Reprinted in many language anthologies.

King, J.B. "The Most Powerful Educational Weapon in Our War on Poverty: Teaching English to Environmentally Handicapped Pupils and to Pupils of Foreign Language Background." In B.W. Robinett, ed. *On Teaching English to Speakers of Other Languages: Series III*. Champaign, Ill.: National Council of Teachers of English, 1967.

Knowlton, C.S. "Spanish–American Schools in the 1960s." Paper prepared for the 1966 Teacher Orientation Conference, East Las Vegas, New Mexico. Mimeographed.

Kurath, Hans. *Word Geography of the Eastern United States*. Ann Arbor: University of Michigan Press, 1949.

Kurath, Hans, dir. and ed., *et al. Linguistic Atlas of New England*. 3 vols. in 6. [Sponsored by the American Council of Learned Societies and Assisted by Universities and Colleges in New England.] Providence: Brown University Press, 1939–43.

Kurath, Hans, and Raven I. McDavid, Jr. *The Pronunciation of English in the Atlantic States*. Ann Arbor: University of Michigan Press, 1961.

Labov, William. "The Logic of Nonstandard English." In Alatis, ed. *Report on the Twentieth Annual Round Table Meeting on Linguistics and Language Studies*. 1970a. Pp. 1–43.

———. "The Reflection of Social Processes in Linguistic Structures." In Fishman, ed. *Readings in the Sociology of Language*. 1968. Pp. 240–251.

———. *The Social Stratification of English in New York City*. Washington: Center for Applied Linguistics, 1966.

———. "Some Sources of Reading Problems for Negro Speakers of Nonstandard English." In Baratz and Shuy, eds. *Teaching Black Children to Read*. 1969. Pp. 29–67. Reprinted from Frazier, ed. *New Directions in Elementary English*. 1967. Pp. 140–167.

————. "Stages in the Acquisition of Standard English." In Shuy, ed. *Social Dialects and Language Learning.* 1964. Pp. 77–103.

————. *The Study of Nonstandard English.* Champaign, Ill.: National Council of Teachers of English, 1970b.

————. "Variation in Language." Chapter 5 in Reed, ed. *The Learning of Language.* 1971. Pp. 187–221.

Landar, Herbert. *Language and Culture.* New York: Oxford University Press, 1966.

Lawton, Denis. *Social Class, Language and Education.* New York: Schocken Books, 1968.

LeFevre, Carl A. *Linguistics and the Teaching of Reading.* New York: McGraw–Hill Book Company, 1964.

Lenneberg, Eric H. *Biological Foundations of Language.* With Appendices by Noam Chomsky and Otto Marx. New York: John Wiley & Sons, 1967.

Leopold, Werner F. "Patterning in Children's Language Learning." In Saporta, ed. *Psycholinguistics.* 1961. Pp. 350–358.

Lewis, M.M. *Infant Speech: A Study of the Beginnings of Language.* Second Edition. New York: Humanities Press, 1951.

Lewis, Sinclair. *Babbitt.* New York: Harcourt, Brace & Co., 1922. Reprinted in many subsequent editions and copyrights.

Lloyd, Donald J. "Our National Mania for Correctness." *The American Scholar,* Vol. 21, No. 3 (Summer 1952), 283–289. Reprinted in Leonard F. Dean and Kenneth G. Wilson, eds. *Essays on Language and Usage.* Second Edition. New York: Oxford University Press, 1963. Pp. 306–311.

————. "Snobs, Slobs and the English Language." *The American Scholar,* Vol. 20, No. 3 (Summer 1951), 279–288. Reprinted in Wilson, ed. *A Linguistics Reader.* 1967. Pp. 99–106.

Loban, Walter. *The Language of Elementary School Children.* Champaign, Ill.: National Council of Teachers of English, 1963.

McCarthy, Dorothea. "Psychological Concepts Essential for the Effective Teaching of the Language Arts." In Gregory and Tingle, eds. *Foundations for a Curriculum in Written Composition, K–6.* 1967. Pp. 106–137.

McDavid, Raven I., Jr. "A Checklist of Significant Features for Discriminating Social Dialects." In Evertts, ed. *Dimensions of Dialect.* 1967. Pp. 7–10.

————. "Dialect Differences and Social Differences in an Urban Society." In Bright, ed. *Sociolinguistics.* 1971. Pp. 72–83.

Marckwardt, Albert H. *Linguistics and the Teaching of English.* Bloomington and London: Indiana University Press, 1966.

Mencken, H.L. *The American Language.* The Fourth Edition and the Two Supplements, abridged, with annotations and the new material, edited by Raven I. McDavid, Jr., with the assistance of David W. Maurer. New York: Alfred A. Knopf, 1963.

Metz, F. Elizabeth. "Poverty, Early Language Deprivation, and Learning Ability." In Evertts, ed. *Dimensions of Dialect.* 1967. Pp. 14–18.

Miller, George A. "The Psycholinguists: On the New Scientists of Language." In Wilson, ed. *A Linguistics Reader.* 1967. Pp. 327–341. Reprinted from *Encounter,* Vol. 23, No. 1 (July 1964), 29–37.

Moffett, James. *Teaching the Universe of Discourse.* Boston: Houghton Mifflin Company, 1968.

Morley, M. *The Development and Disorders of Speech in Childhood.* London: Livingstone, 1957.

Mukařovský, Jan. "Standard Language and Poetic Language." In Paul L. Garvin (selec. and tr.), *A Prague School Reader on Esthetics, Literary Structure, and Style.* Washington: Georgetown University Press, 1964. Pp. 17–30.

Mukerji, Rose, and Helen F. Robison. "A Head Start in Language." In Evertts, ed. *Dimensions of Dialect.* 1967. Pp. 19–22.

Nisbet, John. "Family Environment and Intelligence." Chapter 23 in Halsey, Floud, and Anderson, eds. *Education, Economy, and Society.* 1961, 1965. Pp. 273–287.

Nist, John. "American English Writing Systems." *The Encyclopedia of Education.* New York: Macmillan & Free Press, 1971a. Vol. 3, pp. 366–373.

———. "English Structures." *The Encyclopedia of Education.* New York: Macmillan & Free Press, 1971b. Vol. 3, pp. 323–342.

———. "Handicapped English: A Linguist Looks at the Language of the Culturally Deprived." Speech and Hearing Association of Alabama *Letter,* VI (Monograph, June 1969), 11–23.

———. "Handicapped English: An Outline." Unpublished paper presented to the American Speech and Hearing Association, Chicago, Illinois, November 1969.

———. "Introduction." In Nist, ed. *Style in English.* 1969b. Pp. 5–8.

———. "Language: Communication and Communion." *College Composition and Communication,* XVII, 2 (May 1966), 50–54.

———. "Linguistics and the Esthetics of English." *COSTERUS Essays in English and American Language and Literature,* I (1972), 183–205.

———. *The Phonology of Modern American English.* Amsterdam: Editions RODOPI, 1973.

———. *Speaking into Writing: A Guidebook for English Composition.* New York: St. Martin's Press, 1969a.

———. *A Structural History of English.* New York: St. Martin's Press, 1966.

———. "Teaching the Esthetic Dimensions of English Poetry." *English Teaching Forum,* IX, 1 (January–February 1971), 21–25.

O'Neil, Wayne. "The Politics of Bidialectalism." *College English,* Vol. 33, No. 4 (January 1972), 433–438.

Orwell, George. "Politics and the English Language." *Shooting an Elephant and Other Essays.* New York: Harcourt, Brace & World, 1945. 1946, 1949, 1950. Pp. 77–92. Reprinted in many language anthologies.

Osgood, Charles E. "Some Effects of Motivation on Style of Encoding." In Sebeok, ed. *Style in Language.* 1960. Pp. 293–306.

Peirce, Charles Sanders. "The Icon, Index, and Symbol." *Elements of Logic.* Volume 2 of *Collected Papers.* Cambridge, Mass.: Harvard University Press, 1960. Pp. 156–173.

Piaget, Jean. *The Language and Thought of the Child.* Tr. M. Warden. New York: Harcourt and Brace, 1926.

Piaget, Jean, and Bärbel Inhelder. *The Psychology of the Child.* Tr. Helen Weaver. New York: Basic Books, 1969.

Plumer, Davenport. "A Summary of Environmentalist Views and Some Educational Implications." Chapter 14 in Williams, ed. *Language and Poverty.* 1970. Pp. 265–308.

Ponder, Eddie G. "Understanding the Language of the Culturally Disadvantaged Child." In Evertts, ed. *Dimensions of Dialect.* 1967. Pp. 23–29.

Reinecke, John E. *Language and Dialect in Hawaii: A Sociolinguistic History to 1935.* Edited by Stanley M. Tsuzaki. Honolulu: University of Hawaii Press, 1969.

Roberts, Paul. *Modern Grammar.* New York: Harcourt, Brace & World, 1967, 1968.

Rockas, Leo. *Modes of Rhetoric.* New York: St. Martin's Press, 1964.

Rodriguez, Armando. "The Mexican–American—Disadvantaged? Ya Basta!" In Aarons, Gordon, and Stewart, eds. *Linguistic–Cultural Differences and American Education.* Spring/Summer 1969. Pp. 35–36, 160.

Rosenthal, R., and Lenore Jacobson. *Pygmalion in the Classroom.* New York: Holt, Rinehart & Winston, 1968.

Sharpe, Johnnie M. "The Disadvantaged Student Trapped Behind the Verb 'To Teach.' " *College Composition and Communication,* XXIII, 3 (October 1972), 271–276.

Shugrue, Michael F. *English in a Decade of Change.* New York: Pegasus, 1968.

Shuy, Roger W. "Bonnie and Clyde Tactics in English Teaching." In Aarons, Gordon, and Stewart, eds. *Linguistic–Cultural Differences and American Education.* Spring/Summer 1969. Pp. 81–83, 160–161.

———. "The Sociolinguists and Urban Language Problems." Chapter 16 in Williams, ed. *Language and Poverty.* 1970. Pp. 335–350.

Skinner, B.F. *Verbal Behavior.* New York: Appleton–Century–Crofts, 1957.

Sledd, James. "Bi–Dialectalism: The Linguistics of White Supremacy." *English Journal,* Vol. 58, No. 9 (December 1969), 1307–1316.

———. "Doublespeak: Dialectology in the Service of Big Brother." *College English,* Vol. 33, No. 4 (January 1972), 439–456.

Smith, Henry Lee, Jr. *English Morphophonics: Implications for the Teaching of Literacy.* Monograph Number Ten. Oswego, New York: New York State English Council, 1968.

———. "Language and the Total System of Communication." In Hill, ed. *Linguistics Today.* 1969. Pp. 89–102.

Steinbeck, John. *The Grapes of Wrath.* New York: Viking Press, 1939. Reprinted in many different editions and copyrights.

Stewart, William A. "Continuity and Change in American Negro Dialects." *The Florida FL Reporter,* Vol. 6, No. 1 (Spring 1968), 3–4, 14–16, 18.
———. *Language and Communication Problems in Southern Appalachia.* Washington: Center for Applied Linguistics, 1967.
———, ed. *Non–Standard Speech and the Teaching of English.* Washington: Center for Applied Linguistics, 1964.
———. "Sociolinguistic Factors in the History of American Negro Dialects." *The Florida FL Reporter,* Vol. 5, No. 2 (Spring 1967), 11, 22, 24, 26.
———. "Toward a History of American Negro Dialect." Chapter 17 in Williams, ed. *Language and Poverty.* 1970. Pp. 351–379.
———. "Urban Negro Speech: Sociolinguistic Factors Affecting English Teaching." In Aarons, Gordon, and Stewart, eds. *Linguistic–Culture Differences and American Education.* Spring/Summer 1969. Pp. 50–53, 166.
Swain, Emeliza, and Emily B. Gregory. "The Concept System." Chapter VII in Gregory and Tingle, eds. *Foundations for a Curriculum in Written Composition. K–6,* 1967. Pp. 88–95.
Thompson, Hildegard. "Teaching English to Indian Children." In Evertts, ed. *Dimensions of Dialect.* 1967. Pp. 64–71.
Torrey, Jane W. "Second–Language Learning." Chapter 6 in Reed, ed. *The Learning of Language.* 1971. Pp. 223–265.
Trager, George L. "Paralanguage: A First Approximation." *Studies in Linguistics,* XIII (1958), 1–12. Reprinted, with notes and additional bibliography, in Hymes, ed. *Language in Culture and Society.* 1964. Pp. 274–288.
Trager, George L., and Henry Lee Smith, Jr. *An Outline of English Structure.* Fifth Printing. Washington: American Council of Learned Societies, 1957.
Tucker, C. Allen. "The Chinese Immigrant's Language Handicap: Its Extent and Its Effects." In Aarons, Gordon, and Stewart, eds. *Linguistic–Cultural Differences and American Education.* Spring/Summer 1969. Pp. 44–45, 170.
Twaddell, W. F. "Meanings, Habits and Rules." In Wilson, ed. *A Linguistics Reader.* 1967. Pp. 10–17. Reprinted from *Education,* Vol. 69, No. 12 (October 1948), 75–81.
Van Riper, Charles. *Speech Correction: Principles and Methods.* Third Edition. Englewood Cliffs, N.J.: Prentice–Hall, 1954.
Vigotsky, L.S. "Thought and Speech." In Saporta, ed. *Psycholinguistics.* 1961. Pp. 509–537. Reprinted from *Psychiatry,* Vol. 2 (1939), 29–54.
Warren, Austin. *Rage for Order: Essays in Criticism.* Ann Arbor Paperbacks. Ann Arbor: University of Michigan Press, 1959.
Weeks, Robert P., ed. *Commonwealth vs. Sacco and Vanzetti.* Englewood Cliffs, N.J.: Prentice–Hall, 1958.
West, Robert. "Speech Pathology." Chapter 8 in Reed, ed. *The Learning of Language.* 1971. Pp. 307–331.

Whitehall, Harold. *Structural Essentials of English.* New York: Harcourt, Brace & Co., 1956.

Williams, Frederick. "Language, Attitude, and Social Change." Chapter 18 in Williams, ed. *Language and Poverty.* 1970. Pp. 380–399.

———. "Some Preliminaries and Prospects." Chapter 1 in Williams, ed. *Language and Poverty.* 1970. Pp. 1–10.

Williams, Frederick, and Rita C. Naremore. "An Annotated Bibliography of Journal Articles." Chapter 20 in Williams, ed. *Language and Poverty.* 1970. Pp. 416–456.

Wolfe, Thomas. *Look Homeward, Angel.* New York: Charles Scribner's Sons, 1929. Reprinted in many different editions and copyrights.

Young, Florence M. "An Analysis of Certain Variables in a Developmental Study of Language." *Genetic Psychology Monograph,* No. 23 (1941), 3–141.

INDEX